OUTSTANDING CRITICAL ACCLAIM FOR *FLIGHTS OF PASSAGE*

A Book-of-the-Month Club
~~~~~~~~ Selection

(more)

D0188087

"An honest and honorable, as well as sometimes very funny, account of a young pilot's initiation by the great *rite de passage* of war. Hynes's description of learning to fly, and of the consequent application of the lessons in the theater of the real . . . checks with my own experience of the same things at place after place. Truly, as Hynes says in his preface, our generation shares a secret: simply the war itself. I was much moved by this book, which evokes my memories in concert with the author's."

—Howard Nemerov, author of
War Stories

"Hynes's prose betrays a mature intelligence. It is deceptively simple and consistently enchanting. . . . His book conveys memorably the sense of flight and the descent back to ordinary life."

—*Time*

"*FLIGHTS OF PASSAGE* is not a standard story of courage in war, but rather a tale of the dogged and mortal persistence to pass many versions of "the Test" that training and combat and even sex presented to a young man preparing for war. An introspective, winning, and vivid recollection sketched by a gifted observer."

—*Library Journal*

FLIGHTS of PASSAGE

Samuel Hynes

POCKET BOOKS

New York   London   Toronto   Sydney   Tokyo

Sequences from this book have been published in *Four Quarters,* *TriQuarterly,* and *The Sewanee Review.*

 POCKET BOOKS, a division of Simon & Schuster Inc.
1230 Avenue of the Americas, New York, NY 10020

Published by arrangement with Frederic C. Beil/Naval Institute Press
Library of Congress Catalog Card Number: 87-70233

ISBN: 0-671-67410-2

First Pocket Books printing April 1989

10 9 8 7 6 5 4 3 2 1

for John Graves and Les Conner

Preface

Every generation is a secret society. The secret that my generation—the one that came of age during the Second World War—shared was simply the war itself. We grew up on active duty. I entered Navy Flight School when I was eighteen, and I was not twenty-one until two weeks after the war ended, and most of the young men I flew with were roughly my age. The years that in peacetime we would have spent in college, we spent instead first in learning to fly, and to fight a flying war, and then in fighting it. Our secret made us different from those who were older or younger than ourselves, or who were not in the war. I can't formulate the differences in terms that seem adequate to the experience, but perhaps I can recover something of the experience itself.

This is the story of a fairly ordinary flying war—of the training and the fighting, and of the growing up that went with it. I have tried to tell it with the voice of the young man who lived it, and to see it with his eyes, and not to impose upon it the revisionary wisdom of age. I have not improved upon events, but have told them, insofar as memory allows, as they happened. Only here and there have I changed a name, or disguised a circumstance, where not to do so might have troubled an old companion.

Sequences from this book have been published in *Four Quarters*, *TriQuarterly*, and *The Sewanee Review*, and I thank John Keenan, Reginald Gibbons, and George Core, the editors of these journals, for their help, and for permission to reprint those pieces.

Princeton, New Jersey

Chapter 1

My father was a tall, country-looking man. When he walked, with his long farmer's stride, he swung his hands with the palms facing back, so that he seemed to be paddling his way through some fluid more resistant than air. Because his arms were long, and his overcoat was cheap, a good deal of wrist protruded from his sleeves, making his enormous hands looks even more like paddles. As he walked beside me that cold night in March, 1943, through the empty Rock Island station and onto the platform, he seemed to be propelling himself forward swiftly but against his will, toward the edge of his familiar world, where he would have to stop, but I would step over.

He had missed his own war—had been drafted in 1918 but was left waiting in a New Jersey camp until it was all over. I remember the pictures in the family photograph album—a yellowing snapshot of a smiling young man in a private's uniform, sitting in the doorway of a tent, and another, a posed portrait taken by the town photographer in LaPorte, Indiana, of the same young man standing stiffly at attention, looking very determined, but still a farmer dressed up as a soldier. Now he was too old to fight, though at fifty-six he was bigger, stronger, handsomer, and more eager than I would ever be. He loved his country in a simple, old-fashioned way, and he loved his sons; it must have been almost unendurable for him that they should go off to war, and he remain at home. Still, he would go down to the station with me, though he wouldn't say much, certainly wouldn't kiss me goodbye, or express any feelings right out.

The platform was dark, except at intervals where standing lamps shed pale disks of light at their bases, and as we moved from dark into light and back to dark our shadows slipped back and forth, before and then behind us, his tall, mine shorter and slighter. At the end of the platform, under a lamp, a yeoman was reading orders from a clipboard, and boys in civilian clothes were shuffling into crooked lines. I stopped awkwardly and shook my father's hand. It was the first time I had ever done that; a boy didn't shake hands with his own father. He put his other huge hand on my shoulder, as though he would still protect me while he could. Then he let go, and I went on and joined a line with the others. The yeoman began to call muster: ". . . Baird, Berg, Eichman . . . Johnson, Milch, Spitzenberger. . . ." The names were midwestern-sounding, German and Scandinavian, most of them, the kind of names you'd expect to find in Minneapolis. I had grown up with such names, and I felt a little reassured by their familiarity. I picked up my suitcase and went to board the train. On the steps I paused to look back. My father was far down the platform, his long arms swinging, his head bent a little, moving rapidly away through the spots of light and shadow toward the dark street.

I don't remember feeling any particular vocation for flying, or any sense that flight school was where I belonged. I was not one of those kids who built model airplanes, I never ran around with my arms stuck out, making engine-noises, I never put goggles on the helmet that I wore to school in the winter. I read *G-8 and His Battle Aces* like everybody else, but I didn't imagine myself in those Spads and Nieuports, shooting down Huns and winning medals. I don't think I imagined myself as anything at all.

Still, in the thirties airports were romantic, and drew boys to them. None of the kids I knew had ever been in a plane, or expected ever to be in one; planes were for watching, not for riding in. On sunny Saturday mornings my friends and I would make sandwiches and fill our sour-smelling Boy Scout canteens, and ride our bikes out through the thinning Minneapolis suburbs and between the first farms, to the airfield. Along the highway, just before you came to the commercial part of the airport, there was a sign pointing down a narrower road to the Naval Reserve Air Station, and we turned there and rode toward a tin-roofed hangar with U.S. NAVY painted on the roof in big yellow letters.

Across the road from the hangar a small hill had been partly dug away—perhaps for gravel or fill—leaving a grass-covered knob, like a head with hair on it, with its sandy face toward the field. We lay on the grass on the top of that slope and ate our sandwiches and watched the navy biplanes landing and taking off. If the wind was right they would take off over our heads, passing so close that we could see the grease and oil streaks on the cowlings and the spurts of flame from the exhaust stacks, and could watch the wheels draw up as the planes roared over us. It made us feel daring, to be lying there in the path of the booming planes.

When we had eaten we sometimes went down onto the field and hovered around the hangar. (There never seemed to be any guards to chase small boys away.) Inside it was cool and shadowy. I remember the light coming down, soft and unfocused from the high ceiling, and the soft cries of the swallows that nested in the roof beams, and the smell of hydraulic fluid and oil. Planes in for repair were scattered around the hangar floor, half-dismantled, surrounded by cowlings and tools, and mechanics worked beside the open engines. Sometimes one man would speak a word or two to another, or tap a tool on an engine, but the sounds were muted and lost in the tall emptiness under the roof; and the effect was of a careful quietness, as though the hangar were a church, and the mechanics priests engaged in some ritual that we were too young, and too earthbound, to understand.

But for all the romance of the Navy field, I didn't want to be a pilot. All I wanted, when I rode out to the airport on those distant Saturdays, was the presence of that romance. I wanted to hear the engines and see the planes climb out of sight, and to watch the mechanics at their priestly tasks. I was not, even in imagination, a pilot; but I was a true believer in the religion of flight.

The young men on the train that night were from Minnesota and the states around. Most of them came from farms, or from little towns, places I had never heard of like Blue Earth, Minnesota, and Bonesteel, South Dakota. The most citified were, like myself, from Minneapolis, which was not much more cosmopolitan than Bonesteel. We were all yokels. For many of us it was the first time away from home, the first time out of the home state, the first time in a Pullman car. Everything was new and strange—the berths with their green curtains, already made up for the night, the smoking room at the end of the car, the yeoman with his clipboard giving orders. We were subdued by it all, and there was none of the shouting and singing and drinking that a troop train would have had. We were shy of each other, and nervous about behaving properly (none of us knew how an aviation cadet was supposed to act), and frightened by the mystery into which we were moving.

Among all those strangers were two boys I had known in high school and during my few months at the university. They became my friends, but that night on the train they were only familiar faces, comforting simply because I had seen them before. I knew Joe Baird because he was an athlete. He had played end on the university's freshman football team. He was tall, and so broad-shouldered and narrow-hipped that he looked top-heavy. When he moved, he moved very delicately, walking on his tiptoes, carefully, as though holding back his great energy and strength out of a protective concern for the world. His friend Wally Milch was a straw-haired, pink-faced Minneapolis Swede—the kind of boy who at eighteen still hadn't shaved, and didn't look as though he'd ever have to. He had the face of a sweet-tempered child, and that's what he was. Like Joe, he was kind and generous by instinct—it seemed easy for him to be a nice guy—and funny out of simple good feeling.

The three of us crowded together onto a lower berth for a while, talking and giving each other such encouragements as we had, and I went to bed feeling a little better, and a little sad for the others, the country boys in their plaid mackinaws, with their high-sided haircuts and their shy manners, who were absolute strangers that night. But though I was better off than they were, my own apprehensiveness would not go away entirely, and I lay awake for a long time, watching the snow-patched Minnesota fields and the dark, lonely little towns pass, and trying to imagine what was coming. The life of flying was so mysterious that I could not construct an image of it; I couldn't even visualize it enough to imagine failing at it. It was as though the darkness through which the train rolled would go on forever.

We were headed south, to Texas and Oklahoma. There we would be scattered among little towns, each of which had a college of sorts and an airport. At the college we would be instructed in subjects thought suitable for pilots—physics and aerology and military history—and at the airport we would be taught to fly Piper Cubs. We weren't exactly in the Navy yet—the program we were entering was called *Civilian* Pilot Training—but we weren't exactly civilians either. If we passed this first testing period, the yeoman on the train explained, then we would be sent on into the real Navy flight training; "But if you wash out," he went on, "it's Great Lakes!" To "wash out" meant to fail; it sounded as though you turned colorless and just faded away, like a guilty spirit. Great Lakes was the Navy training station where such failures were reassigned, and would-be flying officers turned into enlisted men. I didn't yet know how to fail, but I had learned the vocabulary of failure.

Early in the morning of the second day we stopped somewhere in Oklahoma, and Wally and Joe and some other boys got off. I heard Joe ask the name of the college they were going to.

"Panhandle A&M."

Joe laughed his whinnying laugh. "You're kidding." And it certainly did sound like a joke, a made-up name for the worst school in the world. But it was a real place.

The rest of us went on, across the flatness of north Texas, to Dallas, and changed to another, dustier, older, and pokier train, and crept back north a bit, and stopped at last beside a station with a sign that said "Denton."

"Fall out!" the yeoman shouted, and we stumbled out of the train onto the platform, and stood blinking in the bright sunlight. From around the corner of the station a man appeared dressed in the uniform of a Navy lieutenant junior grade. He was, apparently, our Commanding Officer; but even in the uniform he looked like a schoolteacher. He stood still for a moment, staring abstractedly through his glasses, as though he were running over in his mind a speech that he hadn't memorized. "Ten-shun," he said apologetically. "This way—uh—cadets, for the bus to North Texas State Teachers College." It sounded a little better than Panhandle A&M. But not much.

Everything about Denton, Texas, and the life we lived there was strange to us; we lived in strangeness as though it were an environment, or a climate. Perhaps that is why memory offers only fragments and images of that time— often very vivid, but only bright, broken pieces. The town itself was strange, like no town that any of us had known back home. It spread out around us in a random-looking sprawl of one- and two-storied buildings, dust-colored and flattened-looking, as though the weight of the Texas sky had pressed it down into the earth. The trees were different from the ones back home, and the flowers bloomed too early, and the soil was the wrong color—reddish and sandy and dry. The people we met spoke a soft-slurring speech that at first we couldn't understand. Shopkeepers welcomed us as though we were old friends, and when we left they said, "Y'all hurry back, heah?" The black shoeshine boy who kept his stand on the main street grinned and greeted us cheerfully, and played a jazz tune with his rag on our shoes. Pretty girls smiled as they passed. It was all very friendly—friendlier than it would have been in Minneapolis or Bonesteel—but it was unfamiliar, a foreign country in which we were only tourists. I felt more at home back in my dormitory room, where Midwestern was spoken.

But even there life was strange. I had never slept in a room with anyone but my brother, and now I shared one with three strangers—Ike, Bergie, and Johnson. There were common showers and common toilets, and a common mess hall where we ate together at long tables. It was all pleasant enough, and I suppose it wasn't much different from life in a college dormitory, but I hadn't lived in a college dormitory, and for me the abrupt loss of privacy and family, both at once, was a shock.

Our airport was a sheep pasture on the edge of town, which we shared with the sheep. It had no runway, only grass, which the sheep kept trimmed. It was not even flat— it sank in the middle and rose steeply at the far side, where it ended in a grove of trees. At the corner of the field by the road was a small hangar and a shed that was called the Flight Office; beside the hangar four or five Piper Cubs were parked. That was all the equipment there was, except for a windsock, once red and yellow but faded now to an almost invisible gray, which drooped on a staff near the fence. It wasn't much of an airport, or much of a school, but I took my first flight there, and soloed there, and I have the sort of affection for the place that I have for other beginnings—for the first girl, the first car, the first drink.

First flight: what images remain? I am in the rear seat of a Cub, and my instructor is taxiing to the takeoff position. The wheels of the plane are small, and it rides very low, so that I seem to be sitting almost on the ground, and I feel every bump and hollow of the field as we taxi. The wings seem to flap with the bumps, and the whole machine seems too small, too fragile, too casually put together to be trusted.

The instructor turns into the wind, runs up the engine, and I feel the quick life of the plane. It begins to roll, bumpily at first, as though we are still taxiing. The nose is high, I can't see around it, and I have a panicky feeling that we are rushing toward something—a tree or a sheep or another plane; and then the flow of air begins to lift the wings, the tail comes up, and the plane moves with a new grace, dancing, touching the rough field lightly, and then not touching it, skimming the grass, which is still so close that I can see each blade, and I am flying, lifted and carried by the unsubstantial air.

At the end of the field the grove of trees is first a wall, a dark limit, and then sinks and slides, foreshortening to a green island passing below us. The plane banks and I can see the town and the college—but below me, all roofs and tree-tops—and beyond it there is distance, more and more distance, blue-hazy and flat and empty, stretching away to the indistinct, remote horizon. The world is enormous. The size of the earth increases around me, and so does the size of the air; space expands, is a tall dome filled with a pale, clean light, into which we are climbing.

Below me the houses, each in its own place, look small

and vulnerable on the largeness of the earth. I stare down at first like a voyeur, looking into other people's lives. A truck drives along a road and turns into a yard; a woman is hanging out clothes; she stops and runs to the truck. Should I be watching? Does she feel me there above her life? The world below exposes itself to me—I am flying, I can see everything!

I don't remember doing any flying myself on that first flight. I must have tried, and I could invent what the instructor said and what I did, but I don't remember it. What I remember is the way the world changed from the familiar, comfortable space I had always lived in to the huge, empty world of the flier.

As the days of marching and flying and just hanging around passed, the strangers in my room became my friends. Ike, a big, gentle, countryish boy from South Dakota, was like my father, and that made friendship easy. He walked with long, galumphing strides (it came from walking between the corn rows, Johnson said), and he talked like a yokel in a movie. He was the only person I ever knew who really said "Golly." (But it was more like "Gawlly"—he always spoke as though his mouth was full of water, and he didn't want to spill it.) He didn't talk much, though; he was ill at ease with words. He communicated in other ways—by smiling, or by touching. He would put his arm around a friend's shoulder without embarrassment, in a way that the rest of us couldn't. I envied him his natural affection.

Bergie came from South Dakota too—from a town larger than Ike's, he explained, though in South Dakota that didn't seem to make much difference; they all seemed like country boys to me. He was as tall as Ike, but slender and dark where Ike was blond and broad; and he had a small, deeply seamed face, as though he had been born smiling and had never stopped smiling long enough for the furrows to smooth out. He spoke in a rapid tumble of words that were sometimes hard to separate; but when he sang, which he did whenever he wasn't required to be silent, his voice was pure and clear, and very high, almost like a boy soprano's. Even on first meeting, he looked and acted like a friend—so open, so decent. I liked him at once.

Johnson was a smoother character than Ike. Like almost everyone else in the group he was blonde, but he had not allowed his hair to be cut in the standard crew cut; it was parted high up on the side, and slicked back. He knew the current slang, and the campus fashions; and he had a worldly, knowing smile (Ike's smile was all trusting innocence). He would have been a city slicker—the kind who swindles rubes like Ike—if he had come from anywhere but South Dakota. How, I wondered, could you be a city slicker in a state that had no cities? But Johnson had been to the state university there, and he had been in a fraternity (he even wore his pin on his khaki shirt until the CO noticed it). He regarded the country boys with pitying disdain—hayseeds, he said, with the cow shit still on their shoes.

After a week or so we trusted each other enough to bring out the pictures of our girls that we'd been hiding in our dresser drawers. Ike's was a cheerful-looking, long-faced girl with an elaborate movie-star hairdo. "She runs the beauty parlor," he explained, "back in Bonesteel." Johnson had two—a Pi Phi, he said, and a Tri Delt. I brought out my picture of Alice. She was a girl I had met during my first week at the university. She was pretty and in a sorority (both good), but she was a Catholic (bad). We had been going steady for a couple of months, and the night before I left we had sat in my father's car parked on a bluff by the river, necking a lot—but not going-all-the-way (whatever *that* was)—and talking romantically about our future. She was my girl, and I assumed that I'd marry her some day. Right now I didn't want to—what I wanted to do was to take all her clothes off, look at her, touch her, and find out what going-all-the-way meant—but I expected to want to later on. I wasn't sure that her picture would impress my roommates, but Johnson examined it with an experienced eye, and said she reminded him of an Alpha Phi he knew, and Bergie raised his eyebrows, making the furrows in his brow even deeper, and whistled appreciatively. Ike said "Golly!"

On the other side of town, at Texas State College for Women, hundreds of girls lived lives made celibate by the draft and gas-rationing. TSCW had been the traditional territory of boys from Texas A&M, and those boys were now out of reach. We rode past the campus every day in the bus that took us to the airport, and looked at the girls, moving in twos and threes along the campus paths under the trees that were just coming into leaf. Sometimes we waved, or shouted something, and they waved back, some cheerfully, some wildly, as though they were drowning and we were the lifeboat crew. It was a little scary, seeing them so eager; I wasn't sure that the things I had learned about girls back in Minneapolis would be adequate for this situation.

After a couple of weeks of training we were given a Saturday-night liberty, and Ike and Johnson and I caught a crosstown bus for TSCW. None of us was quite sure what we should do when we got there, and for a while we just walked around, sticking together like a rifle platoon.

But finally we spoke to a girl, and she had friends, and in a few minutes we were paired off.

At first my new date seemed very different from what I was used to. She had more names, for one thing—her name, she said, was Jo Belle (or maybe it was Mary Beth, or even Lalla Rookh), and when she spoke her voice was like homemade fudge. But beyond those variations she was just another middle-class American college girl.

Where should we go? We could go into town to a movie, she said, or we could dance at the Union. But I said I only had until eleven, so we had a coke and went out onto the dark campus. There was an outdoor theater nearby, Jo Belle said, that was right pretty.

It was still March, but the evening was warm, and we sat on the grass at the back of the theater, under some bushes. Jo Belle was soft and warm, and soon we were lying back, kissing and whispering. But we were still strangers, and we were shy of each other. I wasn't sure how much groping she would tolerate, and she wasn't sure how far I expected to proceed. So it was mostly fumbling there under the bushes, and "No" and "Please" and more "Nos." I suppose all that she wanted, really, was just to touch a young male, to be assured that at eighteen she was pretty and desirable. I wanted to be led into a darkness that I didn't understand. You could call it sexual need, all right, but it was more than that. It was a desire to know, not to be ignorant of what was there, under a girl's clothes. Sex was a journey of exploration. Girls were Africa and I was Stanley. Which way to the Congo? And what did you do when you got there? Adults knew. I wanted to know too.

Then it was ten-thirty, and I was back on the bus with Ike and Johnson, remembering how her body felt under the starched cotton, and lying about how I had made out, and all the time my genitals feeling like cannonballs. I was no more ready for women than I was ready for war. Sex was another military skill that I hadn't yet acquired.

I didn't advance my knowledge of sex much at Denton, but I learned a little about flying. My teacher, a man named Moreland, was one of three flight instructors—leathery-faced, laconic Texans, cropdusters, I suppose, in peacetime, or dollar-a-ride fairground fliers. You'd find them, when they weren't flying, lined up in chairs propped back against a sunny wall of the hangar, watching the planes take off and land, and occasionally making a terse comment: "Should'a used some power there," or "He done landed ten feet in the air." If you were scheduled for a flight, you'd find your instructor in his chair, and he'd tilt forward and rise, and stand for a minute looking at the sky, as though the thought of flying hadn't struck him until right then, and he'd walk out to the Cub, and you'd trail along behind him.

The Piper Cub, with its large square wing and slender fuselage, is like a kite with a small engine in it; it will float on an air-current, settle lightly to the ground with no power at all, and bounce forgivingly away from a bad landing to give you a chance to try again. In heavier planes the engine dominates, pulling the plane along, but in a Cub it is the wings; the engine seems to do no more than hold you hovering in space. It was a wonderful plane to begin with, friendly and safe.

At first we did simple things—turns and climbs and gentle glides. I was all right while the plane was flying straight and level, but I felt insecure and vulnerable when it banked, and I could feel myself leaning away from the turn, trying to keep my body vertical to the ground, as though I might get some support from the earth if I were loyal to it. "Relax, son," Moreland would say, "fly with the plane. The ground ain't no use to you up here." And gradually I learned to move instinctively with the plane, and to let the world tilt as it would. For, once you are really flying, it is the world that tilts, not the plane; it's the horizon that tips up when you turn, and settles back when you roll out, sinks when you climb, and rises when you dive. The plane remains a steady thing, a part of yourself, or so it seems—and you are not really flying the plane, you are flying the world.

"Now you take it," Moreland would say, and he'd let go of the stick, and I'd clutch it with my right hand, grab the throttle with my left, and shove both feet onto the rudder pedals, and the plane would jerk and yaw about the sky. "E-e-e-easy movements," Moreland would plead, "easy movements, that's all she needs," and I would try to relax, and move the stick gently forward, and the nose would sink, back and it would rise, left and the left wing would drop. It wasn't exactly the feeling of flying that I was getting then; it was the feeling of mutual responsiveness, my life touching and merging with the life of the plane.

Once I could perform these simple flying movements we went on to the next step, which is a kind of nonflying, or antiflying—stalling the plane, so that it virtually stops in the air. You pull the nose high; the earth and the horizon disappear, the airspeed drops, and you hold the stick back and wait for the shudder; and the nose falls heavily earthward like a stone, or something dead, and you recover speed and are flying again. Or at the top, at the moment of stalling, you kick the rudder in, and the plane falls in a twisting stall that is a spin, and you are looking down at the earth, rotating like a dream of falling, and you *are* falling, and then the recovery, the plane begins to live again, the horizon settles into a reasonable place, and it is like waking after a sickness. I learned to do these things because I had to, but I hated them; they seemed a violation of the plane and of the life of flying.

When we had learned one set of skills, or at least had flown the prescribed number of hours, there were check-rides, to determine whether we were ready for the next set. These were tests, but not like any test that I had taken at school or university. You couldn't cram for it, and you couldn't fake it. You weren't even being tested on something that you had studied, really, but on what you were. If you were a flier, you passed; if you weren't, you washed out—fell out of the air, and became a lower order of being.

It became clear that some people were natural fliers, and some weren't. The athletes usually were; they used their bodies easily and naturally, and they seemed to make the plane a part of themselves. Ike was one of those. He didn't enter a plane so much as put it on, like an odd suit of clothes, and you could see already that the only trouble with the Cub was that it was too small for him, that he belonged in a full-sized, serious plane, like a Corsair or an F6F.

I wasn't a natural pilot—or an athlete. I had to think about flying all the time—left aileron, don't forget left rudder, back on the stick, keep the horizon there, watch the airspeed—all this to make a simple 360° turn. But Ike did it all intuitively: "I just roll her over," he'd say, "and around she goes." I wondered if it was significant that the plane was a female for him, and only an *it* for me.

I wasn't a natural, but I learned to control the plane, and myself with it. But there were some young men for whom even this was impossible. In some, fear of the air was as deep and as irrational as fear of water or of the dark is in others; it kept them tense and helpless in flight, jerking the plane about with sudden, desperate gestures, skidding into turns, overcorrecting mistakes, bouncing on landings, never making those easy movements that are all she needs. One cadet, a big, stolid farmer who was older than the rest of us, was airsick on every flight. He returned each day, grimly, to try again; but he never got over whatever it was that gripped his belly, never reached the point at which movement in the air, you and the plane moving together, becomes a liberating, joyous action. I remember Ike walking back from the flight line with him, his arm around the sufferer's shoulders, saying, "Golly, it's not so bad," and the farmer's face sweaty and strained and despairing. Then one day he was gone, washed out and shipped off to Great Lakes.

But the rest of us, those who had not failed, began to enter the pilot's world, a world in which weather is an environment, clouds are three-dimensional landscapes, and the earth is—not exactly two-dimensional, but panoramic, patterned, and expansive. We began to get a pilot's sense of the earth, how it goes out to horizons beyond horizons, how it is marked by man and nature—the straight lines of roads and fields and railroad tracks, the irregular lines of rivers, the dark patches of woods—and how, in spite of those marks, earth can deny location and leave a flier lost above unknown landmarks.

I asked Moreland one day if we could climb to ten thousand feet. To be two miles above the earth seemed to me something remarkable, something more than merely flying. It was a fine, clear day—it must have been in April—and as we climbed, slowly because the Cub engine didn't have much power, the earth opened out farther than I had ever seen before, extending in a vast circle, hazy at the edges and, it seemed, faintly curving away toward the horizon. I thought, if Columbus could have climbed two miles high he'd have known that his theory was true, and he could have saved himself the trip to America.

Since we were over Texas, the most striking thing about that expanding circle below us was its sameness. To the southeast lay Lake Dallas, and still farther off I could see the smoke of Fort Worth, but in every other direction the land spread its redundant flatness unbroken to the horizon. And since it was all the same, there was no knowing how far away that horizon was; we might have been looking north all the way to Canada, it would have looked the same. It was just earth, and space, and weather.

Weather is the pilot's nature, air is his ocean, winds are his waves and streams. Wind makes the plane fly—the flow of air over the wing literally holds it in the air—but it also blows you off course, tosses a light plane about in a landing run; it can get you lost, or kill you. When the northers blew down across those flat Texas fields, planes like ours could take off and land almost vertically, but they could also get hopelessly lost downwind, blown like a bird or a scrap of paper out of sight. On the windiest days we kept the Cubs tied down, rocking and bouncing against the ropes. But off to the east of us, at the Army field where artillery spotters were being trained, the little observation planes would go on flying, barely moving into the wind and, when they put their enormous flaps down, seeming to land moving backwards. And then they too would be grounded, and the sky would be empty, swept clean by the streaming wind.

By early May we had all finished the CPT course. We

could get a Cub into the air and back down again; we could march together if the commands weren't too complicated; we had a smattering of knowledge of aeronautics and weather. We were ready to graduate, and like any graduating class we gathered to have our picture taken on the steps of our dormitory. The boys in that picture look tanned and fit, and much too young for a war. Some of them are grinning into the camera, some are clowning around. It's the sort of picture that you might find in a high-school yearbook—the baseball team, or a fraternity. Nobody seems to regard the occasion as a very solemn one. After all, we weren't really in the Navy yet.

It seemed a million miles from Texas to Georgia, and every mile just the same. I remember sitting in a hot, stationary train, looking out the window at a cotton gin and a mule and a pine tree, while we waited for a more urgent train to pass; but I don't know whether we were in Louisiana or Mississippi or Alabama or Georgia. It was May, and already it was like high summer back home. A black man sat on a wagon, waiting like us for the train to pass; he looked back at me, but without interest. I had seen the cotton gin and the mule and the man on the wagon a hundred times in the two days that it took us to ride that slow southern train from Dallas to Athens, Georgia. It was like a punishment in some myth: we were condemned to ride forever through the same southern landscape.

Athens, in its way, was like another myth—the fall of Icarus, if he had landed on red Georgia dirt. For a few weeks we had been pilots—well, sort of pilots—and now we were back on the ground, at a place called a *pre*flight school, as though in the Navy's eyes we not only weren't pilots, we never had been pilots. As we rode into the school's grounds we passed a symbol of our situation; a worn-out fighter plane had been set in concrete in front of the administration building. It was the only plane in the place, and it looked sad and humiliated, grounded and stuck there as a decoration, far from any airfield.

The school occupied part of the buildings and grounds of the University of Georgia. Our quarters were in two converted girls' dormitories that faced each other across what had been a lawn, but was now a grassless, pounded parade ground. The architect of these buildings had obviously been much influenced by *Gone With the Wind,* and had designed two Taras, with tall white columns and a commanding sweep of steps (and after all, what else would you build for southern coeds?). But there was nothing romantic, or collegiate, and God knows nothing coeducational, about the life we lived there.

I felt at once, almost before I had unloaded my gear, that this was a place dominated by two qualities: it was very military, in an oddly phony way, and it was very tense. On the baked clay between the two Taras cadets were marching as we arrived, practicing for a parade. We had marched and paraded at Denton, but never like this, not rigid with concentration, eyes staring forward, arms swinging, sweating in the Georgia sun. A lot seemed to be at stake. As we carried our bags into the barracks, a voice came down from a window across the way: "You'll be sorry!" It was what old hands always shouted to new ones, but this time it seemed to be more than that, as though he really knew that we would be, that what would happen to us there would make regret a certainty.

Later, at our first muster, we got the official version of that warning. We stood on the parade ground in platoon formation, and above us, at the top of the steps between the white columns, an officer stood and told us how the next three months would be, and why.

"We're here," he shouted, "to prepare you to be naval officers. You'll be taught things in ground school that we think an officer should know, and you'll learn the discipline of close-order drill. But most of all we'll be seeing if you can take it. If you can't take it, now's the time to find out, not when you're Out There, with lives depending on you." He spoke with feeling, and you could almost forget for a moment that he was a schoolteacher or a football coach dressed up as an officer, and think that he must have been at Midway or the Coral Sea, that he knew what he was talking about. He stood silent for a time, running his eyes back and forth along our ranks, as though watching for someone to speak or move, or perhaps looking for weaklings, the ones who couldn't take it. Then he barked "Dis-missed," and the echo bounced back from the other Tara, "-missed," and we turned slowly back into human beings.

Back in the barracks I found some of the boys who had left Minneapolis with me. Joe Baird and Wally were there, full of unlikely stories about Panhandle A&M, the flying and the Oklahoma girls, and I told them a few lies about Jo Belle and Denton. But then we were scattered again, shoved once more into rooms with strangers. I had a roommate from New Orleans, one from Virginia, and one from New Hampshire. I knew nothing about any of these places, and I had no way of understanding what these strangers were like. I couldn't read the Virginia or the New Hampshire signs of background or class or manners, and they couldn't read my Minneapolis signs. We circled each other cautiously, like sniffing dogs. But though we shared nothing of the past, we shared everything in the present—a room, toilets, mess hall, classrooms, parade ground. And more than that we shared a hatred of the whole program, and a determination to survive it.

At preflight we stopped being half-civilians and became a military unit, the Twenty-fifth Battalion. We were given regulation short-back-and-sides haircuts, and regulation uniforms: khaki for working days, whites and blues for dress, like officers; and our civilian clothes were packed and sent home. We posed for official pictures in our new whites, and the Navy sent them to hometown papers, and they came back as newspaper clippings stuck in our parents' letters: "Local Boy Begins Pre-flight Training."

Ground school began (*"Ground* school," Joe grumbled, "it's always *ground* school, as though we ever got *off* the ground in this place"), and we learned how to behave in a military classroom. You sat and waited for the instructor, and when he entered, the first cadet who saw him coming yelled "ten-SHUN!" and you jumped to your feet and stood stiffly until the instructor said "At ease," and you could sink back into your seat. If the instructor called on you, you jumped to attention again and began your recitation with "Sir!"—an exclamation more than a form of address. "Cadet, what is the armament of the Scharnhorst-class cruiser?" (Leap to attention) "Sir! The armament of the Scharnhorst-class cruiser is. . . ."

I suppose it all must have been modeled on the customs of the Naval Academy at Annapolis, and perhaps it worked there; but it seemed extravagant and a little comical to be always leaping up for these schoolteachers, and to stand backed stiffly up against the wall whenever one of them walked down the hall. This was called "bracing the bulkhead." The terminology was part of the nautical atmosphere, and part of the joke—the wall of a converted women's dormitory at the University of Georgia being called a "bulkhead," for God's sake!

The whole of the life was like that. We never walked anywhere, we marched—to meals, to classes, to church on Sunday (where we sang the hymn about God protecting those in peril on the sea), even to the movies. And we drilled, close-order drill, hour after hour on the fierce parade ground in the sun. If you were a great success at drilling you might get to lead a platoon or even a company; or you might even be made Cadet Commander and run a whole parade. But that glory went mostly to cadets who had been in ROTC or had gone to military school; the rest of us stayed in the ranks, and tried not to fall down, or turn right when everybody else turned left. Because you could wash out just as easily for bad drilling as for bad flying; the football coaches believed that if you couldn't drill you were uncoordinated, and if you were uncoordinated you obviously couldn't fly.

Sport was another, even better test of coordination, and in that steaming Georgia summer we competed with each other in every kind of sport. We played football and ran races, both dashes and distance; we boxed and we wrestled, slipping from each other's sweaty grips like wet soap. They were all *games* when other, ordinary people played them, but for us they were Tests. Every competition was Judgment Day, and if you lost it seemed a moral failure, a revelation of a weak character that would make you useless, dangerous even, "Out There." It wasn't, of course, *The* Test—that would come at the heroic moment, the true and final occasion for action. I felt—surely we all felt—a boy's desire to do that one thing that really mattered, that was adult, that required courage and skill. I was being trained for it, the Navy would see that I was ready for it (or would cast me aside because I wasn't), and when it came I would move through it easily and without anxiety, and would come out the other side into an eternal state of heroism, which would also be adulthood. Flying would provide and demonstrate the skill, flying in combat would show the necessary courage; but only the successful attack—the bomb well placed, the enemy plane destroyed by accurate gunfire—would be the true consummation. Sometimes I had secret doubts: Would I ever be ready? Would I know when I was? The Navy's endless Tests were there to reassure me. I was passing, I was winning—surely it was all preparation, it was all right and necessary.

Not everyone could win, of course, not everyone would get his wings and his commission and fly into combat; there had to be losers, and so, though we liked each other, we began to look on even our best friends as competitors, as opponents. I boxed with my roommate, and though I didn't want to hurt him, because I liked him, I found myself pressing in, pounding at his guard, hitting harder and harder because an officer was scoring us, and one of us would win; and afterward I felt ashamed that friendship had been weaker than the need to win, to pass the Test.

Not everybody minded it. Joe Baird, who could do anything effortlessly, and who never lost his temper, ran and boxed and climbed ropes all day, and would come into my room afterward, still on his tiptoes, to joke and chatter, as though the whole ordeal was just a summer camp. And Ike was the same: he just went on smiling and saying "Golly," and doing what was required of him with placid ease. The actions that for the rest of us were torments of physical strain and psychic tension were for them simply exercise. Their bodies had been lean and fit at the beginning, and they simply stayed that way, while their friends grew thinner and more irritable by the day, and more daunted by the effort that tomorrow would demand. But it was more than just physical conditioning. Joe and Ike were serenely happy people, *above* the Test; whatever the competition was, they simply weren't in it. I admired and envied their state of mind, but I never attained it.

What I dreaded most was the obstacle course, a race run over, under, and through various painful difficulties. The obstacles included most of the things I couldn't do— a long rope to climb, a log over a ditch, which had to be inched across straddling (it was known as the Nutcracker), a high wall to be scaled. I would lie awake at night thinking, Tomorrow is Thursday, I'll have to run the obstacle course, and this time I won't make it. And when I slept I would run it in my sleep, and fail at The Wall.

There was only one way to get over the wall (which was probably about eight feet high, though it seemed higher). You had to run at it full tilt, leap and catch a momentary foothold on its smooth side, grasp the top before your foot slipped, and hurl yourself headfirst over, turning in midair to land on your feet. If you failed to do this perfectly there was nothing to do but go back and start your run over again, while all your friends and opponents dashed past and over it and out of sight. It was humiliating, and I think that's why it was there—to make defeat seem worse than anything, worse than dying. The obstacle course was a moral exercise. It tested your willingness to undergo any strain, any effort, for the sake of a chance at a commission, and to avoid the shame of losing.

I made a new friend at the wall when, as I was hanging headfirst over the top, gasping for breath, I heard an angry southern voice say, "Aw, fuck it!" and saw a cadet named Taylor walk around the wall and jog off toward the next obstacle. I knew he could have got over—he was a good athlete—but he'd had enough; he just didn't see the sense of it. This approach to life made Taylor good and consoling company during those trying months. He would collapse on my bunk after a day of unreasonable trials and groan, "Every muscle in muh fuckin' body is screamin'," and then he would go over the day's activities in vivid, angry detail—the recognition class on Italian fighter planes ("*Italian* fighter planes, for Christ sake! There *ain't* any Italian air force except on those goddamn slides"), the signal-flag practice, the lecture on saluting, the film on venereal disease titled *She May Look Safe, But.* . . . It was all chicken shit to Taylor. "Old Taylor," some other southerner said, "he thinks like a nigger. Even walks like a nigger. Maybe he *is* a nigger." But he said it with a kind of admiration. He saw that Taylor was a born outsider, a natural anarchist caught in a system that had nothing for him, and that his anger and his sly evasions were the only self-defense he had.

I thought I had no memories of that time, because it had nothing to do with flying, and because I hated it so; but names and faces come back: the roommate from Virginia, with his soft Tidewater accent, who said "hah-oos" for "house"; the methodically tidy New Englander whose housekeeping got us past a white-glove inspection; Hawk Henry, an ex-enlisted man who was the only cadet in our platoon who could give orders with style. ("Eyes in the boat!" he would shout as we marched past the CO, "Eyes in the boat!" It seemed a very salty way of telling us not to gawk around.)

One evening remains, still evocative of how it felt to be

young then, and going, however slowly, toward war. We had been marched across the campus, down a cinder trail through a pine wood, to the university's auditorium to see a movie. We sat by battalion, and while we waited for the film to begin we chanted, battalion by battalion, how long we had to go: "Twenty-third, one more week!" "Twenty-fourth, three more weeks!" We were the Twenty-fifth—five more weeks! Then the movie started. It was *Casablanca*.

When we returned late to our barracks, marching along the dark path through the pines, no one talked, but every once in a while someone would whistle or sing a phrase from "As Time Goes By." We were not so much thinking about the film as floating on its emotions, feeling the sadness of Humphrey Bogart, who had given up Ingrid Bergman for the Cause. We didn't really understand what the Cause was, exactly, what high principles linked the French at Casablanca to us at Athens, Georgia. But we felt the emotional link; it had to do with separation and loss, and at eighteen, in a strange place among strangers, we knew something about that. In the barracks we went quietly to bed. There still wasn't much talking, but as I fell asleep I heard one last cadet, alone in the shower, singing, "You must remember this, a kiss is just a kiss. . . ."

The days of those painful months will not separate themselves into this day or that one. But I remember the weather. There were two kinds. Rain: it fell heavily from purple-black, low, pregnant-looking clouds, straight down, windlessly, for days at a time. The red dirt of the parade ground was marched and kneaded into mud like dough, and puddles stood in the paths between the buildings. We were wet from morning until night, and the next morning our clothes had not dried, and it would still be raining, and the voice of the Officer of the Day would come over the barracks loudspeaker: "Now hear this. The uniform of the day will be raincoats, with condom-type cap covers." And we would hunch out into the waiting rain for muster. And sun: it burned down, indifferently, out of a coppery, cloudless sky that seemed to be stretched very low, just over the parade ground and the football field. It burned through clothes, it burned through short Navy haircuts, into the scalp, into the skull, and made your brain feel hot and dry. I played a sixty-minute football game under that sun, and it was like a year on Devil's Island.

But then, the whole thing was a kind of penal servitude, three months at hard, meaningless labor. Far from increasing our endurance, preflight drained it. Our faces grew tanned, and our bodies lean, but we were strained and tense, keyed up beyond any useful level. It was an ordeal that did nothing for us, certainly didn't make officers, or even men of us, a pointless ritual to a god called "Attitude." I sensed this, and resented it, though I didn't understand what was wrong with it then. But my resentment must have surfaced, because the football coach who commanded my company called me into his office to say, with loathing in his voice, "Cadet, you'll never make an officer. Your Attitude's all wrong." Perhaps it was. Certainly it was different from his.

The most surprising thing about preflight school is that we managed to survive it, and as friends. I don't think we learned much there, but we did learn one lesson that was valuable to us all. We learned to hate our enemies—not the Germans and the Japanese (nobody ever mentioned them), but the nonflying, Attitude-talking martinets who commanded us, and the military system that they represented. After preflight we would never quite join the Navy; we had joined instead a smaller, more independent and anarchic group, the community of fliers. The Navy was our antagonist, muscle-bound and dumb like those football-coach officers; but because it was dumb we could beat it. With a little imagination we could circumvent, muddle, and exploit the regulations, and we could fly. "Fuck the Navy," Taylor said as we packed to leave Athens. "That's all, just fuck the Navy." We were moving on, out of the chicken shit, back to our proper element, the air.

Chapter 2

Memories of flying are almost always memories of landscape. It isn't that you think *I am flying over this state or that one*, but that you are moving above a landscape pierced by a mountain, or patched with woodlands, or edged by the sea. The earth is always there below, apart and beautiful (no land is ugly from the air), revealing its private features in a way that it never does to the traveler on its surface. A pilot can see where a road goes, what is over that hill, the shapes of lakes and towns; and I suppose this knowledge of the earth's face is a part of the feeling of domination that a pilot feels when his plane reaches a commanding altitude and he looks down on the world that stretches out beneath him.

At the Naval Air Station at Memphis there was, most of all, the river, a broad presence lying to the west of the airfield: black in the morning light, a vast reflector at sunset, gray when the sky was gray, but always there. The impression it gave, from the air, was of absolute flatness—

an odd impression, perhaps, for what would you expect a river to be except flat? Still, the earth from the air retains its contours and remains three-dimensional (it never really looks like a map or a patchwork quilt); but the river was relentlessly two-dimensional. It didn't seem to move or to have any irregularities at all—it just lay there, like an old mirror, revealing nothing, only reflecting.

Beside the river, the Naval Air Station looked temporary, raw, and ugly. A year before it had been a Tennessee farm, with a big old frame house surrounded by oaks, and a pond where cattle stood and drank. Bulldozers had come in, and the trees and the pond were gone. In their place were rows of impermanent-looking gray buildings and two paved circular landing mats, and around the whole Station a high wire fence, along which military police patrolled with guard dogs. It was a place without a single thing to please the eye, and I was always glad to take off from it and to see the river and the farmland outside.

Life at the Air Station was lived in the constant presence of planes—the sound of engines testing, warming up, taking off. There were planes overhead all day; and at night, as you walked back from the movie or a beer at the Slop Chute, red and green running lights passed in the dark sky, and the flicker of exhaust flames. You went to sleep to the sound of flying, and woke to the first morning takeoffs. Planes became a part of your subliminal life, only thrusting up into consciousness when an engine faltered, and you rushed off to a window or stepped in the street to look up at trouble.

At Athens we had lived four in a room in our women's dormitory with the columns. But Memphis was a real naval base, and we were housed there in regulation enlisted-men's barracks, barnlike two-story frame buildings with one long room on each floor. In each of these rooms double-decked bunks were lined up symmetrically on either side of a central aisle—room for eighty cadets, maybe more. It didn't seem possible that I could ever fall asleep in a room with eighty people, and at first I lay awake at night after the lights were out, listening to the sounds— the street sounds, the airfield sounds, and the sounds of sleeping. The dim exit light at the end of the room only made the shadows deeper, the sounds more anonymous and remote. Then I was sleeping too.

In a barracks, life begins anonymously. Every bed is like every other bed, lockers are identical, all arrangements are symmetrical (hang your towel, folded once vertically, on the lefthand end of the foot of your bed; do not display personal photographs; shoes must be placed in the locker in pairs, toes in). There is one common toilet room (no doors on the stalls) and one shower room. No individual is to be distinguished from another.

But gradually personality seeps in and fills the spaces between the identical beds, and makes the barracks into a human community, and the anonymous others into people. So I remember how, first of all, there were only the individual voices: a drunk Georgia cracker at the other end of the long room, babbling to himself in a shrill, incomprehensible whine; a couple of country boys on their bunks harmonizing a mournful church song; a Texan telling a long dirty story. Then, after a while, some of the voices became persons, and some of these became my friends.

In the service, friends often come by the accidental conjunctions that the system imposes. Because my name came between the next-to-last of the H's and the first of the I's I got to know Spanish John (above me in the double-decker bunk) and T (on my left). The three of us became friendly, took our liberties together, got drunk together, shared our money and our news from home, encouraged each other when the work or the flying got tough. Once, while drunk in Memphis, we had our portrait taken together by a classy photographer, and there we still are, looking young, and soberer than we were, with faces like blank pages.

T became my close friend, and remained so. He was an odd-looking guy—short, thin, and undernourished-looking, nothing like what you'd expect an Aviation Cadet to be. He carried his shoulders hunched forward, and his head slightly on one side, as though he had been interrupted in a shrug. His walk was a kind of shuffling dance; he seemed to hear a jazz tune that nobody else heard, and he sang wordless Louis Armstrong riffs to himself as he walked—"bah-bah zoo-zee bah, yeah, yeah." He looked frail, but he could do everything that I could do, and slightly better. When we boxed he landed three punches while I was landing two, when we swam he finished his laps first, and when we flew he seemed always to pass his check-flights sooner and with less trouble. But though he was good at what the Navy demanded of him, he never seemed altogether involved in the business of being military; even in the middle of a platoon he didn't seem to be actually *marching*. Like Taylor, he had a streak of the born anarchist in him; perhaps he had learned it from the southern blacks who played the music he heard in his head.

Spanish John wasn't really Spanish; we took the name from a petty gangster in a story by Damon Runyon, because John seemed to us like that kind of guy. He was a tough kid from a New Jersey slum, and he seemed to know more about adult life, or at least the drinking and the sex parts, than the rest of us did. He regarded us as childish innocents, and his mouth wore an habitual smile

33

of disdain; his eyes were restless and watchful, alert for an opportunity to outsmart authority and to beat the system. I didn't like him as I liked T, but I was impressed by his city-shrewdness, and I accepted the companionship that the alphabet had imposed.

Another new friend was the story-telling Texan, who was called Rock, no doubt because his face looked as though it had been carved in red sandstone—or perhaps not carved, but simply eroded. The skin of his forehead and cheeks was red and dry looking, and scored with deep lines, like a dry gully, and his nose thrust sharply outward, and then turned suddenly down and slightly to one side, like a crooked beak. I asked him about the nose. "Met a Mexican once," he explained. "Meaner than me." Rock had endless stories to tell, about Texas, about his college years at A&M, about women and drinking. He would flop down on his bunk, drop his shoes on the floor, and remark that that reminded him of the time he bought a pair of twenty-dollar boots and then got drunk. "Got me to bed, and in the middle of the night I had to piss so bad, and was so drunk, that I *dreamed* I got up and went to the can, and went back to sleep. Woke up in the morning, and there was my twenty-dollar boot, full of piss right up to the top."

Sometimes you would meet someone just by accident, hanging around the flight line waiting for a flight, or over a beer, or in the barracks. Bud was an accidental friend; we had been at the same university the fall before, but we met for the first time in a chow line in Memphis. Bud had an ironic view of life that was a great consolation in the military world. He didn't expect life to be rational, or effort to be rewarded; he didn't expect success, I don't think he even wanted it. He was content if the human comedy was occasionally funny. Bud was incapable of assuming a military posture, or a military appearance; however he was dressed—in flight gear or in dress whites—he looked like a lost Marx Brother. Such a guy is a natural subversive; Bud denied and defeated the Navy way of doing things, simply by existing. And he helped his friends to preserve their individualities, because he would only deal with the world in individual terms.

Bud was much preoccupied with sex. His problem, as he saw it, was a simple physiological one: "My balls are too big," he explained. But though he was interested, the girls weren't, and his life at Memphis was a long series of failed conquests. Perhaps because he found the sex so elusive, he also found it poetic, and he spoke of sexual matters in lyric metaphorical terms. The female organ was "the bearded clam" or "the mossy doughnut," and when I came in from a date he would look up brightly and ask: "And did you soak the social sausage?"

I don't think Bud's metaphors were obscene—he really was a sexual poet. But much of what we all said and sang *was* obscene. Obscenity was a kind of intimacy, a shared language like the common toilet and the single room we slept in, a step past conventional reticences. We took that step because we had to live an intimate collective life, and this was one way of accepting it. Our common vocabulary connected us with each other, and separated us from the world out there, and Back Home. There were limits, though. You used obscenities with each other, but not too freely; you could call your friend a bastard, affectionately, but you couldn't call him a shit. You never used any really obscene terms when you were speaking of people you were fond of—your family, for instance—and never in the company of girls, unless they were clearly tramps. And you didn't use it indiscriminately. Fucking couldn't *always* be the adjective; that was the way enlisted men talked, and we were going to be officers.

Obscenity was masculine; anyone who objected to it, or simply didn't use it, must therefore be feminine—a queer, a pansy. In a bunk just down from mine lived a gentle, Bible-reading Georgia boy named Newton. He was the politest cadet I ever met, in that formal, old-fashioned way that some southern country folk have, and the most fastidious. He would wait until midnight to go to the toilet or take a shower, so that he could be alone there, and he would leave the room when the talk got too coarse. He must have hated us and the way we lived; but he wanted to belong, too, and so he kept coming back, and hanging around. We teased him, called him "Newt the Fruit," and hinted, if he seemed to have made a friend, that unnatural acts took place in the shower after lights out. The mood was meant to be joking, and I think many of us felt some fondness for him, but his manner was outside the limits of our world, and so we had to keep him outside, too. I don't think he was homosexual, what we took for femininity was simply his gentleness (T said he was just a Good Ol' Boy who loved his mamma). But we were beginning to think in a—what shall I call it?—a military way; perhaps we had learned the preflight lesson after all, and were developing the right Attitude. We didn't actually persecute poor Newton, but we despised him, and that is worse than persecution when you're nineteen, and want to belong.

The planes at Memphis were Stearman N2s's, open-cockpit biplanes that were painted yellow and were known as "Yellow Perils." In fact they were anything but perilous; they were probably the safest and strongest airplanes ever built. They could be flown through acrobatic maneuvers that would disintegrate a fighter, they could be dropped to a landing from a stall twenty feet in the air, and they could be ground-looped with no more damage than a bit of scraped paint. I did all these things to the planes, and they (and I) survived. And in the process I learned a bit more about flying.

What I learned, first of all, was the intense delight of flying an open plane. I'm not sure that I can explain why it is so different from a closed cockpit, but it has to do with the intimate presence of the air itself, the medium you fly in, streaming past and around you. You can thrust your whole arm out into the slipstream and press back against the flow of air; you can lean to the side, and the air will force the tears from your eyes and rush into your lungs. And you can look straight into space, down to the earth and up to the sky, with nothing between you and the whole world. The plane is not a protective shell, as an automobile is, but an extension of your own body, moving as you move; and your head is the brain of the whole stretched and vibrating organism. Flying alone in an open plane is the purest experience of flight possible.

But from the Navy's point of view our learning was a bit more programmed and less lyrical than that. Each of us was assigned to an instructor, a flying officer whose task it was to guide his pupil through the stages of the training program and to prepare him for the periodic Tests, the check-rides. The instructors were flying tutors, each with his own style, though with one common syllabus.

Primary flight instructors were of two kinds. One lot had been private pilots before the war—amateurs, mostly, who had flown light planes on weekends. They had been hustled into the flight program and assigned to bring beginners like ourselves up to roughly their own level of competence. So long as they did this more or less efficiently, they would be allowed to remain where they were; but they would never be promoted to *real* planes, the combat planes that we aspired to, they would never join the fleet, they would never do any fighting. Pilots in this category had a special designation—they were called Voluntary Reservists (USNR-V) rather than simply Reservists, like the rest of us. They were on the whole a complacent lot, content to fly all day and then go home to their wives and children like any bank clerk; they were easygoing and undemanding in the air, asking only that you did nothing while flying that might get them, and you, killed. You could recognize them by their expression, and by their generally unmilitary bearing.

The other kind were pilots who had been through the same program that we were in—had gone all the way through Pensacola or Corpus Christi and had been commissioned like any service pilot, and then, instead of going on to operational training and fleet duty, had been sent back to a primary base to instruct novices in Yellow Perils. These men—at least the ones I came up against—were angry and bitter; they hated their job, and the cadets they taught, and the fat, comical-looking airplanes they flew. They seemed sadistically demanding, especially in checkrides, and we feared them, without really respecting them (after all, they had never flown fighters).

Ensign Dewberry, my instructor, was USNR-V. He had a round face that always seemed to be freshly polished, and he smiled a lot, not at anything in particular, but as though he had been smiling a while ago and had forgotten to stop. When he flew he wore a flying suit that was too short in the arms and legs, so that his khaki pants and shirt sleeves stuck out at the ends. The effect was oddly temporary, as though he was only playing at flying for a minute or so, and would then revert to something more appropriate and civilian.

We met each day at the schedule board in the hangar, where flight assignments were posted. He would be standing there, with his parachute slung over one shoulder by the leg straps (something we were told we must never do), staring dreamily at the board, and when I approached and saluted he would turn, still smiling but without any sign of recognition, and say "Hi." Usually he forgot to salute. We would drift out to the flight line, and he would comment vaguely on the weather, and ask me what we were supposed to be doing on this flight.

There was no radio in the N2S, and once in the air we could communicate in one direction only, through a tube that ran from a mouthpiece attached to Dewberry's helmet, down inside the fuselage, and up to earpieces on my helmet. As I took off I could hear Dewberry humming to himself as he gawked around at the sights, like a yokel on his first five-minute ride at the state fair. Sometimes he'd point to something that had caught his eye, and looked up in the mirror above his head, and I'd nod furiously to show that I saw what he saw. It was all very amiable, but sometimes I felt that I was teaching myself to fly, while in the front seat a cheerful but simple-minded stranger nodded encouragement.

Together Dewberry and I rode through twenty-five or thirty flying hours. We began with the basic things that I thought I had already learned in the Cubs at Denton—takeoffs and landings—but now we did it differently, because this was *Navy* flying. Some of us would fly from carriers some day, and so we learned to get the plane into the air fast—no more of those long, tail-in-the-air rushes, like a galloping cow, that had been the CPT style—and we learned to land in a full stall, the tail wheel touching the ground first, so that the landing hook (if we had had one) would always catch the arresting wire (if there had been an arresting wire on the Memphis mat). Between flights, back in the barracks, T would explain how it should be done. "Puh-TOW," he would say, flapping one hand down on the other, heel-end first, "that's all you got to do, just puh-TOW!" It looked easy, but it wasn't; but after a while I could do it, and it was very satisfying to feel the plane stop flying just as you touched the mat. Puh-TOW!

Then we went on to an altogether new kind of flying—acrobatics. Acrobatic flying is a useless skill in its particulars—no combat pilot will ever need to loop or slow-roll—but it is one that extends your control of the plane and yourself, and makes extreme actions in the sky comfortable. In acrobatics the sense of flying is extended to its extreme limit; flying a plane through a loop or a Cuban-eight is the farthest thing possible from simply driving it. When you reach the top of a loop, upside-down and engine at full throttle, and tilt your head back to pick up the horizon line behind you, you are as far outside instinctive human behavior as you can go—hanging in space, the sky below you and the earth above, inscribing a circle on emptiness. And then the nose drops across the horizon, your speed increases, and the plane scoops through into normal flight, and you are back in the normal world, with the earth put back in its place. It's that going out and coming back that makes a loop so satisfying.

After a while, that is. At first it was terrifying, like being invited to a suicide that you didn't want to commit. "This is a loop," Dewberry said casually. He lowered the nose to gain airspeed and then pulled sharply up. The earth, and my stomach, fell away from me, and we were upside-down, and I could feel gravity clawing at me, pulling me out into the mile of space between me and the ground. I grabbed at the sides of the cockpit and hung on until gravity was on my side again. Of course I knew that I had a safety belt that would hold me in my seat; but my body didn't know it—*if you're upside-down in space*, my body said, *don't be a fool, hang on!*

"You seemed a little nervous that time," Dewberry said, when the plane was right-side up again. "You've got to have confidence in that seat belt or you'll never do a decent loop. So this time, when we get on top, I want you to put both arms out of the cockpit." And I did it. It was like stepping off a bridge, but I did it, and the belt held, and the plane came round. And after that I could fly a loop. It was, as I said, satisfying.

Not always, though. There was an instructor named Harris who was famous for his fondness for loops. It was said that if you could do a good loop for him you could pass any flight test, whether it was supposed to involve loops or not. He would fly you through one of his own beautifully executed maneuvers, and as he pulled out he would say through the speaking tube, with evident self-approval, "And that, cadet, is how a loop should be flown." Since the speaking tube was only one-way, the cadet couldn't reply, but he was expected to assume an expression of reverent admiration. Then he could try one himself. One day the cadet in the back seat forgot to fasten his safety belt, and at the top of the loop he fell out. Harris pulled the plane on through, and began his speech: "And that, cadet, . . ." glancing up in his mirror for the appropriate look of admiration. No cadet. He turned and flew sorrowfully back to the field, wondering how to break the news to the CO that he had dropped a student. By the time he had landed the cadet was trudging toward the hangar, carrying his opened parachute.

The next time out, Harris drew a student from my barracks called Gus. Gus was the shortest cadet in the Navy, and he flew with his seat raised all the way to the top (you could raise and lower it like a barber's chair). Harris began his favorite maneuver, first diving to pick up airspeed and then pulling up sharply. As he did so, the ratchet on the back seat slipped, and centrifugal force thrust Gus forcibly down to the bottom of the cockpit, where the seat stuck. Harris completed the loop, and once more began his routine: "And that, cadet, . . ." Meanwhile Gus was bent over, groping for the seat lever. Harris glanced at his mirror. My God! He had lost another one!

I found all acrobatic maneuvers pleasurable: the slow-roll, in which the plane is rolled around its length-wise axis; the snap-roll, a quick rotation that has a wonderful suddenness; the Immelmann, the first half of a loop with a half-roll at the top. The more things you can make a plane do, the more you are flying it; though that's not quite right—you don't make a plane roll, you coax it, ease it, fly with it through the whole maneuver. It becomes a natural series of muscular adjustments, like walking or running, but more conscious.

For some acrobatics instructors these natural movements were no longer enough; they were decadents, bored with ordinary maneuvers, only thrilled by exotic variations. They would fly a loop wrong-way-round, beginning upside-down and reaching the top right-side-up—a maneuver that put the pilot on the *outside* of the circle and forced the blood to his head, and that would tear the wings off a less sturdy plane. Or they would fly outside snap-rolls, a much more violent version of the ordinary kind. Or they would ride a falling-leaf—a sort of controlled stall that loses altitude very fast—too close to the ground, and come out with a roar just over the trees. I found all these maneuvers perverse, contrary to the nature of both planes and pilots; but I could understand why some instructors did them. The bitter ones knew that the war would be fought and finished some day and that they would still be there, in the Yellow Perils, and that we wouldn't. We would go on to fly the fighters and the bombers, to see Pacific islands and learn what combat was like, and whether we could pass the Test. But they would never know. Like most perversions, theirs was the product of despair at never knowing the real thing.

Time passed, and we began to have some feeling for the movement of the plane, some sense of the harmony that exists between a pilot's body and his machine—what pilots mean by "flying by the seat of your pants." We had come to be at ease in space, even when upside-down, and we had learned to return to the surface of the earth without anxiety and without disaster ("it ain't the air that kills you," the old-timers told us, "it's comin' back to the ground"). There was only one natural threat left—the night.

In darkness, instincts weaken. The horizon is scarcely there, up is less certainly up, and down may not be exactly down. The earth, by which daylight offers a comforting variety of possible emergency landing fields, becomes threatening at night. Darkness hides hills and trees, and swallows every flat surface. There is no hope for you down there at night, and it is reasonable that you should feel fear, flying in darkness.

I didn't know anything about that kind of fear yet when I reported for night flying at Memphis; it was just one more preliminary Test, one more way of eliminating the unworthy. The exercise was simple, Dewberry had said, anyone could do it. You simply took off between rows of lights, followed the taillight of the plane ahead of you around the traffic pattern, and landed. Then you taxied back to takeoff position and did it again. The only trouble was that you did it in the dark, and so everything had to be learned anew. The cockpit, which by day had become a familiar, secure place, at night was a black hole. Engine instruments showed only as dim greenish lines of phosphorescense; switches were invisible, and had to be found by touch. Just getting the engine started was a new and difficult process, and taxiing was a game of blindman's buff. Then you had to take off without swerving into a runway light, and find and follow the taillight ahead of you. But the night sky is full of lights, and if you chose a star instead of a taillight (and occasionally someone did), you would fly in a straight line forever, waiting for it to turn.

Darkness, which makes most of your familiar plane invisible, makes one feature dramatically visible. The exhaust stacks, which in daylight are just pipes sticking out of the right-hand side of the engine, are red mouths spitting fire at night. If you're flying in a left-hand landing pattern you'll be looking over the left side of the cockpit and won't notice the stacks; but one cadet looked over the other side, saw those streams of flames and thought his plane was on fire, and bailed out. The plane went on without him until it ran out of gas and crashed in Arkansas.

On my first night solo flight the darkness seemed immense and hostile, and the spots of light scattered across it were mysterious and uncomforting. Memphis was a dim halo that seemed to come out of the earth itself, the airport beacon winked and went dark, and the solitary lights below me seemed lonely and apart. Even the red and green running lights at my wing tips seemed separate from me, and a long way off. There were no certain distances, either on the earth or in the air, I wasn't sure where I was, and the plane was a stranger that made odd noises that it didn't make in the daylight. I was eager to be back on the ground.

Not eager to land, though; landing at night was the worst part of night flying. It was like jumping into a dark pool, when you just have to take it on faith that there's really water down there. The runway—the hard, paved comforting reality—was invisible; there were only the two rows of lights and a black space between them. As you turn into the landing approach the lights run together and form two perspective lines, and you thump down between them; but for me that last moment, when I cut the power and waited for the thump, was a moment of complete despair. My confidence as a flier fell from me, I wasn't flying the plane, I didn't know where the ground was; the plane would just have to get down on its own.

During those months in which we were learning to fly the Navy way, we were also learning what it meant to be cadets. It meant, among other things, being a segregated minority, separated both from the enlisted men and from the officers. We ranked neither above the one group (enlisted men did not salute us or address us as ''Sir,'' and they made a considerable show of their contempt for our ambiguous status) nor below the other (officers were more our elders than our betters, since we would eventually join their ranks). We were just apart. It was impossible to imagine hanging around with either an enlisted man or an officer; we hung around only with each other, lived together, ate together, flew together. I cannot recall one instant of that time when I was not with another cadet, except when I was flying solo, and occasionally when I managed to be with a girl, nor one instant when I was with an adult male who was neither a cadet nor an instructor.

Our segregation was extraordinarily complete. Even when we went on liberty we moved in cadet groups; every liberty was a party, and it was always an all-cadet party. There had naturally been no parties at preflight school. We were given no time off there and were never allowed off the grounds, and anyway we were always too tired to do anything very riotous, even if pleasure had been allowed. But now our lives were different. We had our evenings and our Saturday nights, and Memphis was a wild liberty town within easy reach. And we were recovering our energies and our sexual appetites.

A party really began in the barracks head, with the showering and the shaving lotion and the dress uniforms, everybody changing—changing his clothes and his frame of mind, thinking about drinking and girls instead of flying. It was like Saturday night in a fraternity house, I imagine, or in a college dormitory. Then the liberty bus into town, through the dejected little town of Flemington, on past the fields and the unpainted sharecroppers' shacks, and into Memphis—first the shanty town of Negro houses and finally, at the center, the white, romantic city.

The bar of the Peabody Hotel would be full of Navy uniforms, and there you might meet some friends or try to pick up an enlisted Wave. The Waves seemed safer than the civilian women, who might be whores (we remembered the admonitions of *She May Look Safe, But . . .* , the Navy's cautionary VD film), and we assumed, or pretended to assume, that because they were Waves they must be easy and experienced. There must have been Wave officers around, too, but I never met one; they wouldn't have associated with cadets, and anyway they were probably too old (I had just turned nineteen, and I was easily frightened by "older women" over twenty-one).

On an upper floor of the hotel there was a Service Club, where you could buy setups for the bottle you had bought (blended whiskey, most likely, unless you had taken a cab out into the Negro district, where liquor stores sometimes still had a bottle of Scotch on the shelf), and where you could dance with the Wave you had picked up, and try to get her drunk before you passed out yourself. Or you could wander the streets and find other places, where there was music and dancing, or go down to the other hotel, an ancient antebellum pile beside the river called the Gayoso, where there was usually a party going on in someone's room.

The parties passed in a blur of drunkenness and confusion. I am in a room with twin beds and a large number of cadets and girls. There are bottles and a bowl of melting ice-cubes on the dresser, and glasses on every table. All the glasses have been used, and have yellow dregs of drinks and cigarette butts in the bottom, but you can always empty them out the window and make another drink. A girl has locked herself in the bathroom, and her date is asking people what to do. At the window Gus is dropping paper bags of water onto passersby on the sidewalk below.

Taylor lies on a bed with a girl who is drunk, but not drunk enough to be seduced in a room full of people. She has smeared her brown leg-makeup onto the legs of his white trousers. T is sitting on the floor, backed into a corner, with an inverted wastebasket between his knees, drumming softly on it with his fingertips, and humming a jazz tune, almost inaudibly—"If you see me comin', hise yo' window high. . . ." At the door Spanish John explains to the house detective that it's all right now, and gives him some money. Then I am on the bus again, and the shacks pass in the cold half-light, and I am walking up the company street toward the barracks, trying not to stagger, and over on the airfield engines are beginning to warm up for the first morning flight.

One photograph survives from these Memphis nights. It is one of those large, glossy pictures that wandering photographers used to take in night clubs: a party picture, with a table full of bottles and drinks in the middle, and all around it people facing the camera, trying to look as though they're having a good time. The photograph has dimmed and darkened with time, so that it has a remote, underwater look, but I can still make out the faces: three rather ugly Waves, in uniform, looking hearty, as though they might burst into a sea-shanty at any minute; Spanish John, eyeing one of them hungrily; Bud, owlish and melancholy, even though he is smiling; and myself, grinning foolishly around the stem of a brand-new pipe. We are in the Creole Room of the Hotel Peabody. The Waves are going to drink more than we can afford. It will only be worth the effort and expense if they sleep with us. Why else would you spend money on a Wave? They know that, and are determined to leave us at the party's end, broke but un-screwed. Spanish John is optimistic; he believes that no girl can resist him for long. I am hopeful, but uncertain about how the act is actually performed. Bud sees it all—that we will try, that we'll fail, and that it doesn't make any difference.

There were nice girls in our lives, too. Being middle-class is more than a social station, it's a kind of destiny. A middle-class boy from Minneapolis will seek out nice middle-class girls, in Memphis or anywhere else, will take them out on middle-class dates and try to put his hand inside their middle-class underpants. And he will fail. It was all a story that had already been written.

I picked up a pretty girl who worked in a record store, and made a date with her, feeling rather wicked and dashing because I was moving so fast—a seducer at work, a carefree, careless Navy man ruining a virtuous maiden. I should have known when I called for her that I had already lost. The white frame house, the dress with the flouncy skirt, the introduction to the folks ("Don't be too late, dear")—it was all like an Andy Hardy movie. I took her to a beer cellar where there was music, and we drank and danced, and while the jukebox played "Pistol Packin' Mama" I tried to play the role of the irresistible lover. She drank her beer calmly and without apparent effects, and said over and over, "No, let's dance," patiently and without rancor, as though I were subnormal, or a child, but not dangerous.

Our courtship went on all that fall, and I grew quite fond of her, but I never came near reaching the goal that I had imagined, that first afternoon in the record shop. We didn't go off to the Gayoso, or even in the back seat of a parked car; we danced, and though I wasn't very good at that either, at least I had done it before. I suppose I had known all the time that I wouldn't make her. That's really why I went back, because I knew that she wouldn't let me reach the Test, the Big Sex Game where I would have to perform, and would know whether I was a winner or a loser.

At the same time, like everyone else, I went on writing to Alice, the girl back home, letters that I hoped were full of passion and erotic stimulation; and she wrote cheerful, but not very erotic, replies. One of the things that girls from back home did was to come and visit you. It gave you a kind of status among the other cadets if a reasonably pretty girl would make a trip just to see you, and to be paraded around. Every weekend you would see cadets, dressed in careful whites, walking awkwardly around the base showing the sights to girls in frilly dresses. And to their mothers; there were always mothers, it was a chaperoning time. So I invited Alice down from Minneapolis, and she (and her mother) came.

They stayed at the Peabody, in a double room. I had a room on the floor above. My plan of action was simple: get rid of the mother, take Alice to my room, and pass the Test. But first there were formalities. I took them both to dinner, on the roof of the hotel—the Starlit Roof, it was called. A band played, and a master of ceremonies sang and told off-color stories, which Alice's mother received with thin-lipped disapproval. We ate. And drank—not too much, though, I mustn't appear out of control, I mustn't let my lechery show. I danced with Alice, and felt her mother's eyes follow us around the floor. (Was I dancing too close? Were my intentions obvious?) I even danced with the mother, steering her stout, corsetted form like a wheelbarrow among the other dancers. At last the band played "Goodnight, Sweetheart" and the mother, who had her own sense of fair play, said she would be off to bed.

But she would stay awake until Alice came in, that was clear.

But why go on, when the rest of the story is so predictable?—how we got to my room, how we fumbled and embraced, how she would go *that* far (after all, she'd come all the way from Minneapolis, she must have had something in mind herself), but no further, how she struggled, how I pleaded and lost, and at last sullenly delivered her at her mother's door. It had all been a charade, an acting out of middle-class morals, an allegory. I represented Lust, Alice was Innocence (or maybe True Romance), and her mother was the dragon Virtue. Alice went as she had come, a good girl. "How'd you do, man?" Bud asked me when I saw him on the flight line. "Did you get into Alice's Chalice?" But he knew the answer already; her Chalice was still the Holy Grail.

As I approached the end of the training program at Memphis, I began to believe that I would make it all the way to the end—through Pensacola, to a commission, wings, a squadron, even to the ultimate Test of combat. Before, these had all been insubstantial fantasies, but now, gradually, they were becoming real and possible. And as success became imaginable, the meaning of failure also became clearer. After a check-ride the instructor would walk silently back to the scheduling board in the hangar and would enter the result with an arrow beside the student's name. An Up ↑ meant that you had passed; a Down ↓ meant failure. Maybe the symbolism had been borrowed from the Roman emporers in the Colosseum; certainly a Down seemed as final and as fatal to us as thumbs down was to a gladiator. But the symbolism had another, more obvious significance: Up pointed to the air, where we wanted to be, and Down condemned you to the earth. The more I flew, the more I wanted to go on flying, and the more terrible it seemed to fail.

When a friend did fail, it was like a death in the family. Bud, the sad-eyed ironist, washed out on acrobatics—he was just too sensible, he said, to learn to fly upside-down—and left for Great Lakes. And a Dartmouth man failed to master small-field landings and also left, though instead of Great Lakes he went to train in blimps, and even got a commission, which we all thought was all right, because he had been to Dartmouth. I was fond of them both, but when they walked out of the Station gate they left my life as totally as if they had died. And in a way they had; they weren't pilots anymore.

When I first came to Memphis it was late summer, and the fields lying eastward from the river were green. The cotton was being picked, and bits of white lay along the roadsides like blown snow. The sun was hot on the landing mat, and even high in the air it was warm. As I went through the training program, autumn came, the fields turned brown and wet, and the days grew shorter. At the end of my time there, in November, darkness fell so early that it overtook the last flight of the afternoon. It was on one of those late flights that I learned a new thing about flying—that it makes the approach of night different. It was late as I flew back from some practice solo, and the sun was nearly set, but the air was still warm and bright. The flight must have gone well, and I was feeling at ease with the plane and, in spite of the engine's steady racket, quiet and peaceful. Below me lights began to come on in houses and farms, and everything that was not a light became dark and indistinct, so that the ground was almost like a night sky. But still I flew on in sunlight. The surface of the plane seemed to absorb and hold the light and color of the sunset; brightness surrounded me. It was as though the earth had died, and I alone was left alive. A sense of my own aliveness filled me. I would never die. I would go on flying forever.

Chapter 3

I went home that fall, after I had finished the course at Memphis, to see my father. He and my stepmother had moved from Minneapolis to a grim industrial suburb of Chicago, where my father had a job in a factory that made military engines. It was shift work, and it was hard on him at his age, but it was "helping the war effort," and he was the kind of man who accepted such slogans. Maybe he had had trouble finding work; it wasn't the kind of thing we would have talked about in our family. Reticence was a primary virtue in our house, above cleanliness and godliness even.

His shift was off at four in the afternoon the day I arrived, and I walked down to the factory to meet him. I was wearing my Navy blue cadet uniform, and I thought I looked pretty good, almost like an officer. I stood near the factory gate, waiting and eyeing the stream of young girls coming out as the shift changed. Then I saw my father, his handsome, ruddy face and soft white hair tall above a circle of girl workers. They were giggling and flirting with him, and he was smiling and teasing back, in his gentle, courteous way. I waited for him, and for them, too; after all, I was nearly an officer, and in uniform. But they never turned, they just went on flirting, and finally he saw me and came over, picking his way gently among the girls, as though they were flowers he didn't want to step on.

I stayed at home for nearly a week. We talked—"had a good visit" was the family phrase—and we ate the familiar, wholesome, country-style meals, and we listened to the news. Montgomery was moving against Rommel in North Africa; the Nazis were stopped at Stalingrad; Marines were attacking in the Solomons. My father listened in strict, attentive silence, as though the broadcast were a sermon, and I knew that he was wondering where the war would be when I got to it, and that further back in his mind, too far back really to be a thought, was the question of whether I would be killed.

On the last day, my stepmother took a photograph of my father and me standing together in the front yard. I look self-conscious and a little vain in my uniform; my father looks proud but ill-at-ease, as though he is wearing the wrong clothes for a formal occasion, and knows it. Then I caught the train back south.

For many of us, Pensacola was the first experience of a living past. Bonesteel has no history, and Minneapolis hasn't much. We had lived our lives in a floating present, where nothing was very old, nothing expressed past values or recalled past events, and achievement was what you did today. In our brief Navy lives we had moved through a series of hastily improvised installations—a state teachers' college in Texas, a women's dormitory at the University of Georgia, and the raw and ugly Air Station at Memphis. None of these places had had any dignity or any feeling of tradition. They were makeshift, and we regarded them all with disappointment and distrust. Perhaps the resistance that most of us felt to becoming entirely absorbed in Navy life was partly a feeling that we would be joining this makeshift Navy, a system as temporary and ugly as the towns most of us came from.

And then we came to Pensacola, and there was the Navy's past: old buildings—a round powder-magazine that had served naval vessels a century before, and rows of sedately beautiful old houses where the senior officers lived—old, moss-stained walls, old live oaks hung with Spanish moss. The Naval Station had been there a long time. This, I thought, is what tradition means. The past is all around me; the Civil War was fought from here, the first Navy fliers learned to fly here. The atmosphere of the place made the Navy seem as permanent and as value-filled as a national church, or a parliament. At nineteen I didn't analyze or debate the values of military tradition and elitism; I simply surrendered to the tranquility of the Station.

I suppose there is another, even simpler explanation of my response. I was a midwestern boy, coming in November to the Gulf Coast, where the sun shone on the bay, and palm trees lined the Station streets, and the earth was sandy and warm under the feet. Some of the serenity of my image of Pensacola comes from the fact that in memory it is always warm and soaked in sunlight, and there is always the flash and sparkle of light on water. Pensacola was a place that seemed to promise a warm civility, a life that would be happier than it was in my Middle West.

And I was happy there. I was doing what I liked to do—

flying—with young men who became my friends. I had no responsibilities, except to fly and to study flying. No one was dependent on me, and I was dependent on no one. A hostile definition of the military life is that in it everything that is not required is forbidden. But there is another way of putting it. At Pensacola everything that I had to do, I wanted to do, and there was nothing I wanted to do that I couldn't do. It was a simple, preadult state in which we were suspended, but while it lasted it was joyous; like childhood, it remains in the memory as a good, uncomplicated time.

I reported first to the old Main Station, "Main Side," driving in a cab from the town railroad depot along a causeway over the lagoon (the image of bright water comes first from that drive), past the Main Side airfield, with its old-fashioned circular landing mat, and into the Station. Planes took off and landed at the field, and there were always planes in the air, but they didn't disturb the serenity of the Station; their engines were only a background humming, like bees in the warm sunlight. Sailors and officers and cadets walked or marched along the streets, and jeeps and trucks passed; but there seemed room enough to absorb them all, and the effect remained of a quiet, spacious place.

When I checked in at the Transient Quarters, some of my friends were already there: Joe and Wally had settled into the next room, Ike was down the hall, T came in as I unpacked. I felt a pleasure that was also a kind of relief at being back with them. To be with my father, and to feel that strong, steady flow of inarticulate love, was painful; I didn't know what to do with it, and I felt restless and clumsy and resentful. But these young pilots were my *real* family. I was easy with them, we understood each other, they didn't *want* anything.

We shared the Transient Quarters barracks with graduating cadets who were waiting there to be commissioned. And so we saw the rewards—the new uniforms, the wings, the gold bars, all those symbols of the success we aspired to—before we met the obstacles. If this was the Navy's conscious strategy, it was a clever one. The graduates looked much like us; they walked, talked, drank, and played poker like anyone else; but they were different, touched somehow by their achievement. They had made it, they were really naval aviators. We gaped and envied and were condescended to; we listened to their stories and asked respectful questions. But, inside, each of us was thinking: *He's nothing special. I can do it if he did.* We knew at the beginning that there would be no challenges at Pensacola that we couldn't meet.

After a few days we moved out of Main Side to an outlying training field, and out of that remembered sunlight into winter rain. Whiting Field was a new field, a few miles inland from Pensacola, and very different from the Main Station. It had been built, in obvious haste, in the middle of bleak pine woods, near a sad little town called Milton—the kind of southern town where the telephone switchboard is in somebody's bedroom, and the post office is in the general store. It was a town nobody stopped in—why should you? There was nothing there that could possibly be regarded as interesting. It simply existed there at the entrance to the Station to remind us of where we were—not at Pensacola, on the Gulf of Mexico, in the sunlight, but in a Florida piny woods, in the winter, in the rain. Milton existed, T said, for only one purpose: to make sure that the cadets of Whiting Field were always depressed.

Whiting itself had its own kind of depression. It was as temporary-looking as Memphis had been, but whereas Memphis had seemed threatening and prisonlike in its bare ugliness, Whiting was only melancholy. Being new, it was unfinished in all but the meagerest essentials; the buildings were full of the resinous smell of unfinished pine boards, and the interiors were unpainted. The same pine wood stood all around outside, too; the view in every direction ended in a wall of thin, dejected-looking trees. Whatever on the Station had not been paved was still raw earth, and since the winter rains began as we arrived, and continued (or so it seemed) all the time we were there, we lived in mud—red, glutinous mud. We marched through mud to meals, and straggled through mud to the flight line. We followed mud paths to the Slop Chute, and came back, precariously drunk, along those paths in the dripping dark. Mud entered the barracks and the hangars, and even the cockpits of planes. I remember Whiting as a landscape as boring as the time I spent there: gray cloud above, wet red earth below, and between, endless and identical, the impoverished black pines.

At Whiting I learned to fly by instruments, in SNV's, training planes that were neither honest antiques like the N2S's, nor honestly modern like the planes we went on to, but in-between, low-winged, with cockpits that closed, but with fixed landing gear and a shuddering, whining engine—transitional trainers, and like everything else in the world that can be called transitional, profoundly unsatisfactory. They were called Vultee Vibrators, and I never met anyone who enjoyed flying in them.

On an instrument hop you take off with an instructor,

climb a bit, and go "under the hood." A canvas curtain is drawn between you and the world outside, cutting off all sight of earth and air, and leaving you with only the inscrutable, indifferent instruments to look at. You learn how to tell the altitude of the plane by the indicators before you—airspeed, turn-and-bank, altimeter, artificial horizon—and to fly by referring to them instead of to the horizon, as you naturally do in flight. But you don't learn to trust the instruments, because they contradict the information that your own body gives you. Without the testimony of the horizon line, and the solid and visible earth, the exact location of up and down becomes uncertain. Your body says you are leaning, but the turn-and-bank says you are upright. Your body is wrong, and the instrument is right, but it is difficult, perhaps really impossible, to remove the body's message from your mind. If you could do that, you'd separate the mind's experience from the body's in a way that would be psychologically very disturbing. What you learn to do is to suppress the body's version of your attitude, and base your actions on the instruments, and that is what we did, hour after hour, out there above the piny woods. We learned to fly the plane in intricate patterns, at set altitudes; we learned to fly radio-ranges, and to make a landing approach without seeing the field we were approaching; and we learned how to get out of trouble, when the body's bad advice had got us into it.

Trouble, on instruments, is not knowing what you are doing in relation to the earth—how high you are, which way the earth is, what attitude the plane is in. You can get into this kind of trouble very easily in clouds, or in a storm, or at night—any time when the earth is hidden from you—and it will very quickly kill you, spinning you out of the bottom of a cloud, flying you into a hill that you thought was below you or somewhere else, tearing at the plane so violently that it will break. And so we were trained in a new necessary kind of fear, called "Unusual Attitudes." In this exercise the instructor puts you under the hood and then pulls the plane through one violent maneuver after another, while you snap and jerk around the back cockpit like dice in a box, and then says into your earphones: "O.K., cadet, it's all yours." Are you turning or level? Diving or climbing? Right-side-up or inverted? Your senses are so disturbed by the shaking that you don't know, and you must remake your own equilibrium by reading the instruments and doing what they tell you to do. Like all instrument flying, Unusual Attitudes was unnatural, a violation of your reasonable assumption that the ground will always be below your feet, that the earth, at least, can be trusted. But because the exercise was violent and extreme, it made the unnaturalness especially intense, something that took place in the pit of the stomach; it was a nightmare of insecurity, in which earth and air fell, spun, would not stay in place, and in which you were left, blind and alone in chaotic space, to make your world orderly again.

Instrument flying is one kind of flying that can be simulated. In the Link Trainer, a mechanical cockpit with all the instruments and controls of an airplane, you can do anything that a plane can do except take off and crash. At Whiting we spent hours in the Link building, hooded in these nonplanes, struggling with airspeed and direction and altitude, while alongside on glass-topped tables, mechanical crabs traced out our errors and instructors recorded these as passes or failures. It didn't feel like flying—there is no machine that can simulate the flow of air over control surfaces, or the sound of the wind, or the way the stick feels—and it never touched any emotion except anger, and maybe boredom. I remember waiting outside one of the Links while inside, under the hood, Taylor fought the machine, jerking it about as though he would wrestle it into doing what it was supposed to do. The instructor watched his instruments impassively, and finally picked up his microphone: "Cadet," he said, "you are now two thousand feet underground."

The Link might be boring, but there was one machine in that building that was exciting—the Simulated Aerial Combat Machine was like a booth at a fun-fair. It was set up in a room of its own, a cavernous, shadowy chamber like a movie theater. At one end was an elaborate mockup of a fighter plane's cockpit, with a windshield, a gunsight, and all the flight controls. At the other end was a screen, on which films of attacking enemy planes were projected. As you moved the controls of the mock-fighter, the enemy planes moved on the screen, until you got one in your gunsight and squeezed your trigger. All this was accompanied by very satisfying, realistic sound effects— the diving, screaming planes and the chatter of the guns when you fired—and it was impossible not to be drawn into the excitement of the game, not to fly at those twisting images with a hot determination that turned them into realities, and the sound track into bullets. Then it was over, and the house lights went up, and you were left with a score—the number of unbullets that you had fired into the enemy unplanes. The Simulated Aerial Combat Machine was a marvelous, elaborate American game. It made the business of shooting men out of the sky seem a harmless game of skill, something you might do in a pinball palace to pass the time, and win a Kewpie doll.

I learned one other thing at Whiting that had nothing to do with instruments or flying. It was a lesson in the hostilities of ordinary people. Ted Williams, the baseball player, was a cadet in instrument training then. We all knew who he was; we had read the sports pages, and followed the batting averages, like other boys our age. I remembered him from Minneapolis, when he played AAA ball for the Millers before the war; others knew him as a home-run hitter for Boston. He was our first celebrity. He didn't want to be that; he clearly wanted to be just another cadet and to live a military life of perfect ordinariness, but there he was, in the next barracks room or on the flight line, a tall thin guy in a flight jacket, one of us. We all wrote home that we were flying with Ted Williams, and felt a little more important because of him, even if we never spoke to him (I never did).

An interviewer from a Boston paper came to Whiting to interview Williams, and got from him the quite reasonable statement that he wanted to be a fighter pilot, and a story of some small flying mistake—he hadn't lowered his flaps for a landing, something like that. When the piece appeared in the Boston paper, it carried the headline "Teddy Wants a Zero," and reported his "close brush with death." Somehow a copy of the article reached Whiting—I suppose one of those proud parents in Boston, somebody whose son was flying with Ted Williams, sent it—and was stuck up on the mess hall bulletin board. That evening, when Williams entered the mess hall for supper, a chant began: "Teddy wants a Zero, Teddy wants a Zero," on and on, louder and louder, until Williams left his food uneaten and stalked angrily out.

It wasn't his fault, and we all must have known that it wasn't. Sports writers did things like that to decent athletes. What were we punishing him for, then? For being famous? For having an existence out there, outside the Navy? Or simply for being somebody, a person with an identity, when we were all kids, just ciphers?

Though the rain fell, we took our hours of liberty, and went damply into Pensacola, in raincoats and condom-type covers. Pensacola was a small southern town that tried to look Spanish. It had the railroad tracks running through the middle of town, the dejected-looking stores with their wooden awnings over the sidewalk, the black ghetto that you would see in any Alabama or Mississippi town of that size; but it also had a sort of plaza, or maybe it was a boulevard, where the architecture was white stucco and red tile, and there were rows of damp, spindly palm trees. It was also a Navy town, the first I had seen—a place packed with sailors, every other store a uniform tailor, and the ones in-between bars, with a few taxis to drive drunks back to the Station, and a hotel with a whore for the sexually necessitous.

I knew only one cadet who ever patronized the hotel whore. He was an earnest, business-like person from Brooklyn named Green, who went to the whore in a business-like way, as he might have gone to a dentist. He was also the kind of guy who came back to the barracks at Whiting and told us about it. The whore, he said, was busy; it was Saturday night, and the bellhop who provided her customers could bring them up as fast as she could deal with them. When Green walked into her room, she fell on her back almost before the bellhop had closed the door, and lay there waiting, like a side of beef waiting for the butcher. Green prepared himself carefully; he was entering where hundreds had gone before him, and he didn't want to spoil his Navy career with a dose. Once he had mounted her, he was determined to stay; he had paid his five dollars, and he wanted his money's worth. So he hung on for all he was worth, thinking of the cash value of what he was getting in dollars-per-minute, making it last. The whore grew impatient, tried her erotic skills, such as they were, heaved and groaned, but Green rode on. She lost her temper, cursed and raged: "Come on, damn you, *come!* You're costing me money!" But Green was unmoved, until in his head a meter clicked over at $5.00. Then he withdrew, in a dignified way, he said, leaving the whore exhausted and defeated.

We all professed to be amused, but I think the episode, and Green's triumphant telling of it, as though it had been a clever business deal, struck most of us as gross and ugly—the sort of thing you might expect of a guy from New York, who had gone to CCNY and wore a lavender sweatshirt. We were puritans; it didn't matter where we had come from, the whole country between the two coasts shared that tradition of severity, work, and repression. Certainly middle westerners and southerners were alike in taking sex and liquor as two forms of sinfulness, to be indulged in, usually at the same time, and to be punished for, but not to be taken lightly, and certainly not as a business deal with a whore. We probably all wanted sex as much as Green did, but we wanted it in the form of seduction, or true love (which was another name for the same thing), with plenty of emotion, and a lot of guilt afterward. Green had shaken our romanticism as well as our puritanism.

There were, of course, exceptions, cadets who had somehow escaped our puritanical rearing—like Spanish John, whose working-class industrial town in New Jersey was a different world—young men who had had girls early and easily, and whose lives seemed to the rest of us vivid and depraved. We heard their stories of callous seductions restlessly, but with helpless fascination. There was a cadet who, when a girl wrote to him that she was pregnant, and would kill herself if he didn't marry her, replied that Yes, that would probably be the best thing to do. When he heard from her again a few weeks later, he was very annoyed: "That bitch," he complained, "she didn't kill herself!" We all knew that, in that situation, each of us would have married her and ruined our lives. For the Navy forbade cadets to marry, and anyone who did and was found out was washed out of flight training and sent to Great Lakes, to become—most ignominious of conditions—a married enlisted man. So the cold-blooded seducers and the Greens seemed free, in a way that we could never be— free of the consequences of their sexual needs.

Sometimes hometown girls came to visit at Pensacola, as they had at Memphis, and stayed at the whore's hotel, and sometimes they were conquered there, by drink and the sentimentality of wartime, or perhaps by the atmosphere of continuous fornication, and went away pregnant, and then the frightened cadet would go home on leave and arrange a back-street abortion. Even the few cadets who were secretly married were afraid of having a child, afraid that somehow the Navy would discover it and would throw the father out of flight school, and so even legitimately conceived babies were aborted, to save the father's flying career. A Good Ol' Boy I knew from Birmingham did that, took his young wife to a Negro woman with a knitting needle, and then had to return to Pensacola while she nearly died of infection, back home.

If you were afraid of whores, and had no girl, you could

take a bus to Mobile, and there pick up country girls who had come to the city to work in the shipyards, and were careless with their favors. You met them in Constitution Square, an agreeably old-fashioned place then, with its elegant old hotel and its rows of canopied shops. The girls would be walking, two or three together, around the square, looking into the shop windows and chattering in their up-country voices, or simply standing under the street lights, like torch singers about to break into "My Man."

Your approach didn't have to be polished; you simply invited a couple of them to have a drink. After the drink you'd find a cab, and ride out into the anonymous small streets of Mobile, to the girls' apartment—it would be two rooms in the cellar of an old house, or the back half of a bungalow that you entered from the alley, or rooms above a store. The cabdriver would overcharge you because you were drunk, and then you'd be alone in the dark, wondering if you had a rubber, worrying about the clap, while in the other room some friend was fumbling with the other girl, indistinguishable from yours.

That's how it happened, the Big Test, as casually as that. I guess I passed it, in the sense that I was able to perform; but I couldn't have given that girl much pleasure, and I certainly felt none myself. I don't remember her name or her face—I probably had forgotten both the next morning—or what she said or what I said. I only remember the room—a sun porch at the back of the house, shut off from the next room by double glass doors that were covered by curtains, a room so small that a bed filled it, and the girl fell back on it as soon as we entered, and lay there silently in the dark. What did she feel? Hope? Curiosity? Boredom? Despair? I don't know, she was scarcely there for me; I only know what I felt—a kind of numb fatalism, that it was too late now to change my mind.

I could hear my friend in the other room, and I suppose he could hear us, and afterward we were both embarrassed, though the girls weren't, and we joked too much and said good-bye hastily, and were back in the drab street, empty at 2 A.M., no cabs anywhere then, walking back toward the square, sober and depressed. For the next couple of weeks we were anxious, too, nervously watching for the signs of infection that we had seen in the VD movies. It had all been necessary, we all agreed on that, you had to have girls, it was something important, like a part of our training; but I had found less pleasure in it than I did in flying, and I wasn't any good at it, and I think this was true of most of my ignorant friends, too.

Memories of those liberty nights have faded. I don't remember the girls of Mobile, and the nights have run together into one montage of drunkenness, fumbling, and the loneliness of late streets. But I remember standing in a barracks room back at the Main Station, with instrument school finished and the last stage of training about to begin, and hearing someone say, "Smith got killed yesterday." It wasn't, of course, Smith—I've forgotten what his name was—but I knew him. He had been with me at Memphis, and I could picture his face and recall his voice; he was an actual person out of my life. Somewhere in the building someone was playing a piano, and the sound of the music is a part of the story as I remember it: how he had been dogfighting with another student pilot, each maneuvering his plane to get behind and below the other, as fighters would do in actual combat, and how the planes had collided, and one pilot had bailed out, but the other had been caught in his spinning plane.

The reality of death comes to you in stages. First it is an idea—all men are mortal, as in the syllogism. Then it is something that happens to strangers, then to persons you know, but somewhere else, and at last it enters your presence, and you see death, on a runway or in a field, in a cloud of dust and a column of smoke. Though even that doesn't make your own death conceivable. There were times when I was afraid in a plane, when I knew I was in trouble, but I never believed that I would die *then*—it was always something that would happen later. But after that moment in the barracks while the piano played I realized that some of the men I knew would die, that they would be killed by planes, by bad luck, by their own errors. At that moment the life of flying changed.

Pilots are always fascinated by accidents. Any sound of a plane in trouble, a sudden change in an engine's note, a cough or a burst of power or a silence, will bring a whole ready room to the windows. There was a French cadet at Whiting who sat every day in the ready room in total silence. No one had ever heard him speak a word, and we only knew he was with the Free French because he wore an enormous beret with a red pom-pom. One day a plane taking off made an odd, whining sound, and the Frenchman rushed to the window. "Aarrh," he exclaimed, "I thought he was takeeng off in high peetch!" Then he returned to his French silence.

Any story of a crash was listened to avidly, as though it were scandalous gossip, and accident reports were read like novels. The Navy in those days published a monthly magazine that contained accounts, sometimes with photographs, of the month's accidents in Naval aircraft, and we all turned to those pages first. What were we looking for? Some sort of magic, perhaps, by which we might avert disaster by experiencing it vicariously? Or the reassuring feeling that this was one accident that had already happened, and to somebody else? Or did we look for reasons to believe that the difference between those pilots who had accidents and the rest of us who didn't were absolute—differences of intelligence or skill or luck that would protect us? Most of the reported accidents were caused by pilot error, as most flying accidents always have been; and it was clear, from those reports, that most of us could stay alive, at least until we got into combat, simply by not being dumb.

The military life doesn't offer a man many real choices, but at this point in our training the Navy offered two: What kind of planes do you want to fly? And do you want to fly with the Navy or with the Marines? The first choice was easy, or seemed so to the cadets I knew best: to choose any course except single-engined planes—the route to fighters and dive-bombers—would have seemed cautious, unromantic, almost middle-aged, like wearing your rubbers or voting Republican. The second choice was only difficult if you thought about it: if you surrendered to your impulse, you at once chose the Marines. Marines were tough, romantic, and elitist; virtually all Marine officers got into combat, and though they were supposed to be officers and gentlemen, they were, in our minds, fighting men first. I don't think most of us really saw ourselves as fighting men, but it was tempting to think that other people might if we wore the right uniform. For me it seemed a good way of fighting my father's war in his style; he'd like having a son in the Marine Corps. My closest friends—Joe, Wally, T, Rock, Taylor—all made the same choice. We were sent to finish our training at Bronson

Field, an outlying field west of Pensacola, near the Alabama line, where cadets were turned into Marine fighter and dive-bomber pilots.

Like the Air Station at Memphis, Bronson Field had been built on the site of an old southern farm. The road to it, off the highway, was like a farm road, between a pine wood and a pasture, and the field itself had a quiet, sun-baked rural feeling, even with the planes. The farm buildings were gone, and only one reminder of the old life remained; on the other side of the field, out by the gunnery butts, there was a little family graveyard—just six or eight graves, weed-grown and untended, with a wrought-iron fence around them. The graveyard provided instructors with a tired joke, and occasionally it seemed a bit macabre, there at the end of a runway; but most of the time I liked it being there, untouched by our busyness, a continual silent recitation of private human history.

Perhaps it was that we had made the same choice of duty, and held a future in common, or perhaps it was simply the natural selection of like-minded young men; whatever it was, the move to Bronson was the beginning of an intimacy among us so close that I find it difficult to put a name to it. For this final training cadets were divided up into six-man flights, and T and Rock and Taylor and I were all in the same one. We flew together, we took our check-rides together, and we went to ground school together. We shared our barracks rooms, and when we went on liberty we went together. We were responsible for each other—to see that the others got up in the morning and got to meals, that they came back from liberty, that no one missed a flight. We wanted our flight to finish the course with a perfect record—no Downs on check-rides, no flying missed. If we did, we would be allowed to fly together to New Orleans ("the birthplace of Louis Armstrong," T said reverently). But it was more than that; we wanted our record to be perfect, because the flight itself, the way we felt about each other when we flew together, seemed perfect. So we worried about each other, and even Taylor, the wildly irresponsible Taylor, would turn up to rouse us if the weather changed. I remember waking on a morning that should have been rainy to find him standing in the center of my room shouting, "Come on, you guys, it's blue as shit out there!"

When the time came to buy our officers' uniforms we went together to the expensive, dishonest uniform shops of Pensacola, and there we bought greens and tans and trench coats, all said to be tailor-made but in fact mass-produced in New York. When we got them back to Bronson we immediately dressed up for each other; there was no point in pretending to be modest, we all felt exactly the same extravagant pride in what we were about to become. For the moment, in that barracks room in our ill-fitting new uniforms, we felt transformed—elegant, romantic, elite; surely when we were at last made officers, and put on these clothes for good, we would be changed as completely as our uniforms changed, we would be different people, we would be adults. It was like the feeling I had when I was a child, of what it would be like to become twenty-one. It would be like walking through a door, and closing it behind you.

We went on liberty together, and drank and pursued girls, abetted each other's attempts at seduction and helped each other home when we got drunk. It was all a collective activity, like formation flying. After one trip to Mobile I developed the symptoms of gonorrhea, and the whole flight was worried, not about my health ("Shit, man," Taylor assured me, "a dose of the clap ain't half as bad as piles") but about the flight. "If you turn yourself in," T said, "they'll ground you, and what'll *we* do?" The flight was a unit, and it couldn't function as a flight with one member in the clap shack. But if I didn't turn myself in I would become sterile, blind, palsied, and insane, like the guys in the VD movies. I reported to the sick bay, and was grounded as T had predicted, and lay in my bunk for a whole day, sweaty with fear, while I waited for the results of the test. I didn't sleep, I didn't read, I just lay there. I would be dropped from the flight program—that was clear. What would I tell my father? I would be sent to Great Lakes. I thought about the outer darkness into which I would be hurled—the strangeness, the statusless obscurity, the boredom of being an ordinary seaman. In flight school I belonged—to the world of fliers, and to my flight; I knew what to do there, I lived in an agreeable, entirely familiar world. But out in the drab world of enlisted men I would be a stranger, a nobody, ignorant and alone, and, worst of all, grounded.

But it wasn't the clap, after all. The doctor said it was only overexertion, and he advised me to stay out of Mobile for a while. That night I bought beer for the flight at the Slop Chute, and T explained to the other cadets that I had just passed through a medical crisis.

At Bronson we flew SNJ's—training planes that were like real combat planes, but slower, smaller, and safer. They had, most importantly, retractable landing gear. When a plane takes off and the wheels come up, it has cast off its connection with the earth and become adapted to the air (birds do the same thing with their legs). The pilot can't see that the wheels are up, but knowing it makes a difference. The SNJ also had a closed cockpit, like a fighter, and it could be mounted with a machine gun, and could carry toy-like practice bombs. It could execute any maneuver that a fighter could, and it was an excellent acrobatic plane. Because it had a variable-pitch propeller, it even sounded like a fighter—it took off with a whine that faded in the air to a sort of stammering whisper—wh–wh–wh–wh. Flying SNJ's was like trying on officers' uniforms; it made us feel almost like adults.

The sudden Gulf Coast spring came as we began to fly from Bronson. Wisteria bloomed on the houses in the little towns, and the air was soft. We seem, in memory, always to have been high in a sky of tropical blueness, with perhaps some bright fair-weather clouds below us. We are making gunnery runs on a towed sleeve, or diving on a target at the edge of the sea, or we are tail-chasing, playing like children or birds, up the sides of tall clouds that are blinding-white in the sunlight. I remember flying alone among cumulus clouds on a fine day, and hearing two of the Mexican students who also trained at Pensacola talking on the radio, one calling, "Hey, Cisco, where are you?" and Cisco: "I'm over here, behind thees leetle cloud. Come chase me." It was all like that, like play, *Come chase me;* it was games, and we were children. Gunnery and bombing were only follow-the-leader; you kept score, and somebody won and somebody lost, but nobody got hurt.

In gunnery practice one member of the flight takes off towing a canvas sleeve at the end of a long cable. The rest follow him to a proper altitude, and make attacks on the sleeve as though it were an enemy plane. A gunnery run is a beautiful gesture, as graceful as a ballet movement— a long descending S-curve from a position above and to the side of the target that brings you into position, and ends in a burst of firing. As plane after plane repeats it, it seems choreographed, symmetrical, aesthetically perfect.

To the pilot in the towplane, the experience is not quite so aesthetic, though. He can see the planes entering their runs, can hear their guns and see the tracers' tracks. And when an attacker gets too intent on the target, and slides round behind the sleeve, the towpilot can feel the tracers reaching for his own plane, and his own vulnerable flesh. And it's his own friends who are back there, taking shots. I remember the voice of Taylor, plaintively: "Hey you guys, stop shootin' up mah ass!"

Bombing was another kind of game, a sport rather like throwing darts—the same target of concentric rings, the same scoring according to how close you came to the bull's-eye. You approached the target in a steep glide, weight thrown forward against your seat belt, the plane bucking as it accelerated, wind screaming a higher note, earth rising toward you. As you dived you had to bring the target into your bombsight, jerking the plane over with stick and rudder, holding it for an instant to drop your bomb, and then pulling up in a steep bank to look back and see the puff of smoke that showed where the bomb had hit. The dive was like taking a dare, and the pullout was safety, the dare taken, the Test passed.

That spring at Bronson was full of games; flying, together or alone, we seemed possessors of the empty, golden air. But the emptiness wasn't always joyous. Once, flying alone, I wandered above a bank of cloud, and learned how it feels to be separated completely from the earth, how anonymous and signless clouds are, and how uncomforting the sun is when it shines down on unbroken, trackless whiteness. This kind of experience, of separation from the comfortable and the familiar, is a part of the price of flying. The pilot has to accept the stretches of loneliness and isolation, when the earth is erased by cloud or darkness, or is facelessly strange or hostile, when his will to fly has thrust him into void space.

I felt this separation most intensely on the navigation flights that were a part of the final training program. First we flew, in flights of three planes, out over the Gulf on a triangular course that, if we were proper navigators, would return us precisely to the field. Since there were other planes involved, this was not really a separating experience, though it did offer one new kind of feeling that was disquieting—the feeling you get when the last bit of land disappears behind you, of the shapelessness and endlessness of space. Below you is the flat and uninformative sea; all around you the air extends its emptiness. Why go one way rather than another, when it is all the same, and goes on forever? People have committed suicide by flying straight out to sea, and I can understand that it could have a right feeling, that it would be a gesture that would express the feeling of suicide, as well as a way of dying.

The other navigation flight was flown alone, and overland. This time, too, the pattern was a triangle—inland to one town, across to another, and back. No doubt the solitariness was a part of the flight's strange feeling, but it was more than that. I was flying over the pine woods of Florida and south Alabama, a surface that stretched unbroken to the horizon, as flat and featureless as the sea. The Gulf behind me became what the land had been before, a friendly and familiar landmark. When I lost sight of it I felt as though I had flown out of measurable space into the boredom of infinity.

I could see the shadow of my plane sliding along below me on the tops of the trees, and its insubstantial, steady movement seemed a part of the emptiness. Occasionally a railroad track appeared, making a diagonal mark across the pines; but railroads are as identical as pine trees, and it did nothing to alter my mood. I checked the calculations on my plotting board, and I watched the clock on the instrument panel, and at the predicted time the right town appeared, an island of tin roofs and a water tower floating in the sea of pine trees. But I could feel no necessity in that appearance; it might as well have been some other town, or no town at all. I turned, found the second landmark, and headed south. When I could see the Gulf once more beyond the trees I felt that I was reentering the real, distinguishable world.

At the end of our training we came again to that other kind of unreality, night flying. It was even more alarming at Bronson Field than it had been at Memphis, because we took off over the Gulf, and so had no comfortable human lights below us, but only a darkness more absolute and bottomless than the sky. A few lights—a town, scattered farms, a car on a road—would have given some sense of depth, of where the earth was; but in that blind blackness the earth seemed to have fallen away, and left below me the other side of the sky.

Our instructions were to leave the traffic pattern and fly away from the field, into the outer training space called simply "the area," and then to return, reenter the pattern, and land. I flew cautiously out over what I thought must be the south end of Alabama—though it was alien and unidentifiable—and when enough time had passed, turned back toward the flashing beacon that was home. But nothing looked the same, the approach was different at night, none of the usual landmarks were helpful, and I reached the field in a state of disorientation and uncertainty. But it was the field, all right, and I swung round the pattern and began my landing approach. Lights seemed to flash from all directions, and the radio sputtered bursts of hysterical static in my ears, but I couldn't understand what was said because of a horn that was blowing somewhere behind my head. Then I touched down—not with a bounce and a roll, but with a screaming, scraping cry of anguished metal that ended suddenly as the plane stopped. Then there was only the horn blowing, and the siren of the crash-truck approaching. I had landed wheels-up. The horn I had heard was the warning horn, which blew if you cut off power before you lowered your wheels, the lights were signal lights from the tower, the radio hysterics had all been for me. But I had simply concentrated them all out of my consciousness, and I had wrecked my first plane.

The consequences were complex, but not particularly unpleasant. By a curious piece of official reasoning it was decided that I had not failed the flight, since my task had been to leave and reenter the pattern, and I had done that quite satisfactorily; so there was no downward-pointing arrow on the flight-board, and our flight still had a perfect record at Bronson, and would get the cross-country flight to New Orleans. But if I didn't get a Down, what was to be done with me? Clearly the Navy couldn't simply ignore that wrecked plane. I was sent to a Navy psychiatrist.

The psychiatrist was a disappointment. I had been reading Freud, evenings in the barracks, and I knew what to expect: a beard, a German accent, and a lot of questions about sex and dreams. But this one looked like a farmer and talked like a Georgia cracker. He peered at me gloomily through his gold-rimmed spectacles for what seemed to me a long time, and then said: "Cadet, Ah don't want to know why you didn't put your wheels down. Ah want

78

to know why all those other guys *did*." I had no answer; it seemed unreasonable to me, the way the whole night-flying system was arranged, that anybody should have thought to lower his wheels, ever, and I said so. The psychiatrist brooded over that for a while. "But it works for everybody but you." I had to admit that that seemed to be so.

"If Ah was to make a report on you," he said at last, "you know what would happen—Great Lakes, and the night run to Murmansk." I tried to imagine that fate. "Cain't do that." He looked up and smiled. "Mah professional advice to you, cadet, is—put your goddamn wheels down. Dismissed."

There was nothing very memorable about the flight to New Orleans—we simply flew over, landed and looked around for a while, and flew back. But it felt memorable. We were flying *to* somewhere, and this was the first time any of us had ever done that. Up until now, the planes we flew had not been vehicles for transportation, we had never gotten anywhere in them, except back where we started. There was always the invisible elastic, one end attached to the plane, the other firmly fastened at the field; and though you could stretch it out for an hour, it then snapped you back and landed you where you had begun. But now we were in transit, flying from Florida, first over Alabama and then Mississippi, and landing in Louisiana. Mobile Bay, and then Mobile passed below us, Biloxi was off to our left, the coastline curved away to the south, and then we could see Lake Pontchartrain, and the Naval Air Station, New Orleans.

The other thing I felt during that flight was how large and empty the air is, away from a flying field. We didn't see another plane after we left Pensacola, and our little flight of four seemed tiny and vulnerable in all that space. If a plane slid away from the formation, it immediately became very small, a speck you could lose if you took your eyes from it. I thought for the first time of what it would be like to be flying like that, so separate and exposed, out where the war was, where the speck at the far end of a vision might be a Jap fighter. Vaster and emptier than the widest prairie, the air offered no place to hide, nowhere to run to. But our air remained empty, and as we returned the elastic began to pull once more. We were reentering the familiar: Mobile Bay appeared, Perdido Bay was just ahead, we began to respond to habit, wheels went down, and we swung in a stretched-out file around Bronson and landed.

It was our last flight as cadets, and I climbed down from my plane a little sadly, and stood for a moment, looking at the place where I had found such content. High up, over the field, two planes were dogfighting; at that distance it seemed a desultory, leisurely activity, a kind of slow-motion dance in the air. Across the field, beyond the graveyard, cadets were firing machine guns into the butts, making an irregular crackling sound. Everything seemed warm and comfortable in the sun, and everybody seemed happy. "Come on," Taylor said, "I'll buy you a fuckin' beer. To celebrate." I wasn't sure a celebration was the right thing for that moment, but I picked up my parachute and walked back with him across the mat toward the hangar. We might as well have a beer.

Chapter 4

After the ambiguous life of a cadet, the life of an officer promised to be simple: money, status, and freedom would be ours, the high living come at last. An officer could marry and move off the Station, or he could live in Bachelor Officers' Quarters, where black servants would make his bed and clean up after him. He could give orders to enlisted men, and he could drink in the Officers' Club. Enlisted men would salute him. And women—women would fall on their backs before him, stunned by his golden glory. We left Bronson and moved back to Main Side for the last time in a state of dazed expectation, and when the day came we dressed in our new green uniforms, pinned on the bars and the wings, and marched off to be transformed.

The commissioning ceremony at Main Side was more like a high-school commencement than seemed quite right, everyone dressed up in unfamiliar costumes, and the Commanding Officer like the high-school principal, making a speech about duty, and handing out diplomas and shaking hands. One striking difference, though, was that Tyrone Power, the movie actor, was in this class—he had been training in multiengined planes while we were training for fighters—and so there were photographers and reporters around, but not for us. "Shit," Rock said angrily, "I can fly better than him. Take *my* picture, you bastards!"

We felt a little superfluous until the ceremony was over; our new glory had been diminished before we got it. We walked together back to the barracks, Rock and Taylor and T and I, and enlisted men saluted us along the way, and I felt embarrassed, saluting back, as though I had been caught doing in earnest what we had played at, back at Bronson. It still seemed like a game, that diploma and handshaking hadn't changed anything. No door had closed behind me; I didn't feel like an adult.

The flight was breaking up, going on to different operational training stations, some to fighters, some to bombers. We had had to make a choice, back at Bronson; and most of my friends had applied for fighters—naturally enough, I suppose, that was where the excitement and the glory were—and some of them were ordered to Jacksonville to train in Corsairs. But others were disappointed, and would be training in dive-bombers with me. I hadn't even tried to be a fighter pilot, and I'm not sure why I hadn't. Perhaps I didn't think I was good enough for Corsairs. They were said to be very hot, very hard to fly—if you stalled in your landing approach you rolled over, or so the old-timers told us, and you couldn't get them out of an inverted spin. Or perhaps it wasn't that, exactly; maybe I just didn't see myself as that heroic figure the Fighter Pilot. Whatever the reason, I decided that the fighter test was one I didn't have to take, and I chose dive-bombers without pausing, as though there was no choice to make.

Before we reported to our new stations we got a few days' leave, and the whole flight went to Birmingham to T's wedding, traveling together up from Pensacola in a Greyhound bus that meandered through the Alabama spring as though it had no certain destination. The trip was a ritual, we all felt it, it was like the flight to New Orleans. It was the last time we would all be together, and the last time we would all be bachelors. I wondered which would divide us from each other more, the different combat roles we'd play, or the entrance of wives into our world. When we thought ahead, the game-playing days seemed to be ending, we could see responsibilities coming. An officer was supposed to be a leader, to care for his men, to share in the conduct of the war. And if he were also a husband? It began to seem that what the Commanding Officer had handed out to each of us was an assignment to adulthood, ready or not.

T's sister Liz met us at the bus station. She was wearing a dress with Degas dancers on it, and she was like a dancer, too, pretty and gay, and light in her movements. She laughed and teased her brother, and she greeted his friends prettily; and when she turned, her hair swung, and the Degas dress swirled to her body. It was all like a dance. And she was very Southern, with her formal manners and her soft speech that seemed to be all vowels. I had never met anyone like her in Minneapolis.

Nor like her family—her mother, who was friendly and fussed, and said "I swanee," and "Our fathers!", and her grandmother, a matriarch with the commanding presence of a Confederate general, and her stepfather, who was fat and easy, and spent most of his time calming his wife down, saying "Now 'Lizbeth, now 'Lizbeth." Nor like her town, so hot in April, so leafy and blossoming, the streets so crowded, so many Negroes everywhere. There was too much life there; I was charmed but I was also confused by it all.

That first night there was a bachelor party for T, and we all got drunk and made speeches about how great it had been, and how we would always stick together; but even drunk we knew that only the first part was true. The next day we went to the wedding, in a Methodist church that was all varnished pine and ugly red and blue windows, and I was Best Man. Through the ceremony I felt hung over and distracted, and while the preacher rambled I stared absently at the window above the altar. It was Christ the Good Shepherd and the lamb in it looked like somebody I knew back home, but I couldn't remember who. Alice's mother? Then the ring part of the ceremony came, and I couldn't find the ring in my pockets, but then I did, and it was all right.

In the evening we went, rather self-consciously, to the Birmingham Officers' Club, the first Officers' Club that any of us had ever been to. I took T's sister, and we danced and drank and talked, the way you do on a first date with a nice, pretty girl (and especially if her brother is there). The next day I rented a car and we drove around town, to the pool and the country club, and she showed me the statue of Vulcan and the steel mill where her uncle worked, and when we stopped at night we held hands and kissed. It was very romantic. I was a flier on the way to war, and she was a Southern belle. Our roles seemed fixed, as though we had been cast in a sentimental movie, or a story by Scott Fitzgerald. We were convinced that we felt deeply about each other.

Then the leave was over, and I was in another train, with T and Taylor and the others, moving on to another airfield, sentimentally sad, but relieved to be out of the civilian world of mothers and relations and fond neighbors, and even of dates with nice girls. We sat in the dusty, red-plush coaches, sweating into our new uniforms, down the length of Alabama to Flomaton, that odd, obscure intersection in the piny woods that all Southern trains seem to reach sooner or later, and across to Jacksonville, where the Corsairs were, and where Ike left us, and then south again, down the east coast of Florida. The land turned from red clay to bright sand, and sometimes the train ran so close to the shore that we could see the wide white beaches and the breaking waves, like pictures on travel posters, indolent and inviting. I had never seen the Atlantic Ocean before—or any other ocean—and I tried to respond to it; but there was too much of it, I couldn't think of anything to think about it.

Toward afternoon the train turned inland and stopped at Deland, a town twenty miles or so from the coast, behind Daytona Beach. It was a small college town—very pretty, I thought, with its Spanish-style buildings, and its palm trees and little ponds; it seemed very green and cool-looking after the bright coast. I thought of Denton, the other college town, and wondered if I had changed enough since then. Would I be any better with the Jo Belles of this place?

The Naval Air Station at Deland was neither green nor cool-looking. It was sun-baked space in the woods, with a plain, functional airfield in it. As we drove in I saw only standard Navy buildings, a single long landing strip, and a tower, and parked by the tower, rows of SBD's—no other kind of plane, just SBD's. NAS Deland existed for one purpose—to teach new pilots like us how to fly those planes.

Assignments here, to dive-bomber training, had been a furious disappointment to guys like Taylor, who dreamed of flying Corsairs and thought of fighter pilots as the aristocrats of the air; but I didn't feel like an aristocrat, and I felt pleased and easy when I saw the planes in their rows. The SBD was a slow, sturdy, dependable plane that I thought I could probably fly well enough. Old-timers said that you could lose a cylinder, or two feet of wing, and still get it home. It had no particular style, and you certainly wouldn't call it beautiful; but it had its own aura of achievement. It had been the Navy's dive-bomber through most of the early part of the war, and Marines had flown it at Guadalcanal. It worked well, carried the bombs (slowly) to the targets, could be dived with great accuracy, and would then fly you back. I didn't think I wanted anything more than that from the plane I flew into combat. "But Christ," Taylor said, *"look* at it! It looks like a pickup truck. But a Corsair, man, that fuckuh's *beautiful!"* And of course he was right, that fucker was beautiful, and the SBD wasn't. Still, I was content with its plainness—a matter of temperament, I guess.

The planes on the flight line were old; they had come from fleet duty, and they were still painted in what was then the standard fashion for naval combat planes—the upper half dark blue, the lower half a blue that was nearly white. The theory was that this scheme camouflaged the plane when seen either from above (against the dark water) or from below (against the light sky). I don't think it worked any better than gray or brown or white would have—I certainly never had any trouble seeing a plane against either the sea or the sky—but it seemed symbolically right for Navy fighting planes to be painted the colors of the sea and sky, and I liked the look of it. It seemed serious and warlike.

Like the planes, our instructors were combat veterans, and they too made the field seem closer to the reality of war. These were the first pilots I had met who had been to the Pacific theater, had seen the islands, and Japanese planes in the air, had dropped real bombs on real enemy targets, and had been shot at. They had passed the Test. All the excitement that I had gotten from movies and stories hung about these men, and made the plainest and quietest of them extraordinary, touched by heroism and romance. When they talked about the 'Canal or the Coral Sea, it was like Spanish John talking about sex—they had been somewhere, and had had feelings there, that were beyond my imagining. I couldn't conceive how it would feel to be at fifteen thousand feet, above a ship or an island, and then to dive through the antiaircraft fire toward the target, and drop and pull away. But I knew it would be a great thing, and that it would make me different.

I met the Navy lieutenant who was to be our instructor sitting in the bar of the BOQ, sipping Southern Comfort through a straw. He was a Cherokee Indian from Oklahoma, and he had a profile like the Indian on the penny; like every Indian in the service, he was called "Chief." The Chief had flown dive-bombers at Midway, and he was a good, intelligent pilot. He led our flights carefully, and taught us how to approach a target, the best position from which to enter a bombing run, how to dive. He dropped his bombs accurately, and he taught us how he did it. And he also taught us how to pull out, how to take evasive action and get the hell out of there. There were two goals in his flying—to carry the bomb to the target, and to carry himself back home—and he was good at both of them, but his flying had no personal style; he was like a driver who has never had an accident, but doesn't like to drive. Perhaps the experience of combat, early in the war when losses were high and achievements were low, had taken the joy of flying out of him. He didn't talk much about it, or the war, or anything else. He just sat in the bar when the day's flying was over, quite friendly if you approached him, but content to be alone as though he were waiting for it all to end, patiently, but without much hope, sipping his Southern Comfort. Strictly speaking, this was illegal. Indian's weren't allowed to drink liquor; there was a Federal law against it. But the lunacy of denying alcohol to a man who was fighting your war must have struck the local bartenders, and the Chief was never refused a drink.

The main thing the Chief had to teach us was to dive an airplane straight toward the earth, and to drop a bomb while diving. This is the most unnatural action possible in a plane, a kind of defiance of all life-preserving instincts. As a maneuver it is no more difficult than a loop or a slow-roll, but psychologically it is a violation of life. You begin a dive-bombing attack in an echelon, a diagonal line of planes stretched out and back from the leader, letting down from twelve or fifteen thousand feet in a steady, accelerating glide. Then the leader signals, pulls up sharply, rolls, and drops suddenly, like a bird shot in flight, and each plane follows, rolling nearly over at the start, so that the pilot pulls the nose of his plane onto the target from an inverted position. The plane is diving vertically now, or nearly so, and your weight is no longer on your back and seat, but forward, against your seat harness, and on your feet on the rudder pedals. You have your dive-brakes open to make the descent slower, but still the earth that you see through your bombsight seems to rise to meet you very fast. As speed builds up, the flight characteristics of the plane change, the target slides away from your bombsight, and you have to fly the plane back to it while holding the dive. The sudden change of altitude hurts your ears, and you yell to relieve the pressure, and to help the psychological pressure that is also building up. You glance at your altimeter, which is unwinding swiftly toward zero, kick the plane onto the target, press the button on the control stick that releases the bomb, and pull out, banking up so that you can see where your bomb fell.

Diving was a violent experience, always. You could - burst an eardrum in a dive (I saw T walk back from the flight line after a flight, with blood seeping from his ear); and you could lose consciousness in the pullout, when the force pulling the blood from your brain was many times the force of gravity. But what made dive-bombing sometimes fatal was not the dive, but the target. Down there below you was a bull's-eye pattern of concentric circles painted on the ground, and up here, on the bombsight set in your windshield, was a similar pattern drawn in lines of light. The problem was to bring them together, so that one was centered on the other, and then to drop. But air and airplane conspired to make this difficult and momentary, and the pilot might try again and again to get on target, slide away, try, slide, and dive into the center of the target still trying.

In Florida in 1944 one dive-bomber pilot died every day. We heard about them at dinner, in the officers' mess— a guy at Jacksonville, someone we had known in flight school killed at Vero Beach, another at Lauderdale. The account of every crash was embellished with details: how the plane buried itself in the bull's-eye, how the wreckage covered the target, how the body was gathered up in a bushel basket and sent home in a coffin that had to be loaded with engine parts to give it sufficient weight. It was a kind of accident that any of us might have, a momentary hypnosis that no intelligence or skill seemed proof against.

As any war movie will tell you, the prospect of sudden death draws men together. Those of us who had been friends before—Joe and T, Rock, Taylor, Wally, and I—were closer still at Deland. It was partly, perhaps, because of the way dive-bombing is done. A dive-bombing attack is always a group attack, and we flew constantly at each other's wing-tips, followed each other in dives, rendez-voused after the attack, flew back together in divisions of V's. So bombing became a form of comradeship; you had a good feeling about those other planes strung out below you in the dive, joining up in sections as you pulled out.

So the old friends became closer, and we made some new ones—pilots who had trained at Corpus Christi instead of Pensacola, or had simply been in another flight at Bronson, party-goers, drinkers, comedians, eccentrics. Taylor found a wild accomplice in a Portuguese from New England called Puta. And T and I took up with a guy who had played shortstop for the Saint Paul Saints. I liked him because he could talk about Minneapolis, and T liked him because he was an athlete and could talk comically about life in the minor leagues, and we both liked and trusted him because he was a good, steady flier.

The pilots in the flight who couldn't fly—who were too stupid, too clumsy, or too frightened—became outsiders and enemies. We had one such in particular, a faded-looking Southerner with hair so pale that he was called Cotton-head. It wasn't exactly that Cottonhead couldn't fly, of course—he had graduated from flight school, and he could get the plane off the ground and down again—but he flew as though he or the plane were spastic, skidding and jerking, slowing and speeding in unpredictable and unnerving ways. Taylor, who often flew with Cottonhead, would throw his helmet into his locker after a flight and rage, "That fuckuh. I look at him up there and I think, 'He's gonna kill me if I ain't careful,'" and he would itemize Cottonhead's misdeeds for the day—the sudden throttling back, the ungainly roll into the dive, the slow, stretched-out approach to a landing. It was like living with a bomb, Taylor said. Our distrust of Cottonhead in the air made us avoid him on the ground, as though he carried danger with him everywhere, and might explode or crash into us at meal-times, or in the bar. He must have lived a lonely life at Deland, but there was nothing to be done about it; he was excluded by an instinct below self-preservation, the same instinct that made the rest of us closer than friends. In the squadron photograph that was taken at the end of our training there, we stand in an informal group in front of an SBD; it is clear that we are friends, that there was joking going on when the picture was taken, that as soon as the posing is over we'll all go to the bar. All except Cottonhead, who stands at the edge of the picture, not far from the rest, but separated, like a man with a smell, or a fatal disease.

Another kind of fellow-feeling developed from the fact that the SBD was a two-man plane, which in combat carried a gunner. We began to fly with an enlisted crewman in the rear seat, and occasionally flew gunnery flights in which he fired his machine gun at a sleeve, while we simply drove. We had all flown other people before, but they had always been instructors or other student-pilots—people who could fly, and who had a set of controls to fly with, if necessary; but now we had men riding with us

91

who had no controls, and wouldn't have been able to use them anyway, and who depended on us to keep them alive. They weren't our own crewmen yet. All the names in my logbook are different, and occur only once—Nugent, Redlinghafter, Beeken, Poe—and there was no sense of a common enterprise. I simply felt responsible—to them, to their mothers, to life.

May passed into June, and the Florida sun burned down. The concrete of the runway and the flight line burned, the air quivered with heat above the burning earth, and when we took off to eastward, over the beach and the ocean, the water below was metallic and blinding, the color of heat. A cockpit was a furnace. Every metal surface was hot to the touch, and the engine blew back parched air that smelled of burning gasoline. We flew in nothing but our cotton flight suits, and whenever we weren't at high altitude we were sweating; the suits became black with sweat-stains, and rotted from our shoulders, and our cotton helmets shone with sweat.

In the afternoons thunderstorms built up and swept across the field and erased it in pelting rain. Coming back from a flight over the ocean, we would maneuver among the storms to find that the field was hidden at the bottom of a dark column of rain that seemed to hang like a curtain from the bottom of a thunderhead. We would fly around and wait for the storm to pass, circling aimlessly out over the piny woods in the burning, improbable sunshine. When we landed, the field would be bright with sun, and the strip already steaming; the earth would be hot as ever, and the sweating would begin again.

But it wasn't really enervating, it wasn't like that other summer in preflight school. We were not held in the heat, made to bear it incessantly as though it were a moral exercise. When we had flown, we could go back to our quarters in the BOQ, shower, have a drink, and lie around half-dressed and talk. T and I had a phonograph in our room, and some jazz records, and we would lie there, cooling off, and listen to that music: the Benny Goodman Quartet playing "Runnin' Wild," Nat Cole's "Sweet Lorraine," Mezzrow-Ladnier's "Comin' On With the Come On," Peck Pecora and his Back Room Boys. And eat oranges. The country around Deland was orange-growing country, and you could buy a tall sack for a dollar just outside the Station gate. There was always a sack in the closet, and orange peelings under the bed. There were black enlisted men, called mess-boys, whose job it was to clean out the peelings, but if they came in while we were there they would mostly just hang around, listening, and have a drink if we were having one (it was part of the resistance to Navy Regs to assume that a mess-boy who appreciated jazz wasn't a mess-boy). And sometimes when I came in from a flight the phonograph would be playing, a blues, maybe, "Don't the moon look lonesome . . . ," and one of the mess-boys would be sitting alone there on the edge of a bed, or leaning on a broom among the unswept orange peelings, listening, and maybe thinking of other places, better times.

When the sun went down and the air cooled, we went sometimes to Daytona Beach. It was a good time to go to a resort: civilians had no gasoline and no time for holidays, and the hotels and bars were nearly empty. And it was off-season, early summer then. There were girls around, though: Waves from the air stations, casual party girls, even a few nice girls. The shortstop from Saint Paul met one of the nice ones, and dated and courted her, and got no further than the rest of us did with nice girls. I remember him coming into the room late one night after a date, and T asking, "How was it, man? Did you get in?" "Ah," said the shortstop sadly, "it's always the same with me. Cheek-cheek-forehead, that's all I get, just cheek-cheek-forehead." He's one of us, I thought, even if he did play shortstop for the Saints.

The steaming summer air seemed to create an atmosphere of feverish sexuality. There was a Wave from the Air Station who took a leave and spent the whole time in a hotel room in Daytona, taking on all comers, or so the story went. Taylor and his pal Puta had found her, and told us about her. "Shit, man," Taylor said, "she ain't very good-lookin', not what you'd call a beauty. In fact"—he began to laugh his high-pitched, wildman laugh—"she's downright ugly. But who cares?" Puta said nothing, but made an obscene Portuguese gesture, winked, and laid an index finger alongside his nose—a movement that apparently expressed satisfaction.

We went to see her, as you might go in a party to the zoo to look at a rare new species; five or six of us trooped into the room in the cheap tourist hotel, and had a drink, and just looked at her. There she was, in bed all right. She was a big, husky girl, and Taylor was right—she wasn't very good looking. She might have been a farm girl or a singer in a church choir, except for the look that never left her face—a despairing, defiant look, the look of someone who had got to a place too far to come back from. She lay in the bed, her big body covered by a sheet, and stared back at us. Nobody touched her or suggested any sexual act. Partly we were shy in front of each other, I suppose, but it was something else, too. I remember what the atmosphere was like, now; it wasn't like a zoo—it was like a sick room in a hospital. We were visiting a patient, she was sick and we were all well, and we drew back from her sickness. It wasn't a matter of VD, but of the look on her face. When we had finished our drinks and clowned around self-consciously a little, we left. I looked back from the door and she was just lying there, watching us go, not saying anything.

The hard-drinking, all-night Daytona parties usually ended on the beach. The sand would still be warm from the sun, and it never rained at night. You could go down there with a bottle and a girl and fall asleep under a pier, or just on the sand of the beach, and wake to see the sun rising red and burning out over the ocean, and feel the day's heat beginning. And you'd stand up and brush the sand from your clothes, and start back toward the base, feeling a little stiff, and emptied of feeling and desire. If Taylor went along, the trip back was part of the party, though, and he would touch even the morning quiet with wildness. I remember walking with him in the Daytona dawn toward the bus station. Ahead of us an all-night cafeteria still had its blinking neon sign on, though it was already daylight, and Taylor began chanting in time with the flashing light—"Eat! Eat! Eat!"—until his shouts woke the sleeping citizens, and heads were stuck out of windows to protest. Taylor shouted obscene replies, and we went on, contemptuous and free, along the hot and empty street.

Daytona was like an occupied city. There seemed to be no laws that governed the behavior of Marine pilots; nothing was prohibited; there were not even any proprieties. Many of the girls there were camp-followers, sluttish and obliging. It was said that an enlisted man had gotten syphilis in his big toe while sitting in a booth of a beach-side bar opposite such a girl in a bathing suit. Hotel clerks would register any couple under any name; bartenders were always willing to ignore the fact that none of us was old enough to drink legally; the police might scold, but they never arrested us. Taylor once destroyed the awning of a store while trying to climb it to get to a second-story window where he had seen a girl. No one suggested that he should pay for the damage, and certainly such a thing didn't occur to him. The town had surrendered to a barbarian invasion.

For me it was a disturbing life—too free, too irresponsible, too wild. I was frightened by a world without rules. I wanted to be middle-class again. Others among us might have felt the same, because after a while nice girls began to appear, back-home girls, mostly, and the parties changed into dates, and we all felt more secure. T's wife came down and found an apartment in Daytona, and his sister Liz came to visit, and I began to take her out. It was fun, it was innocent, it was like a game—to dress up like adults and go out to order meals and drinks in grown-up places. We were both nineteen, and we knew no more of the world than any sheltered child does. We scarcely knew what drinks to order, and it seemed impertinent to say to an adult bartender, ''Two gin rickeys'' or ''A sloe gin fizz, please.'' Most of the time we behaved like nineteen-year-olds; we lay on the beach all day, or played in the surf, or dawdled along the boardwalk. Sometimes if it rained we browsed in bookshops, and tried to be literary. I bought Virginia Woolf's *Haunted House* there, and felt rather avant-garde. At night there were hotels—old-fashioned, clapboard-sided places, short on their usual resort customers, and happy to receive whoever turned up. An ocean wind blew all night long through the open windows, lifting the curtains and cooling us where we lay. In the dark there, with the wind blowing, there seemed to be no time, no future, no war, no adults, and no children. Only two people touching, entering that dark world that was beyond my imagination, and altogether different from it.

In the evenings we went to the Casino on the Daytona Pier, and danced and courted. The Casino was an old barn of a place, thrust out over the ocean and open on three sides so that the ocean breezes could cool the dancers. A band played the tunes that Glenn Miller was playing then, and we danced, or sat at a table in a corner and held hands and looked out at the dark water. We were sitting there one night when a sudden roar of engines drowned the band, and I looked out and saw the running lights of three planes coming toward me up the beach out of the darkness, and low—lower than the level of the casino floor. It was like looking down the barrel of a loaded gun. They would certainly hit the casino; they were too low, too close to pull up; we'll be killed, I thought angrily, just when I've met this marvelous girl. And then they were up and over our heads in a shaking roar, and I could see their taillights through the opening at the other side of the casino, receding up the beach. It was Taylor and a couple of friends, just saying hello.

It began to be clear that our flight was divided into the Sane and the Crazy. The Crazies buzzed the Casino at night, or flew night-time tail chases, or tried night loops; the Sane flew their flights as they were instructed to, and tried not to kill themselves. Perhaps it was a distinction between the frustrated fighter pilots, who flew suicidally to prove to themselves that they should have been chosen for Corsairs, and the rest of us, who flew because we liked to, but also flew to stay alive. Or maybe it was something else. Maybe we were afraid, and they weren't. Taylor often said that he *knew* nothing would happen to him, and whatever crazy thing he tried, nothing did; he was a brilliant pilot, but he seemed to be protected by something more than his brilliance. I wasn't brilliant, and I didn't feel, ever, that I could take chances. Or maybe they were afraid, too, but in a different way, of different things. Death isn't the only terror. I don't know; I never understood the Crazies, though they were my friends.

Two planes crashed in the swamps during our training at Deland—one flown by a Sane, one by a Crazy. We were practicing carrier-landings, using a landing strip out in the pines as the carrier. An area the size of a deck was marked out on the strip, and at the end of it a Landing Signal Officer stood with his paddles and steered you slowly in to a heavy, thudding landing. Then you took off again, followed the plane ahead of you out over the swamp, and in your turn made another approach and thumped down again. It was all low, slow, wheels-down flying; and in that heat, with those old, combat-tired planes, there were bound to be engine failures.

The Sane was a sober-sided young man from Yale named Stanley. He was the only Ivy Leaguer I ever met in the Marine Corps, and he seemed out of place, as though he had wandered in while looking for Naval Intelligence. His manners were correct, and rather formally old-fashioned, and he was always clean and pressed and well-groomed. He was the sort of young man who manages always to look as though he gets more haircuts than you do. I liked him well enough; he just seemed a little exotic, that's all. Stanley was on the downwind leg of the pattern when his engine stopped. He made the classic emergency landing, as described in all the manuals, and in many lectures that we had heard—straight ahead, full-stall in to the tree tops, shoulder harness secure, canopy open. He walked briskly away from it, and was brought back in a jeep to the ready room, where we were all anxiously waiting for news. "Christ," Joe said, "what will Yale say if we've killed their only Marine?" Stanley began his account as though he were back at Yale, delivering a lecture on crash-landings: "I perceived that my oil pressure was dropping, and so I immediately set about preparations for. . . ."

The Crazy, in the same predicament, settled toward the trees, but at the last moment decided, as he put it, that "those bastards were wrong" in the emergency instructions they gave, and pushed the nose of his plane down into the trees instead of stalling in flat. He ploughed through an acre or so of pines, and was knocked in the head by a trunk before what was left of the plane came to rest. He climbed out, carrying with him his cockpit microphone, and was found, after a good deal of searching, stumbling through the swamp shouting curses into the mike—at God, the CO, and the designer of the SBD. When he was brought back in the ambulance, he was still clutching the microphone, and as he passed us at the BOQ he hung out of the ambulance window and shouted a reporter's account of his exploit, like H. V. Kaltenborn. He was kept in the sick bay for a couple of days for observation, but the doctor concluded that though he was crazy, he wasn't any crazier than before the crash. When he was released he immediately drove his car back to the wreck and siphoned a tank full of gasoline out of it. He had no other closed containers to fill, but there was all that gas, and it was rationed, so he found a washtub somewhere and put it in his trunk, and filled that too, and drove back to the airfield with a tub of high-octane gasoline sloshing about in the back of the car. He said it made his engine run a hell of a lot better than the SBD's did.

In the end the Marine Corps seemed to recognize the Sane–Crazy distinction. When we had finished our training at Deland and were certified dive-bomber pilots, we were given two kinds of assignments. The Crazies were sent to another Florida training station, where they were assigned to fly target planes for night-fighter training. It was like being sent to Siberia. They would not be preparing for combat, and they had no prospects of ever joining a combat squadron. They would simply be tools for the training of luckier pilots, who would pass on to the world we all wanted to inhabit—a fighting squadron in the Pacific war.

The rest of us, the Sanes, had orders to California, "for aviation duty with MarAirWingSoPac." That last word was what we wanted—duty with the Marine Air Wing, South Pacific. We were going West, to where the real squadrons were put together. It was hard on the Crazies, some of whom were marvelous natural pilots, and I wanted to say something to them, but there wasn't anything to say, really. Taylor was sitting in the BOQ bar when I left, and I went in and just said so long. "So long, man," he said. "Don't crash and burn." I could hear his high, cackling laugh as I walked down the path to the waiting jeep.

Chapter 5

We were on our way to the real war, but first we were given a leave, and I went to see my father. The visit wasn't a success. I had decided that I was going to marry T's sister before I went overseas, and I knew I couldn't tell my father. I was only nineteen; I had less than a year of college, and no prospects after the war; I had known her only a few months, neither of us had any money or any expectations of it—the sensible arguments against such a foolish act were overwhelming. And the arguments for it didn't exist.

It wasn't that I thought I would die in combat; I knew that pilots were killed out there, but I didn't believe, couldn't even imagine, that I would be the one who would meet the anti-aircraft burst, the one in the spinning, burning plane. So I wasn't rushing into marriage before I died, nothing so foolish and romantic as that. No, I think I saw marriage as simply one more Test that stood between me and adulthood, or manhood, or whatever that state was that lay on the other side of innocence. I had passed one Test. I was a Marine officer and a pilot. If I were also married, then there would be only one Test left—the Test of combat. The girl I had chosen was pretty, and we were happy together, but I didn't expect that marriage would be like the days at Daytona. I had seen the way it was for my parents and their friends, I knew that it was bills and decisions and children and quarrels, and above all being responsible for somebody else—a voluntary abandoning of freedom. And I was nineteen years old; I had only just begun to know what freedom offered. Still, I was determined that I must be a married man.

And so I moped around home, and had another picture taken with my father, in front of the house. In this one I am wearing my new Marine uniform; the blouse is too long—the shoulders fit all right, but it was obviously made for a taller man—but it looks new and pressed, and the gold bars are bright on the shoulders. My father is in his shirt sleeves, taller than me, white-haired. He has one hand on my shoulder, in a gesture that was meant to be affectionate, but looks a little threatening, as though he might lift me into the air, or press me down into the ground with one powerful movement. It is a picture of deep, clumsy love.

Then I went back to Birmingham, and we told Liz's parents, and there was a lot of weeping and talk, and Aunt Sister came in and wrung her hands, and then we were married, in the Methodist church at the corner, with the flowers left over from somebody else's wedding. After the ceremony I sent my father a terse, embarrassed telegram; I knew that nothing I could say would explain what I had done, or ease his puzzled disappointment. Liz's family gave us a wedding supper, and we spent our wedding night in the Tutwiler Hotel, and the next day T and I set off by train for California.

Almost immediately (I think it was in New Orleans) I knocked a suitcase against my ankle and did something to a bone. While we rolled through Texas in a hot, crowded train, my ankle swelled. By the time we had reached New Mexico, I couldn't walk; I had to hop to the toilet, and I could only stand in line for meals by leaning on T, using him as a crutch. At night I sat with my foot propped on the opposite seat, not sleeping, just hurting and worrying. I worried about what I had just done—the marriage that I had committed. Suppose Liz was pregnant? I'd have a child before I was twenty-one. How would I support it and her? And myself, for that matter? I had never had a full-time job; I had only been a college freshman in that other world back home. Alone there in the night, rolling through the darkness that was New Mexico or Arizona, the comfortable present-tense security of the military life fell from me, and I looked bleakly beyond, into a gray civilian future. This was what being grown-up was like. It still seemed an imperative that I couldn't dodge; but I wished I had not rushed toward it so eagerly.

I worried about military matters too, as the train swayed and my swollen ankle responded with a jab of pain. What would the doctors do to me in California? Would I be put into a cast? Would I lose my place in the squadron? Would my friends go off to the war and leave me on crutches? I hobbled off the train at Los Angeles in more anxiety than pain.

Railroad stations and bus stations: they were the sad places of the war, the limbos of lost souls. All those troops, far from their hometowns, and miserable-looking in their new uniforms, and the sad, young country girls, pregnant or holding babies, not looking around much, just standing, waiting. Lines everywhere. There was no place you could go that you didn't have to stand in a line first. Piles of duffel bags. And MP's with their white leggings and night sticks, patrolling, representing discipline, *being* discipline in their stiff postures and their sharp uniforms. War could do worse things than this to plain people, but for a sense of the ordinary outrages of life in a country at war, the stations were the place to go.

T helped me through the Los Angeles station and onto a train for San Diego, and off at the other end, and found the liberty bus for the Marine Corps Air Depot at Miramar. People in the stations stared as I hobbled past, and perhaps wondered vaguely if I had been wounded in action; but they had their own problems, and they turned back into themselves. I had my problem, too, and I brooded on it as we rode out of San Diego and up into the hills. I had to get checked in at this new base without revealing that I was crippled, and I had to cure myself before I was discovered. I couldn't go to the doctor at the sick bay, for fear he'd ground me, and I didn't know how to treat myself, or even exactly what was wrong.

When we got there, T did it all. He installed me at the BOQ bar with my foot up on a cushion, and checked me in by proxy ("My buddy ain't feelin' so good," he'd say, "it was a little rough in L.A. last night, y'know"), and he wangled a crutch from a sympathetic corpsman. I was safe until the next orders came.

Miramar was a staging base, just a collection of barracks and mess halls—that was all—on a bare, treeless hill above San Diego. If you entered or left California, in either direction, you had to go through Miramar, and while you were there you did nothing except wait. Orders came, and you went, or they didn't come, and you waited, and drank, and tried to make long-distance phone calls home. In the bar you met pilots on their way to the war, pilots who had just come back, and pilots like us, passing through to California bases for still more training, before we could join those enviable guys who were on their way out.

We must have been impatient, but I don't remember impatience. Or not the kind you feel in ordinary life, when a letter doesn't come, or a girl is late. There were always parties; we carried our permanent party with us, and you could go to the club and drink anytime. But, more than that, existence itself was exciting. Just waiting on that bare California hill was odd and exhilarating. Most of us had never been to California before; it was new, it wasn't like Minnesota, or even like Florida. And the old hands around us in the bar were always willing to tell us war stories. It was there that I first heard the romantic island names: Rabaul and Munda and Bougainville, Espiritu Santo, Emirau. The tellers were like old explorers, or like the sailor in that painting of the boyhood of Sir Walter Raleigh, and we were the listening boys.

It was a whole life, at Miramar—insulated, alcoholic, and idle, but in its way complete. You could go into town on liberty if you wanted to, but not many people did. I think everyone felt superstitious about leaving the base; if you went away, your orders would come and you'd be left behind. And anyway, San Diego wasn't much of a liberty town. Once T and I did make the trip to Los Angeles, on the fancy train that runs up the coast from San Diego; we found that the crutch and the hobble got us onto the train ahead of the mob of waiting sailors and Marines, and we sat in the soft seats of the club car, and drank and looked at Southern California. I suppose it was beautiful, but its mountains and rocks and dry hillsides were too alien still to register as landscape. It looked like a bad place to crash-land in, that was all.

In a couple of weeks our orders came, and by then I could give a fair imitation of a man with two legs, and I was sure I could fly. We rode up the coast again, past Los Angeles this time, to the Marine Corps Air Station at Santa Barbara. It was the first all-Marine field we had seen, and it was different. The Marines are administratively attached to the Navy, but no Marine likes to admit it, and the Navy is generally regarded (by Marines, that is) as a softer, more gentlemanly, less belligerent service. Of my flight school friends it was certainly true that the well-bred ones tended to take Navy commissions; and those like myself who felt provincial, or common, or under-bred, chose the Marine Corps, where those qualities wouldn't show. The Marines that I knew, both the officers and the enlisted men, seemed to be mainly southerners and midwesterners— country boys, red-necks, and yokels. I don't think I ever met a Marine from New York or San Francisco, or a rich one.

The base at Santa Barbara was small, new, and tem-porary-looking, with nothing like the old-school elegance of Pensacola; but that seemed right for Marines. As we drove along the flight line we could see that each area, with its hangars and Quonset huts, housed a real fighter or bomber squadron, with a number—Marine Fighter Squadron 122—on a sign by the road, and sometimes a squadron insignia, a bolt of lightning, or an ace of hearts, a symbol that you could imagine painted on the side of a fighter plane, beside a row of little Jap flags, for the planes it had shot down. The numbers and the insignias, and the rows of fighting planes, made the whole place seem very real, as though the war was being fought nearby, just over the horizon.

Our squadron was VMTB-943, which means V—heavier-than-air-craft, M—Marine Corps, TB—torpedo bombers. The planes we would fly were TBM's, the model that the Navy had chosen to replace the disastrous Douglas Devastators, the torpedo bombers that had been shot out of the air at Midway. The TBM was a big plane—the biggest single-engine plane ever built—and a good one. It could carry a ton of bombs (the SBD carried only 1,000 pounds), and had a range twice that of the SBD, and greater speed. Because it carried the bombs internally, in a closed bomb bay, it had a curious, sagging look along its belly; and to keep this sag off the ground, it had a very long landing gear, which were attached close to the fuselage, so that they seemed to be a pair of long, awkward legs. It looked, on the ground, like some barnyard fowl, and pilots called it the Pregnant Turkey.

Any plane looks awkward on the ground. A plane's environment is the air, and it becomes itself when the air begins to flow over its surfaces, and it responds to the controls; but the Turkey looked as clumsy in the air as it did on the ground. It really did look like a turkey taking off, and whatever you did with it in the air, that thick, pregnant body moved effortfully. It was only beautiful to the men who flew it; for it was a beautifully functional plane. It did what it was designed to do; it had no tricks, would not stall or spin off in a landing approach (as a Corsair would), would fly heavily but steadily through bad weather or through enemy fire. There was no glory in flying Turkeys, but there was a good deal of flying pleasure.

There was pleasure, too, in flying them in a real squadron. It made our activities seem more significant, and our relationships—in the air as well as on the ground—formal, and directed toward a war. I can think of no analogy for the feeling of belonging to a squadron. It wasn't like being on a team. Nobody ever did anything for the good of the squadron, that I heard of; nobody talked about winning, or about loyalty or spirit. It wasn't like a private club—I'd have happily blackballed some of my fellow-pilots, if I could. Perhaps it was more like a family than anything else, with the CO for the father, and the Adjutant, fussing over his records, for Mom. As in a family, everyone moved in his own sphere, was free to dislike and fight with the other members, but yet acknowledged that there were bonds that linked him to this group of human beings, and excluded all others. In the club in the evenings, squadron members would drink together, and I often found myself joining someone I didn't even like because he was in my squadron, rather than drink with an outsider. It wasn't a hostile exclusiveness, just a recognition that ties existed. Ours wasn't even a combat squadron, it was only for training; but still it was a squadron: it had senior pilots who had been in the Pacific, and it could, if required, have gone into combat. It was a whole fighting unit, with a function and a collective set of skills.

The presence of experienced fliers—not as instructors, the way they had been at Deland, but simply as fellow-pilots—made the greatest difference in the atmosphere of Santa Barbara. The fighter ace Joe Foss was there with a fighter squadron, and his presence made the Corsairs on the field seem more serious, machines made for killing men and destroying other machines, and when I passed them on the field I was aware of the machine guns poking from the wings. You could stand beside Joe Foss at the BOQ bar and listen to him making flat, sane conversation. Because he was one of the Sanes, one of the best of them. He was a famous fighter pilot, maybe a great one, because he had studied his plane, and his enemies, and had used the odds carefully. From him you could learn how to survive. But his very sanity made him drab and unheroic, like a schoolteacher or a successful businessman. It was exciting to stand beside a man who had shot down so many planes, but the man himself was colorless. Without his record he would have been invisible.

We stood at the bar in the presence of Joe Foss and told each other stories about another fighter pilot, Pappy Boyington. If Foss was the greatest of the Sanes, Pappy was the greatest Crazy. He was one who would fly over a Japanese base on a quiet day and invite opponents up to fight with him, as though he were a knight in some old poem. Only a world crazy with war could have supported a man like Boyington; yet for us he was the Hero, and I'd have liked to talk with him and drink with him. Foss was there in the BOQ bar, but there seemed no point in actually meeting him. What could he say?

Certainly it is the Crazies in our lives who charm and seduce us. They live their lives free of the restraints, the fears and prudences, that limit our own actions. They gamble with death and scandal, and seem to thrive on the troubles and turmoil that we spend our lives avoiding. They seem, to the Sane, continuously careless; carelessness seems a necessary element in whatever they do, a seasoning to the sauce, an excitement. So the Crazies become legends, and we talked about them by the hour, there in the BOQ bar when the flying was done. We talked about the guy, whose name no one could remember, who had spent all his training time at Santa Barbara flat-hatting his TBM along the coast highway. Flat-hatting is simply flying very low, the lower the better. Your sense of speed increases as you come nearer to the ground, objects flash by faster, and you get a feeling of domination and power, as though you are defeating the friction of the earth's surface. Your sense of danger also increases as you get lower, and that is why flat-hatters are Crazies.

This Crazy had begun to fly low along the coast, over the flat shelf that lies between the mountains and the sea. He would go out on a flight—navigational practice, perhaps, or a gunnery hop—and would spend the time roaring up and down the beach, or inland, over the undulating foothills. Gradually this palled, and he began to concentrate on the highway. Drivers headed south for Los Angeles would meet him headed north, bearing down on them apparently at their own level, and he would thunder over their heads with a roar, so close they could see the streaks of oil along the bomb-bay doors, and the scared face of the radio man at the tunnel window. Sometimes a driver would try to avoid what seemed a certain collision, and would weave frantically back and forth across the road, or drive into the ditch, and when this happened the Crazy was especially pleased. He seemed to have taken it as his mission to empty the highway of cars, to make the world safe for low-flying airplanes.

Complaints began to reach his Commanding Officer. Even in wartime you can't terrorize civilians, unless they are enemy civilians, and the Crazy clearly had to be dealt with. The CO might have court-martialled him, and thrown him in the brig; but he did a more sensible thing—he sent his Crazy overseas to a combat squadron, arguing that that kind of behavior might perhaps have good results out there. At least that's the story we heard in the Santa Barbara BOQ bar. There were various versions of what happened then, and you can take your choice: the Crazy became a hero, attacking and sinking enemy ships against impossible odds; or he crashed on a takeoff and was killed; or he went out of his mind (*further* out of his mind, some would have said) and is still confined to a naval hospital for the incurably insane. I favor the second version—Crazies are careless, and carelessness will kill you in an airplane, sooner or later.

On the flight line, in the ready room, and in the bar we began to get acquainted with the other pilots in the squadron. The most important man in 943 was Jimmy, a sweet-faced captain who looked about sixteen, but had already had one tour of duty in TBM's, and had a Distinguished Flying Cross. His title was Operations Officer, but in fact he was CO and Executive Officer and everything else in the squadron. He planned everything, he trained all the new pilots, and he told the vague-minded CO what to do. Jimmy had been on the famous torpedo run to Rabaul, and he told us about it, one night in the bar.

"Fucking MacArthur," he began. Marines who had been to the Pacific hated MacArthur; he was the Supreme Commander out there, and Marines believed he had exploited them, gave them the worst and most dangerous assignments, wasted Marine assault troops on unimportant islands, and squandered Marine pilots and planes attacking targets that the Air Force was afraid to hit. MacArthur had got the idea of hitting the ships in Rabaul harbor with torpedoes.

The harbor, Jimmy explained, was shaped like a teacup—no, more like a cream pitcher, round, with steep sides, and one narrow entrance like the spout. If you wanted to drop torpedoes, what you had to do was sneak in over the edge of the pitcher—at this point Jimmy began to fly the strike with his hands—and drop down low over the water, and then fly straight-and-level, at not more than a hundred and fifty knots, for not less than one minute, and *then* release your torpedo. If you weren't flying flat and slow when you dropped, the torpedo would porpoise—he made an up-and-down, plunging movement with his hand—or break up when it hit the water. Then you had to fly out the spout.

So there they were, sixteen planes trying to sneak up on Rabaul because MacArthur thought it was a good idea, and the Japs had them on the radar all the way; and when they came over the hill and dropped down to the bay every gun in the place was on them, and they couldn't even take evasive action until they'd dropped. Then they went corkscrewing out the harbor mouth, and when they got outside there were only four of them left. "Just me and George," Jimmy said, "and Black Mike Savino, and Junior Ransom."

Joe wanted to know what they had hit; I could see that he was imagining himself there.

Jimmy didn't know. He'd been too busy trying to get out of there to look back, but George thought they must have hit *something*, there was all that black smoke. But the smoke could have been the other twelve planes, of course.

Not everybody talked about flying. I met a first lieutenant named Harry who talked mostly about sex. He was tan and blond, and very muscular—the weight-lifting type; you could imagine him on a beach, flexing his biceps, or in an ad for a muscle-building course. All his free time was spent chasing women, and when he couldn't chase them he liked to remember conquests from his past. He was a raconteur of bedroom anecdotes, all of which he claimed had happened to him. While we were in Santa Barbara he established a liaison with a dentist's wife, and he entertained us at the bar with stories of her sexual enthusiasms, until one day the doctor came home early from his office, and the affair ended. According to Harry, the dentist walked into the bedroom while his wife was engaged with Harry in a particularly unusual sexual act. Harry looked up, saw the dentist in the doorway, and said: "Don't you know enough to knock before you enter a room?" "Excuse me," the dentist said, and withdrew, closing the door behind him. This seemed very sophisticated stuff to us, and it was somehow all right to laugh, because the husband was a dentist.

There was another first lieutenant who had been a baseball player; a lot of ball players turned up in the Marine Corps, though I can't explain why. Ken Kelleher was a Boston Irishman who had pitched for some team in the International League, and he was full of stories about how he had gone twelve innings against Montreal, and how his knuckleball had mystified the batters. He would go out behind the ready room when he wasn't flying and pitch to anyone who would catch for him. He liked it if you talked to him while he pitched, like a pro: "Come on, Ken baby, chuck me that old apple," stuff like that. Ken was the squadron philosopher, and he had a philosophical aphorism for every occasion. If you complained about some official order he would say, in his Boston accent, "Don't fight it, you cahn't shovel shit against the tide." We all adopted his sayings, long *a*'s and all, and they became a part of the squadron's language.

All of these guys were likable, even Harry was entertaining. But no squadron is made up entirely of likable guys. There was, for example, Sly. He must have had a first name, but it is an indication of his status in the squadron that nobody wanted to know him well enough to know what his first name was, and he was always referred to as just Sly. He was a big, flabby man, with thinning sandy hair, and a lumpy, shapeless sort of face. To compensate for his general unimpressiveness he had tried to grow a mustache, but his facial hair, like the hair on his head, was thin and limp, and the mustache was never more than a straggly shadow on his upper lip. "Makes his mouth look like a pussy," Rock said. (Rock was growing a handlebar mustache that gave him the look of a Texas sheriff.) Sly was unpleasant to look at and he was a bore, and to my mind he was a mediocre pilot; but he too was a member of the squadron, and we flew with him, drank with him, and listened to his boring obscenities. It was all part of squadron life.

The field at Santa Barbara lay north of the town, between the ocean and mountains. Both sea and mountains became important in our lives. The mountains were simply there, a solid obstacle always, lifting their jagged tops toward the vulnerable belly of your plane, denying the possibility of a safe landing if your engine failed. They were like reality, or death—unavoidable, always there. In darkness, or in bad weather, they were especially threatening, for their presence bent the radio range signals and made it difficult to approach Santa Barbara on instruments. But, whatever the weather, I felt mortal when mountains were below me.

From the sea came afternoon fog that lay offshore, solid and definite as a gray blanket, and then drew in over the field as the earth cooled. From the air you could watch it moving, first the offshore islands gone, then the beach, then the ocean-end of the landing strip. It would get that far and still the mountain-end would be perfectly clear, and you could still land there, and roll out toward the sea, into the thick mist. But once the fog had slid on over the entire strip the field would be closed for the night, and planes caught above it would have to find other landing places.

In the autumn the fogs were frequent, and moved in very quickly, as though the earth were pulling a blanket up to its chin in preparation for a cold night. One day, at the end of October, a quick fog nearly caught a whole flight of us too far from the field to get home. We turned and ran, and all of us made it except one. A pilot we called Frenchy had fallen behind, and as we landed we could hear him on the radio, caught above the fog, asking the tower for directions to a field that was clear. He seemed miles away, up there on top in the sunlight while we taxied slowly and nervously through the luminous wetness toward the flight line. We heard him get a heading for El Centro, the Marine field on the Salton Sea, a hundred miles inland behind the mountains, and we heard no more. We kept in touch with El Centro, but he didn't arrive, and after a few hours, when his fuel supply would have run out, we had to assume that he was down somewhere, perhaps dead in the mountains. Weeks passed, and the squadron was ordered to another station, and there was still no word of Frenchy. He had simply disappeared, as though dissolved, plane and all, by the fog.

* * *

Those of us who were married had left our wives behind when we came to the west coast; there was no time for domesticity, we thought, on the way to a war. But we were nevertheless newlyweds, and it was impossible to pretend to be bachelors again. On weekends we went to Los Angeles in a bunch, some married, some single, and got rooms at a shabby hotel across the street from the Biltmore ("next to the best hotel in town," Rock said). We would sleep there, we thought, but we'd live at the Biltmore, where there was an officers' club and a fancy bar, and a lot of women seemed to be coming and going. Toward the end of the afternoon we strolled into the club. The room was already full of officers and women, some of them in uniforms of the Waves or the woman Marines (called BAMS, meaning Broad-Assed Marines), others pretty clearly local camp followers. The married men huddled together at the bar, in a circle, like a wagon train protecting itself against marauding Indians; the bachelors drifted off after women. I watched Puta moving from one girl to another at the other end of the room. He would approach one, speak low for a moment, watch her face, and pass on with a shrug. Some of the faces looked startled, some angry, one or two laughed. In a few minutes he left with a BAM. The rest of us went on drinking.

When we came out onto the street it was dark, and we were drunk. We must have eaten; I only remember a long taxi ride to Hollywood, where, T said, you could hear great jazz. And he was right. All along Sunset Boulevard, in little clubs, were the jazz musicians I had been listening to on records—Illinois Jacquet, Teddy Bunn the guitarist, Howard McGhee—each in a trio or a quartet, up behind the bar. We drank a good deal more, going from club to club, and my memories are blurred; at one point T was singing with a band, in his husky, Louis Armstrong voice, and somewhere else he was playing drums, and we were all cheering him. The musicians didn't seem to mind.

The next day, on the way back to Santa Barbara, I asked Puta what he had said to those girls in the officers' club. "Me, I got a very straightforward approach," he said. "I go up to a girl, an' I say, 'Hey, honey, do you fuck?' Mostly they say 'No,' but the thing is, see, I don't waste no time."

"And what did the BAM say, the one you went out with?"

Puta laughed. "She said, 'I sure do, you smooth devil!' "

On another occasion Puta and Rock and a friend called Mac went hustling at the Biltmore, but could only manage to pick up one girl. "Never mind," Puta said, "I got a system. You guys go back to the hotel and hide in the john. I'll take her in and screw her, and then I'll say, 'Honey, I got to go to the toilet,' and one of you come back and have a piece, and do the same thing." And that's what they did. It worked all right the first time; Rock was about Puta's size, and had a crew cut like Puta's, but Mac was heavier, and had long curly hair, and when he climbed aboard the girl sensed something had changed. She turned the light on, and found the stranger sprawled in her lap, and she began to cry, more and more hysterically. Puta and Rock had to come out of the bathroom and try to calm her before the house detective heard her. Finally her sobs subsided, and she got up and began to dress. As she opened the door to leave she turned to the three still naked culprits sitting on the edge of the bed: "That's the trouble with you fucking Marines," she said, "you don't know how to treat a lady."

As the autumn passed, and we stayed on at Santa Barbara, those of us who were married began to imagine living a married life there. We could send for our wives, we said, though when we said *wives* it didn't somehow seem like the right word. Liz was my wife all right, but when I thought of her it was more as though she were still my best girl, my steady date. But maybe if she and all the other girl-wives came out and actually lived with us we'd all learn how to feel married. Maybe we'd even become adults. T went down the hall to the phone and called his wife in Birmingham, and then I called Liz. Of course we were married, and we should live together for as long as we could, though none of us had any real notion of what living together meant, except from watching our parents, and you can't learn much that's useful about married life from observing your elders.

Joe sat silently on his bunk for a while, which wasn't like him, and then said, "I'm going to call Bev and tell her to come out here and get married, too." And he went down the hall.

The BOQ phone was hung on the wall of the corridor, next to the head. Joe was shy and didn't want us all to hear him proposing marriage, and so he dialed, and then took the phone around the corner of the door, into the room where the toilet stalls were. Wally crept after him, listened, and when Joe had his girl on the phone, slipped behind him and began to flush the toilets. The room was filled with the rush and gurgle of water, louder and louder as Wally moved along the row of stalls. By the time he had flushed the last one, the first was ready again, and he kept the uproar going, a complex counterpoint of flushing. Joe shouted, turned back to the phone, pleaded, returned to soothe his puzzled girl, and finally began to laugh.

Wally was roaring with laughter, too, flushing and shouting, and waving his arms like a mad conductor; and we all came down the hall to watch, laughing too, hanging onto each other helplessly. Eventually Joe managed to shout his speech over the noise, and his girl accepted. We went back to the room and had a drink to celebrate. Joe said Wally was a very funny guy, and made him his Best Man. Somebody said they should be married in the head, with the crappers providing the wedding march.

Liz was on her way, her train already rolling across Texas, or maybe New Mexico by now, and I didn't have a home for her to come to. It was obvious that that was what a husband did, he *provided;* but I didn't know how to go about it, and I faced the problem in a helpless daze—I suppose I saw it as the first in a lifelong series of duties to be done, a process by which I somehow became my father, and I knew that I wouldn't handle the others any better than I was handling this one. Santa Barbara was crowded already with young people like us, every spare room seemed to have a newlywed couple in it. But, even if I could find a room, was that what I wanted? Was that the way to begin being married? Wouldn't it be like living with your in-laws? But if a room wouldn't do, how did I find something better, like a regular house? So I sat around the BOQ moping and doing nothing, until T came in with the answer.

He had found a house, he said. A big one, and expensive; but we could manage it if we got Bergie to come in with us. It had three bedrooms—well, really *two* bedrooms and a sun parlor off the living room—and two bathrooms; we could fit in all right. Spanish-style, he said, a regular hacienda. Even the address was fancy—Calle Boca del Cañon. I thought it sounded fine. Beginning marriage in the company of other beginners didn't seem so embarrassing as with strangers, or in-laws, or just any other adults.

The house in Calle Boca del Cañon was much grander than anything any of us was used to. The living room had a high, beamed ceiling and a stone fireplace that covered a whole wall, and there was a balcony at the end with a view across the roofs of the town to the mountains. On the upper floor was a round bedroom, with a round bed in it, and another balcony. The idea of sleeping in a round bed struck us all as very sexy, the sort of thing that Rita Hayworth might do in a movie, and we flipped coins for that room. T won, and his first child was conceived there. I came third in the toss and got the sun parlor. Liz and I would never be able to go to bed until everyone else did, but it was all right—we had a home.

While we waited for our wives, we moved our possessions out of BOQ and into the house. The possessions were mostly pieces of Marine equipment, the steel helmets and carbines and .38 revolvers and bayonets that had been issued to us at Miramar, for no reason that any of us could work out. There was no place to store all the gear, so we put it in the fireplace. It made the house look like a guerrilla headquarters, or a set from *For Whom the Bell Tolls*.

Then the wives arrived—three tired nineteen-year-olds, none of whom had ever been to California, or traveled that far on a train before (I don't suppose Bergie's wife Fran had ever been out of South Dakota), or run a house—and we began our collective life. It was pleasant, and sometimes even domestic-looking, but it never seemed more than playing at marriage. We were all too young, we had no idea of what marriage meant; it was all laughter and parties and clumsy love-making. The girls wore their college-girl clothes—bobby sox and big sweaters and loafers with pennies in them—and ran out to meet us when we came home, looking like the girls at a sorority house greeting a carload of SAE's. After work we strolled through the shops of the town, and bought things that made us feel adult and married—ashtrays, and potholders and towels. Liz and I found a secondhand bookstore, and bought the complete works of Thomas Wolfe, and T bought some old issues of *G-8 and His Battle Aces*, and read them aloud to us after supper. There was a copy of *Lady Chatterley's Lover* in the house, and Liz read that, too, but she didn't say much about it. I was too shy to read it; I guess I was afraid that if I read it, we'd have to discuss it. Sometimes we went out to dinner, to a Mexican restaurant called El Paseo, where a marimba band played, and people who knew how to rumba danced. It was like the evenings in Daytona Beach, part of the game we were playing, called Grown-ups.

Nobody made any plans. I think we were all frightened at the thought that the war might end, and then we'd have to start being grown-ups in earnest, with children and mortgages and debts. We had learned that much about marriage from our parents. But in the meantime we could have this long house-party in a romantic town with a view of the mountains, in a romantic place where none of us had ever been before.

T came home one day driving an old Ford that he had bought from an enlisted man. We could drive it to the squadron every morning, he said. But in the morning it wouldn't start; and in spite of our efforts it never would under its own power. Every morning the girls had to come out of the house in their housecoats and push us off down the hill, and at the end of the day we would get a mechanic to bring a starting truck from the flight line and get the car going for the drive home. Bergie, the cautious, practical father of the house, couldn't understand how T could have been slickered so completely. "Well," T explained, "that ol' boy was smilin' and thinkin', and I was just smilin'."

While we stayed in Santa Barbara we had squadron parties in our Spanish house. They were like fraternity parties, mostly drinking and singing. All the junior flying officers came—those who were new second lieutenants like ourselves, and the slightly older first lieutenants who had had one tour of duty in the Pacific. Senior officers—the CO and the Exec—and the nonflying administrators never came; I never once had a drink with a Commanding Officer, anywhere. We took this to be a matter of rank, of our seniors preserving their dignity; but probably it was simply a difference in age. The college boys drank with the college boys, and the adults drank with the adults.

Wives came too, all of them young and newly married. Jimmy brought his new wife, a Navy nurse who ran the medical ward at the Station hospital. Liz met a young war widow who lived across the street, and brought her over to meet Nick Nagoda, one of the squadron bachelors; and she seemed interested, but Nick wasn't. Sometimes a bachelor brought his own girl. Wally invited a girl out for a visit from Minneapolis, and they came one evening, and stood around shyly, as though it was their first date, or even their first party.

Those parties differed in one way from fraternity parties (or at least what I had heard about them)—there wasn't much sexuality at ours. Everyone drank a lot, and there was a good deal of stumbling affection, but not sex. What there was mostly was singing; we were never too drunk to sing, and the singing seemed more important than the drinking, which was more important (and less threatening) than sex. The songs we sang were the ones that had been brought back from the war, a separate repertoire of songs suitable for Marines to sing while drunk. Pilots had learned them at Ewa or Santos or Bougainville, or on rest leave in Australia; none had ever been written down, I'm sure, and many had been remade to fit new circumstances. They were a genuine oral tradition, like folk ballads. Most of them were about sex or death, though a few were devoted to despising senior officers and the military life. All were comic, or were intended to be.

Some of these songs had been picked up from British or Australian troops, and were not entirely comprehensible to us, though we liked them. I didn't know, for example, what it meant when I sang:

> I don't want to be a soldier,
> I don't want to go to war;
> I'd rather be around
> Piccadilly Underground,
> Living on the earnings of a high-class lady.

Where was Piccadilly? Why did the guy in the song want to live underground? How was it that a high-class lady earned money?

Others, or parts of others, seemed to have nothing to do with war and soldiering, and for all I know they might have come from any tradition, and almost any date. A song, for instance, that began with this stanza:

> The captain he rides in his motor-boat,
> The admiral rides in his gig;

It don't go a goddamn bit faster,
But it makes the old bastard feel big

was in the anti-senior-officer tradition; but it went on in this rather different vein:

Here's to the sex life of the camel,
It's stranger than anyone thinks;
In a moment of amorous passion
He tried to make love to the Sphinx.
Now the Sphinx's posterior anatomy
Is clogged by the sands of the Nile;
Which accounts for the hump on the poor camel's back,
And the Sphinx's inscrutable smile.

And what has that got to do with war, or flying, or Marines? But we sang it, and everyone joined in the choruses, which were mostly "toora-looras" and "Sing tiddly-aye-o's." Even the wives sang—or at least the party girls among them did. The shy ones sat, holding untasted drinks, and looked at each other or at the floor, waiting for their husbands to take them home. You could see, if you looked at them, the women they would be in twenty years, living lives devoted to not enjoying themselves.

Joe Baird became the squadron song-leader, a sort of mnemonic curator of the collection. He had no particular singing voice—he could carry a tune, like the rest of us, but no more than that—but he loved to sing. I think he felt the community of the singing more strongly even than the rest of us, how affection flowed among young men when they threw their arms around each other's shoulders and sang a roaring bawdy song. It isn't easy for young American males to express feelings for each other, but on those occasions, when we were together—all pilots, all drunk, shouting indecencies to music and laughing—it was all right; and Joe, who had a deep, easy capacity for love, was our natural leader. With a glass swinging in his hand in time to music, and a happy grin on his face, he would finish one song and begin another, all night, inexhaustibly. "There were *cats* on the roof," he would begin, and we'd be singing:

> And cats on the tiles,
> Cats with the shits
> And cats with the piles,
> Cats with their a–a–ass ho–o–o–les
> Wreathed in smiles,
> As they revelled in the joys of fornication.

Where did that one come from, I wonder? Joe sang it with great feeling. There were, of course, a great many more verses, including some vivid ones on the sex life of the armadillo. Even the sweet-faced Wally would join in, and Bergie, too, with his high pure voice like a choirboy's (T called it his "church-in-the-wildwood tenor"), soaring up easily above the rest of us. It was possible, then, to feel comradeship, to be happy together without being emotional, or not visibly, and thus unmanly. They were good parties.

I said that we were playing at being Grown-ups, but that wasn't entirely true. Fran and Berg weren't playing. It was simply in their natures to be an adult married couple, and as the weeks passed they gradually became the father and mother of the house, taking responsibilities and making decisions. Bergie mended broken fixtures and made sure that the phone bill was paid, and Fran cooked most of the meals (neither of the other girls knew how). It was easy to imagine them together after the war, in some little South Dakota town, with a houseful of growing kids—two solid, church-going, tax-paying citizens, as happy with each other as they were now. For the present, their cheerful maturity made it easier for the rest of us to go on being adolescents.

As domesticity flourished in Santa Barbara, as the squadron dug in and made a stable life, other pilots sent for their girls back home, and were married. One of these was a pleasant, rather remote guy from Minneapolis who was considered eccentric because he was a composer. He would sit in the ready room, waiting for a flight, with a sheet of music paper in his lap. Puta, seeing him thus, asked, "Whatcha doin', Gordon?" Gordon said he was writing music. "Aw, how can you be writing music? You ain't got no pianna!"

As the date approached for his girl's arrival and the wedding, Gordon became more and more nervous and remote, and took to going on long walks into the hills above the town. On one of these he wandered into some poison oak, and his legs were soon covered with an itching rash. We sent him off to the sick bay, and there he made the mistake of explaining to the corpsman that he was getting married in a few days and had to get the itching stopped before then. The corpsman replied that there was only one possible cure, and painted Gordon from his ankles to his crotch with gentian violet. And so he was married, in purple.

It reminded Rock of a story. "This guy comes into a hardware store and asks for a can of green paint, and a can of red paint, and a hammer." "Whadya want that for?" the hardware guy asks. "Well," he says, "I'm getting married tomorrow. So I'm gonna paint one ball green and the other one red. And if my wife says, 'That's the funniest looking pair of balls I ever seen,' I'm gonna hit her with the hammer.''

''Poor old Gordon,'' T said. ''He'll be too embarrassed to take his pants off. He's so shy, I bet he'll put his foot in the toilet and piss down his leg, just so he won't make any noise.'' But the marriage seemed to go all right, the gentian violet faded, and Gordon went on composing music in the ready room.

The ready room was our environment, our club, our sanctuary. Every ready room that I was ever in was just like every other one, yet each was unique—the domain of a particular squadron, the place where the pilots spent their time. They were all fitted with the same furniture—red plastic easy chairs with wooden arms, and seats that were always collapsed onto the springs, so that you sat deep down in them, almost on the floor, and green lockers along the walls for flying gear, and metal-and-plastic card tables. On one of these there was always an acey-deucey board. Acey-deucey was the naval pilot's game—a game something like backgammon that can be played for money, if you have any, or just to pass the time if you're broke. Not a great game, not even a very interesting one, but played in ready rooms, ritualistically. There was a Coke machine in a corner, and a blackboard where flight schedules were posted, and messages written. On one wall an aeronautical map of the area was mounted, with a worn, smudged place where the local field was. The other walls were covered with Dilbert cartoons.

Dilbert was a cartoon character invented, I think, by Robert Osborn. He was the image of an incompetent, careless, stupid flier; and his misdeeds were represented in cartoons that amused pilots, at the same time—or at least that was the theory—that they instructed. "Dilbert," the caption would read, "always believed in stretching a glide," and Osborn's cartoon would show a plane, stretched out over a boundary fence like a piece of bubble gum, with Dilbert's complacent lunatic face thrust from the cockpit. In time Dilbert's name entered the vocabulary of naval pilots and attached itself to every incompetent flier, and every squadron that I was in had one. Nobody had a special name for the brilliant pilots. But the brilliant ones weren't going to kill you.

In the ready room pilots waited for their flights. When it rained, they waited for the rain to stop. If they weren't flying, they just hung around—partly because there wasn't anywhere else to go, but partly because it was a pilot's place. You could watch planes take off and land, and you could talk to pilots who had just flown, or were on their way to fly. You could read about accidents in the *BuAer-News*. If you couldn't be flying, the next best things were watching it, talking about it, reading about it.

Failing that, you could get into a card game—the endless poker games, or, if Wally was there, pinochle, the only game folks played back home, he always explained. He was very good at it and liked to play for money. "I've heard of pool hustlers," Rock would say, "and I've heard of poker hustlers. I've seen a man get shot for hustlin' at pool. But Wally's the only pinochle-hustler I ever heard tell of."

Still, we were a training squadron, and we were expected to train. On wet mornings we were turned out of the ready room by the Training Officer, whose job it was to get us to do things that could be put in his records and sent to Washington, as evidence that we were improving our combat readiness. We might drift down the flight line to the Link building and practice instrument flying under the hood, or draw the ready-room blinds and sleep while an enlisted man ran training movies—*What to Know About Air Masses* or *How to Survive in the Jungle*—or go out into the fog and mist and play volleyball with a ball that was clumsy and slick with the dampness. On the coldest, bleakest mornings we were sent to the swimming pool; and there, in that chill chemical bath, we passed endurance tests, swimming round and round the pool (it was understood that it was not cheating to stand up and walk when you came to the shallow end), or practicing how to swim through burning oil, or how to take your pants off in deep water and make them into water wings. ("But think of the embarrassment," Wally said, "our ship is sunk, the rescue ship comes up, and there we all are, floating around in our underpants.") It was all training for extreme, but possible situations. Pilots did go down at sea, carriers were set afire. But I found them hard to imagine as I swam up and down (being sure to walk round the shallow end) and waited for 4:30, when we could get the car started and go home. The hint of danger made our lives exciting, but the danger wasn't a reality, not yet. I wanted to get into combat, and in my fantasies I did heroic things, but the Test would not happen today or tomorrow. Today and tomorrow we would go on training, and there would be a party at night, or a movie.

When the weather cleared, we trained in the air. We practiced formation-flying and navigation, we bombed and strafed, and we started night-flying; and in the process of learning to do all these things in TBM's we had a run of accidents. They were mostly of the usual kinds—a pilot lost control in a landing, and ground-looped, and scraped a wing; an engine failed on takeoff, and the plane slid to a stop, wheels up, off the end of the runway; a pilot hit his brakes too hard while taxiing, and the plane nosed up—the sorts of accidents you have when you're new and uncertain in a plane. Once, while we were practicing bombing runs on an offshore rock, someone dropped a water-filled bomb—weighing maybe a hundred pounds— through another plane's wing, and I heard the offended pilot's rage on the radio. For a moment I felt that shameful excitement that you feel in the presence of a disaster that is close, but isn't happening to you—there was going to be a crash, reality had entered our bombing game. But the wing held together, and the pilot flew back to the base and made an ordinary landing.

One dark, wet morning in October we drove out to the squadron to meet muster. There had been night-flying the night before, but we didn't expect to fly that day. An overcast hung down along the mountainsides like a heavy, torn curtain, and the wind blew gusts of sudden, vicious rain across the field. But we had to muster anyway. When we were together in the ready room, Jimmy came in and told us that Wally was missing. He had been night-flying the night before, had taken off, Jimmy said, at a quarter to seven. At eight o'clock all planes were ordered to return to the field—aerology said there was fog coming in. Wally was the only pilot who didn't acknowledge the order, and didn't come back. Radar stations along the coast had been alerted, but hadn't picked up any signals. By now the plane was down somewhere, probably in the sea. Wally might be alive, in a life raft or floating in his Mae West. Or there might be wreckage, or an oil slick. We would have to fly a search for him.

We would be scanning the sea and the beach, under a ceiling that sometimes came down to a few hundred feet above the water, below the minimums allowed for visual flight. Visibility would be poor, and the flying dangerous, and there seemed little chance that we would find anything. A plane that goes down at sea, unless it breaks up on impact, simply goes to the bottom and leaves no trace. But a search like this for a lost friend was not a search so much as it was a ritual for the dead. We dressed silently in the ready room. I noticed that Wally's flight was still on the schedule board. Beside it he had left a message for somebody: "Don't forget the pinochle game."

I took off with T in the rain and turned north along the beach. We were to search from the Air Station to Cape Lobos, a stretch of about twenty-five miles. The clouds lay low and ragged over the water, and drooped along the hills. We flew just below the cloud base, scanning the surface of the sea and the beach for wreckage. There was only the gray water and the featureless rocks. As we flew the weather got worse, the clouds lowered until we were flying in a thin and narrowing wedge of rainy air just above the waves. We would have to pull up, climb above the clouds, and return to the field; it just wasn't flying weather, hadn't been, really, when we took off. Still, we went on for a while, all our attention now on flying—clearing the sudden outcroppings of rock that jutted from the coastline, maintaining a little altitude, a hundred feet or so now, keeping each other in sight. Finally we quit, deciding at once and without words, and began to climb together.

I felt a mounting uneasiness as we climbed through clouds that seemed threatening and endless. T's plane on my wing was an indistinct shadow, and I was afraid I'd lose sight of it, and then fly into it. The clouds were dark and full of turbulence, and the planes bucked and tossed, and instrument needles swung erratically. Then it became lighter, there was sunlight above us, and I felt an impulse to pull back on the stick, to plunge up to that light; but still we went on in mist, watching the airspeed, the tilting horizon-indicator, the rate-of-climb. When we had burst out at last, into the light, the sky was burning blue above us, and the tops of the clouds were an unbelievable white that was like light itself. It was like flying out of death into life. Wally was dead, but we had performed our ritual of grief. We flew back in a tight two-plane formation, one plane's wing stuck in the space between the other plane's wing and tail, two friends being skillful together, being pilots, being alive.

Chapter 6

In November the squadron moved to El Toro, a Marine field that lay in a broad, shallow valley south of Los Angeles and inland from Laguna Beach. It was a bigger field than Santa Barbara, and a better one to fly from. The mountains were higher, but they were farther away. You could see their snow-covered tops in the distance to the east when you took off, and the land around the field was flat enough to crash-land on if you had to. And because the sea was beyond the low line of hills to the west, there were no sudden fogs to catch you in the air, the way Frenchy Brelet had been caught. No one knew why we were sent there. Some said it was only an excuse for delaying our assignment to combat; pilots were not dying in the Pacific as rapidly as had been expected.

T and I came into Laguna Beach on a rainy Sunday night. We had ridden down from Los Angeles on a bus to see whether we could find a place for Liz to live (T's wife was pregnant, and had gone home to her mother in Bir-

133

mingham). The town had the shut-down look that resort towns have out of season; not only was it closed, but it would be closed tomorrow and the next day and the rest of the winter. The lights were out on the movie marquee and on the gas pumps at the corner. Nothing moved on the main street, not a car, not even a dog or cat, and there was no sound except the hush and shuffle of the sea on the beach; the water must be close, just behind that row of stores.

The only lighted door was a storefront USO, and we went in, feeling a little ill at ease (the USO wasn't for officers, or at least we didn't think it was). A girl of perhaps nineteen or twenty was sitting at a desk, looking as though nothing had happened for quite a while. She was tall and blond, the kind who would be handsome when she was thirty; but at nineteen she was too big and definite to be pretty, and she was simply friendly looking. Her name was Torchy, and she was the daughter of a local dentist. We both liked her at once, and if either of us had been alone with her, he'd probably have flirted a bit, though she seemed too nice to get very far with, and I thought she'd probably be too tall when she stood up. But we were brothers-in-law, and the ground rules weren't clear yet, so we talked about housing, and I got a couple of addresses, and then we went back into the rain, feeling gloomy and married. Knowing one friendly girl seemed to make the town lonelier. We caught the last bus through the canyon to the Air Station, to report for duty.

The duty was more training. By now we were easy in TBM's, but we weren't very skillful in them yet. We began to work seriously at bombing, getting the angle right, dropping, pulling up, and getting the hell out; and we practiced formation-flying. Tactically, good formations were part of good bombing procedures—the better the formation was in an attack, the sooner all the planes would get onto the target and away again—but we began to fly together for other reasons, for the pleasure and satisfaction of it. Turkeys weren't stressed for acrobatics; you couldn't Victory Roll one low over the strip, or loop to a landing, as I once saw somebody do in a Corsair; but they were marvelous for precision flying, being heavy, stable, and powerful. If you were any good you could put your plane two feet from another one and stay there all day.

We began to work especially on formation approaches to landing—the only kind of flying in which we might look better than the fighter pilots (and right over the field, where they could see the show). A group of TBM's would approach the field in a column of three-plane V's, in very tight, very symmetrical formation, the wingmen's propellers inches from the leaders' wing-tips, and as they crossed the downwind end of the runway the lead plane could break away suddenly, up and to the left, into a sweeping vertical bank, lowering wheels in the turn, holding the bank through a full circle, and rolling out just over the runway in time to make a heavy, full-stall landing on one side of the strip, and already the second plane rolling out to touch down on the other side, and the third plane coming in behind the first, until the whole flight was on the runway, alternatively left and right, and the leader was just turning off onto the taxiway. It was a beautiful and astonishing thing to watch, and it was very satisfying to do, all together, like a team or an orchestra.

Section takeoffs, though less commonly done, were also

pleasurable. I think the greatest satisfaction I ever got from flying an airplane was taking off in section (T was on the other wing) on a rather doltish captain in the squadron. He wasn't much of a flier, but his phlegmatic calm was just right for the occasion. He rolled stolidly down the runway and into the air, while we, on either wing, held position as though we were a single, three-fuselaged machine. It was two or three minutes of absolutely flawless flying, the sort of pure act of skill that stays in the mind, in detail as clear as a sharp photograph—the three planes, rising smoothly in the steady air, the flat land below, the clear sunlight.

Our usual bombing target was a circle of whitewashed stones on a bare hillside some miles south of the field. We went back to it day after day, watching our scores, comparing our hits. It began to seem easy, a daily routine that we would do forever, while the war went on without us. Then on a single day two planes crashed on the target, and killed eight men—the two pilots, their crews, and a couple of extra men who had gone along to get their flight time. Both pilots were experienced, both had been in combat, neither should have died. The first dove straight into the ground on a bombing run—fascinated by the target, perhaps, concentrating on making the drop perfect, or maybe just careless about his altitude. There's no way of knowing. He was Nick Nagoda's friend, and Nick volunteered to help the ambulance crew reach the wreck. He flew above them as they crept up the dirt roads, some of them scarcely more than tracks, that led from the highway into the hills, and when they came to an intersection, he dove to show them which way to go, pulled up into a steep turn, and stalled. The plane rolled on its back and plunged into a ravine and burned. I flew over the target a few days later. The two wrecks were still there, very near each other. They looked small, just two tangles of metal, each in a burned spot on a hillside. They didn't seem big enough to have killed eight men. After a while the wrecks were cleared away, but we could still see the burned spots when we used the target. Two dumb mistakes. Even a good pilot like Nick, an intelligent, quick man, could do something dumb in a plane, and when he did, it would kill him.

About this time we finally heard the end of the story of Frenchy. When he found himself caught above the fog, that day at Santa Barbara, he had asked for a heading to El Centro—we had heard that much on our own radios. But either the controller made a mistake or Frenchy did. Instead of flying on a course of 080 degrees, East, he had flown on 180, which carried him due South, still above solid fog, into Mexico. When the fog began to break up, he saw below him the western side of a body of water. It was the Gulf of California; but he took it to be the Salton Sea, and since he was nearly out of gas he made a wheels-up landing on the beach. Then he wrote a letter to his mother and left it in the cockpit of the plane, with an airmail stamp on it, and set out to walk north along the beach to the town that his map showed was not far away. He left all the emergency rations and water in the plane, perhaps because the town looked so close. But there was no town. The Mexican Army tracking party that finally found him said that he had walked along the beach for a couple of days, then turned to wander inland, returned to the beach, wandered back again into the trees, until at last he fell. "He was found in the surrounding desert," the official report said, "dead and mutilated. The numerous wild birds and small animals existing in the vicinity probably were responsible for the mutilation.'' The body could only be identified by checking Frenchy's Navy dental charts. ''Christ,'' T said, ''he was eaten by wolves.''

That month the Navy took away half the squadron's TBM's, and gave us SB2C's instead. These were the Navy's new dive-bomber, bigger and faster than the SBD's I had trained in, but in every other way less satisfactory. The SBD was named the Dauntless, though I never heard it called anything but Speedy–D, and it *was* dauntless; some public relations man had decided to call the SB2C the Helldiver, and it was as showy and as phony as the name, like a beach athlete, all muscle and no guts. It was a long, slab-sided, ugly machine, with a big round tailfin. Unlike most service planes, it was entirely electrically operated (others had hydraulic systems for wheels, flaps, and wing-folding), and the circuits were very undependable, so that you might approach for a landing, flip the switch that activated the flaps, and find that only one flap opened (which would probably roll the plane on its back a hundred feet from the ground); or only one wheel would retract on takeoff; or circuits would get crossed, and the wheels would drop when you wanted to turn on your bombsight. We were all afraid of the SB2C's, and we flew them as though they were booby-trapped. On dive-bombing flights, nobody dived; we settled for gentle glides toward the target, and even gentler pull-ups. And we landed like the Air Force—far apart, flat in the approach, and with plenty of power. ''That thing looks like a coffin,'' Rock said, ''and it flies like a coffin. It ain't worth a pot of cold piss.''

In the end it wasn't the power system's failings that saved us, but those big tails. The squadron's Executive Officer was sitting in an SB2C one morning, pretending to warm it up, but actually using the cockpit oxygen mask to breathe a little pure oxygen, which was very good for hangovers. While he was sitting there, breathing deeply and running the engine at screaming full throttle, the tail of the plane fell off. It just fell off, and blew across the mat, with the mechanic running after it. We all went out from the ready room to look at the plane, sitting there, tailless and disgraced, with the Exec standing by it, looking as though his hangover was worse, and each of us was thinking, *Jesus, that could have happened while I was flying it.* So they were all grounded, and after a while they were taken away, and we went back to TBM's, the planes that we trusted and knew how to fly.

Though VMTB-943 was by official designation a torpedo-bombing squadron, and though we were once more flying torpedo bombers, none of the junior pilots had ever seen a torpedo, let alone dropped one. The CO decided that we must go, a few at a time, to San Diego, to the Naval Air Station on North Island, to be instructed. I went in a flight of six, and almost at once the flight leader's radio failed, and he returned to El Toro, and left me, flying behind him, to lead the flight. The route looked easy—down the valley to Capistrano, past the church the swallows were supposed to come back to, and then south along the beach, over San Clemente, a boom-town real estate gamble of the twenties that had failed. It was a good landmark. From the air you could see the grid of unused streets, and here and there a sad, fraudulent-looking Spanish-style house, with white walls and a red tile roof, and all around it fields of weeds. Then the coast curved, and we slid out to sea and headed for Point Loma, the northern arm of San Diego harbor. I was rather pleased with myself, leading my flight so neatly and efficiently. Then, as we approached Point Loma, little white clouds began to appear in the air to the left of us—the puffs that bursting antiaircraft shells make. Someone was shooting at us. I swung away from the coast and pulled out my maps. I had just led my flight through a restricted zone, a practice area for antiaircraft crews. ''Some flight leader,'' T said when we had landed at North Island. ''Ain't everybody can lead a flight into combat in southern California.'' But nobody was really upset; it was another part of the game, a joke, something to kid me about. It was still impossible to believe that those white puffs might be fatal.

San Diego was in some ways like Pensacola—an old established Naval Station with a serenely permanent look. But it was different. The harbor was a deep-water anchorage, and when you flew over the bay you could see combat ships entering and leaving, and convoys gathering in the waters offshore before sailing to Pearl Harbor and the islands beyond. In moorings along the edge of the North Island Air Station, carriers with famous names were tied up—the *Enterprise,* the *Saratoga,* the *Ticonderoga*—and we looked at them with reverence as we passed, as though they were heroic monuments of battles fought long ago. You felt, in San Diego, that the serious war began here.

The town was rougher than Pensacola had been, full of sailors just in from the fleet, who were sometimes brutally violent when drunk; a fighter pilot I knew had his face ripped open with a broken bottle in a brawl there, and the bars were full of fights and club-swinging shore patrolmen. But the Air Station was calm, secure in the presence of its own past. The landing field was a circular mat, like the one at Pensacola's Main Side, perhaps fifteen hundred feet across, put down in the thirties; it had been big enough for the biplanes of those days, but it wouldn't do for modern fighters, and so a straight strip had been added at the side. But the presence of that outmoded mat, and of the old hangars beside it, and the seaplane ramps along the beach was all part of the special quality of North Island, the feeling it always gave me of a tradition in Navy flying. It wasn't a long tradition—there had been Navy pilots then for about thirty years—but still I liked the sense of the past I got when I read above a hangar door a sign that said Bombing Squadron Two; it was a designation from the twenties.

We went to classrooms in one of the hangars for ground school—the structure of the aerial torpedo, the technique of torpedo attack—taught by a man who had taught me freshman English in college. He invited me home for dinner, and showed me his newborn daughter; and I felt for a little while out of the flying world, and in a world where people read serious books, thought serious thoughts, and in general took life more seriously than Marine pilots did. We ate and drank and talked about Keats, and I had a good time, but I found the presence of the baby disturbing; it seemed a threatening part of the seriousness, a responsibility that lay in wait. They were already entangled in their future, and in time I would be, too.

In the same hangar I met Bud, my melancholy friend from my Memphis days, now a seaman pushing a broom. We went out together that night, and listened to Stan Kenton in a San Diego bar, and drank Irish whiskey. We were still friends, and he was still funny, but we were a little stiff and awkward together. Life had confirmed his melancholy, and his war was a long boredom, something to be expected and endured. But my war was just about to begin, and boredom was a state I knew nothing about.

Next day our planes were loaded with dummy torpedoes, and we were sent out to make practice runs on an elderly World War I destroyer that was operating among the islands off the mouth of the harbor. The point of the attack was to approach the destroyer from the side, flying low and level just above the water (like Jimmy and George at Rabaul), and drop your torpedo fifty to a hundred yards from the target. If you dropped correctly, the torpedo would fall flat into the water—it was like dropping a telephone pole on its side—and the propeller at the back would begin to turn and drive the torpedo toward the ship. The dummies contained no explosives, but they were still big, heavy hunks of steel; and the destroyer skipper was apprehensive and kept his ship heeling and turning evasively as we approached. We launched our attack, raggedly. Some torpedoes fell too far out and never reached the target; others fell crookedly, and sank, or crossed ahead of or behind the ship. Joe, at the end of the flight, was determined to get a hit. He bore in close, diving toward the ship, delaying the drop until he was sure of his aim. The torpedo struck the water just short of the ship, in exactly the right spot. But it struck at an angle, submerged, and a moment later burst from the water like a porpoise, in a leaping arc that carried it across the destroyer's deck, past the astonished crew, and into the water on the other side. The skipper immediately radioed that he was suspending operations, and the destroyer wheeled and steamed for home, smoke pouring from all four stacks.

We turned to antisubmarine warfare, first lectures, and

then a practice flight, to drop dummy depth-bombs on a training submarine off the coast. We circled offshore, watching the surface. The sub was to cruise, just underwater; we were to spot the dark shadow and straddle it with our harmless bombs, thus learning both to locate a submerged sub and to drop on it. But we came upon it unawares, just as it was surfacing, and began our attack as the conning tower rose from the water. By the time the sub was fully surfaced, and had its tower open, the bombs were splashing alongside and the air was full of TBM's. The submarine submerged in a crash-dive, and lay under the water, sulking, and refused to play, or even to answer our radio pleas. We decided we must be qualified antisub pilots; after all, Joe said, we had nearly sunk the goddamn thing. We returned to North Island.

Back at El Toro we found a new Commanding Officer in charge, a fierce, stiff, academy-trained Lieutenant Colonel—a professional son-of-a-bitch, as Rock put it, with a ramrod up his ass. He was the kind of Regular who is sent to overrelaxed outfits run by Reservists, to bully them into shape. He had swept into 943 during our absence, and had found everything out of order. The Sergeant Major had been lax in his record-keeping, and he was now on his way to the war; officers weren't being trained, and so a new training program had begun. There was no one at all in the ready room when I came in that first morning; either all the pilots were somewhere being trained or they were hiding from the Colonel. The clerks in the squadron office were starched and barbered, and seemed in a state of shock.

The next day, taxiing in from a flight, I followed a lineman's signals, swung my plane around to park it in front of the hangar, and ran the tail into the hangar door. I was annoyed as I shut the engine down—the goddamn lineman should have been more careful—and I was prepared to climb down and give him hell, but I saw that this wouldn't be necessary. There was already an officer standing beside him, and though I couldn't hear what was being said, the lineman seemed to be shriveling.

By the time I had gotten down the Colonel had gone, but the lineman was still fixed to the spot. He stared at me as he might have stared at a man on the gallows. "The Colonel wants to see you," he said. "Jeez, is he pissed off."

He was right. The Colonel was pissed off all right. While I stood as stiffly at attention as I could manage, he paced his office and as he marched up and down he poured over me a cold stream of furious abuse. I was a destructive idiot; I had damaged valuable Marine Corps property (much more valuable, it was clear, than I was); I was a disgrace to the squadron, to the Air Group, to the Wing, to the Marine Corps past and present (in the Halls of Montezuma, angels turned their backs and wept), to my nation, my parents, and myself. I realized all this time that, although I was standing still and he was moving, he nevertheless managed to be more at attention than I was. At last he stopped, turned full at me, and delivered the sentence: "You're grounded, Lieutenant. I'm going to send you down to Pendleton for two weeks, to find out what being a Marine is all about."

The old anxieties came flooding back. I was going to be left out. While I was at the infantry camp at Pendleton, the squadron's orders would come; everyone else would go into combat; I'd be left behind. And it would all be my fault. Goddamn the lineman, goddamn the hangar door. And most of all, goddamn the sadistic Colonel, whose harsh face had cracked into a smile of cold satisfaction. I went home gloomily to explain to Liz that she would be a widow for two weeks while I learned to be an infantry-man.

With me the Colonel sent, for no reason that either of us could figure out, a big, ugly, cheerful man from the squadron named Steve Bakos. Steve and his wife lived near us in Laguna, and he drove us down the coast to Pendleton the next Sunday night. In the back of his car was all the useless gear that we had been lugging around with us since we came to the west coast in August, the stuff that had been in the fireplace at Santa Barbara—fatigue uniforms, carbines, helmets, canteens, bayonets, webbed belts. We had never worn any of it and could never have any possible use for it. Some of it I didn't even know how to wear; but it had been issued to us at Mira-mar, and we were responsible for it all each time we moved. It was like having an idiot-child, Steve said, or a senile grandmother—just one more set of worries.

Dressed in this comical gear, I felt like a character in a play, or in a recruiting movie, Freddy the Fearless Leatherneck. I could even imagine my dialogue: "Just let me at them Japs!" and "Don't worry, men, the odds are only ten-to-one against us," and "Tell Mom that. . . ." I tried to look casual, but the stuff was all brand new, and the fatigues crackled when I walked, and I couldn't keep my pants stuffed down into the leather leggings that were attached to my boots. After a while, when we had marched cross-country for a whole day, the crackling stopped, and I began to feel that I was wearing my own clothes, though I never got used to wearing a helmet. I even began to enjoy the course, without under-standing the point of it.

It was one more summer camp, a last version of military training as a game. One night we played No-Man's-Land, a game in which you crawl on your belly in the dark from one trench to another, across a space that is strung with barbed wire. As you crawl along, machine guns fire tracer bullets above you, to encourage you to keep your bottom down, and here and there along the way explosives are detonated in the earth to simulate shell explosions. With the tracers and the noise and the smell of powder it was quite realistic—as realistic, probably, as the trench scenes in *All Quiet on the Western Front*. But it was still a game. Like the Simulated Aerial Combat Machine, it could momentarily persuade you, but in the end, safe in the other trench, you knew that the real thing would be different, and that this wasn't really much help.

Another night we played Commando Raid, crossing a shallow pond in rubber boats, and stumbling around a lot among reeds and mud. The water was cold—even in southern California nights are chilly in November—but the game was fun. We were told that we had lost, but since I had not understood what winning involved, I wasn't disappointed.

Steve and I were both entertained by our two weeks of pretending to be infantrymen, and we went home feeling easier about fatigues and carbines and web-belts, but without really knowing much more about our remote allies, the ground Marines. When we got back to the squadron, nothing had happened except that the Colonel had left for a higher echelon job, and the new Sergeant Major that he had demanded had turned up. There were still no orders, and the squadron was still training, though now that the

Colonel was gone there were more pilots in the ready room, and the acey-deucey board was out again.

The new Sergeant Major was in fact an old one, one of the prewar breed of Marines, a veteran of the Nicaragua campaign and of China duty. He had the typical bulldog look, heavy-set and jowly, and a voice like an angry bass fiddle. He was punctilious about his military courtesies, but he had small regard for the young flying officers around him. "Goddamn it, Lieutenant!" he would growl when he met a young pilot about to walk out the door carrying a bottle of whiskey, "you can't do that!" And he would find a piece of wrapping paper or a paper bag, and cover it up properly.

The Sergeant Major was old, in our eyes. He had been in the Corps all his adult years, and he had no other life. He had never married, and seemed to have no family, and it was said that he had not left the Station since he arrived there. He spent his free time in his barracks room, so the story went, polishing his shoes and his insignia. But he was aging, and his health was failing, and he would be forced to retire soon—943 was his last billet. One night he went into the squadron office, sat down in the Commanding Officer's chair, and shot himself in the head with the CO's .45. The second lieutenant who was Duty Officer that night was quite upset. There was nothing in the regulations to cover an event like that, and Christ, what a mess it made.

Weeks passed, it was December 1944, and still the squadron stayed on at El Toro. We began to evolve a permanent-feeling life. Liz and I had a little apartment in a house at the top of a canyon in the Laguna hills. I came home at night like any married man, and we walked together in the town, or along the beach, and had parties with other young couples. On wet evenings we went to movies—romantic ones like *Now Voyager* and *Laura* and *To Have and Have Not*—and held hands in the dark, as though we were on a date. We climbed on the rocks along the coast, and found shells and starfish. I have a photograph of Liz fooling around, like a kid, with Steve Bakos; Steve is holding two starfish to his chest, like a stripper's bra, and they're both laughing. The picture has the spirit of that time, as I remember it—being young and happy and silly.

Not always happy, though. In Santa Barbara we had been cushioned from the most fundamental of marriage-truths—the endless intimacy of two—by the company of the other couples in the house. That life had been more like a long college party than like a marriage. But in Laguna we were alone in our two rooms together, and the fact that we were still very ignorant of each other became clear. We were not, for one thing, from the same America. I found Liz's easy southern ways charming, but sometimes maddeningly irresponsible and vague; she found my midwestern puritanism strict and cold. So there were quarrels, and cruel words, and tears. But we learned, each of us, who it was that we were married to, and so gradually became what the certificate said we already were—a married couple. And the two rooms in the canyon became a home, a place I came back to for comfort, a refuge.

We spent our first Christmas together in Laguna. The weather was warm and hazily sunny, and we walked down into the town and had dinner at a French restaurant that we thought was a very good one; perhaps it was, we had no way of judging—everything tasted good, everything was sophisticated to us. It seemed funny, spending

Christmas in shirt-sleeves in the sun, a part of the whole unreality of the game of marriage that we played there. But the next day it was cold and damp again, and as I waited by the canyon road for a ride to the squadron I felt like a commuter going to work too early in the morning.

On New Year's Eve we were with Steve and his wife, in their house high up on a hill over the town. Jane was pregnant, and very big; and she moved clumsily but happily around the rooms, in a domestic dream. Steve was happy and proud of her and the baby. He seemed more married than the rest of us, a man cut out for family life. He was a good, dependable flier, as he would have been a good truck driver or a good doctor; but he wasn't in love with flying, the way the rest of us were. The center of his life was in that small house, with his wife and his child. That night we ate, and drank a little—but not too much, because of Jane—and talked about home, about what high school was like, the dances and the music and the clothes we wore, and for a while the war didn't exist. Except for Jane's pregnancy, we might have been two young couples on a double date, or two pairs of newlyweds in some suburb in a time of peace.

When midnight came, we went out to stand on the porch. It was a cold, clear night, and we could see lights far down the beach, and along the road that led up into the canyon. There were distant sounds of celebration, and one church-bell ringing. So much for 1944, I thought. A year ago I was in a barracks at Whiting Field, listening to the rain—a cadet, single, a kid. I hadn't even met Liz. Now I was married, and an officer. Where would I be in another year? Would I be alive? Liz said she was cold, and there really wasn't much point in standing out there in the dark. We went in and had another drink, and walked home through the dark, quiet streets.

January passed, alternately hazy and warm and wet and cold. We flew when we could, but restlessly; the squadron felt trained, and we wanted to get out, before the war ended. In the Philippines the invasion was going well, and when that was over the next one might be the Japanese mainland. If we missed that, we'd have missed the war. But no orders came, and we went on flying, and living our little domestic lives. Other pilots in the squadron met girls, or sent for their hometown sweethearts, and married them, and moved "ashore": even the unlovable Sly got married.

For most of us, the private, physical side of marriage was a mystery, partly sacred and partly embarrassing, that we never mentioned to each other. But Sly had no such reticence about it; he dragged his sex life into squadron conversations as though it was a dirty joke that he'd just heard, that was too good to keep to himself. He would go home for lunch, and then come back and buy a sandwich at the PX, and eat it in the ready room. "Going home for lunch sure gives a man an appetite," he would say with a leer. "Shit," Rock said, "a guy like Sly gives fuckin' a bad name."

We flew at night, out of sheer restlessness, in wandering section-flights up and down the coast. Laguna, with its curve of bay and its one lighted street, looked like a necklace, with a pendant stretching out into the canyon toward El Toro. Los Angeles was a vast saucer of lights. Long Beach was a bright patch. Inland, a vast darkness seemed to stretch out forever, the darkness of the whole American continent; and westward was another and larger void, the dark Pacific. We were impatient to leave that continent for that ocean, but up there at night, alone in the dim light of the cockpit, both directions seemed alien and fearful, and we held to a course along that thin band of familiar lights that was the coast.

When we didn't fly at night there were parties. We met in bars and sang drunkenly with bands, or by ourselves if the band wasn't playing. Joe sang, with great feeling, a ballad about a girl who married a man who had no testicles, and we all roared out the chorus:

> No balls at all,
> No balls at all,
> A very short peter
> And no balls at all,

while the proprietor looked uneasily around at his other customers. Sometimes we ran through the endless choruses of "Fuck 'em All," though in public we made a concession, and changed the refrain to "Bless 'em All." Some of the bachelors rented an apartment in Laguna—it was known as Shades-down Chateau—and had parties there, and got drunk, and sang, and seduced girls. One of the squadron's most aggressive lovers boasted that he had seduced Torchy, the friendly girl from the USO. I felt sad about that—it was like another rainy night in a strange town, a loss.

At the end of the month our orders came; twenty-eight of us were to report to Miramar on February 8, "for further assignment." We were on our way out, somewhere. I took Liz up to Los Angeles and put her aboard a train for Chicago. My father would meet her (he had never seen her) and take her to the train for Birmingham. I knew how it would be—he, who had never had a daughter, would sweep through the crowd and wrap his big arms around her; and she, who had no father, only a stepfather, would feel at once secure and protected by him. With a daughter he could express the feelings that he couldn't show for a son. I felt full of love for them both as I caught my own train, south, for San Diego.

Chapter 7

Miramar again. I was exhilarated but apprehensive. This was what I wanted, what we had aimed for all these months; it was the dream of success, like marrying money. But, like marriage, it was the beginning of another, unknown life, a step into experience that I knew nothing about, and couldn't imagine, and that all the stories of the veterans couldn't help me to feel. What would it be like, flying from a Pacific island, diving on a real target, being shot at, shooting back? It wasn't exactly fear that I felt, not fear of any specific thing, not death or wounds or even being a coward; it was vaguer than that, an emptiness at the center, a void, a drawn breath in a dark room.

There was nothing to do at Miramar until embarkation orders arrived, but no one left the base. We spent our time in the BOQ bar, drinking and making those quick, temporary friendships that you make in bars. A middle-aged intelligence officer was always there, and he taught us to drink French 75's. The French 75 is a drink invented—or so the intelligence officer said—by American troops in France during the First World War. A mixture of champagne and brandy, it makes you very drunk. "But you'll never have a hangover from French 75's," the intelligence officer said. "I know that to be a fact, based on years of research." Nevertheless, we all did. If he didn't, it may have been because he kept a bottle of whiskey under his bunk. I roomed with him, and he insisted on having the lower bunk, because otherwise he couldn't reach the bottle in the morning while lying down.

As we got drunker, we sang our songs, and the intelligence officer added one that stayed with us. We were between songs, just sitting there, sort of limply, the way you do when you're halfway to being really drunk, and have plenty of time, when the intelligence officer raised his French 75 in the air and began:

> Here's to Marianne, queen of all the acrobats,
> She's a big fat slob, twice as big as me,
> Pimples on her ass like cherries on a tree.

There were other, more scatological choruses, and it ended:

> She's the kind of girl that will marry—

The intelligence officer looked around, and spotted Harry, the squadron seducer.

> —that will marry Harry here.

A great joke, we thought, Harry married to a big fat slob, and we sang the song again and again, changing the name at the end sometimes, when somebody else came into the bar.

A pilot just back from the South Pacific taught us a ballad that he had learned from an Australian, about a man who went out with a bloody great rod and came back with a bloody great cod. There was a chorus, "Singing ee-iy—ee-iy—ee-iy—o," something like that. The pilot went on:

He didn't have a place to put the bloody fish,
So he put it in the pot where the old girl pissed,
    (chorus)
In the middle of the night she got up to take a squat,
And the codfish crawled up you know what.
    (chorus)
They worked it out with the handle of a broom,
And they chased it around and around the room.
    (chorus)
There's a moral to the story, and the moral is this—
Always look into the piss-pot before you take a piss.
    (chorus)

We all learned it, and it joined the repertoire. Joe liked to act it out, especially the part about the broom, and he would get to laughing so hard at his pantomime that he couldn't sing.

From time to time someone would leave the bar and try to place a long-distance call. Not that there was anything to say, but it seemed a thing that you did before you went overseas. There was always a wait—the operator would intone through her nose, in an automatic way, "There will be a four-hour delay"—and so the caller would return to the bar, have another French 75, sing another song, until at last, when his mother was on the phone, he'd be too drunk to say anything except "Hello, Ma."

Even the bar and the songs got boring. I got a jeep, drove to a nearby Navy field, and scrounged a hop in a PB4Y, the Navy's version of the B-24 bomber. A flight in a four-engined plane would be something different, at least. Pilots tend to feel about new planes the way lechers feel about women—every one is a new experience, it's all interesting, any flying is better than no flying. But this time it was pretty dull, just flying around, like a long ride on a Greyhound bus. Only the landing was really interesting; getting all that heavy clumsiness down and stopped seemed a difficult and delicate operation, the only part of the flight I wasn't sure I could do. But I was relieved to get in the jeep and hurry back to Miramar to see if the orders had come while I was gone.

They hadn't, but eventually they did, covered with "SECRET" stamps, and written in the odd, condensed language of official military bureaucracy, but saying, when we'd worked it all out, that we would go to Pearl Harbor, and there would be assigned to a working squadron somewhere in the South Pacific. So we were going to make it to the war. We had a last, all-night party in the BOQ, packed our gear into trucks, and were driven, in the half-light of early morning, down to the San Diego docks.

Our transport was a Liberty ship called the *Lavaca*. Rock said it meant "cow" in Mexican, and that seemed appropriate for such a lumpish, uninteresting-looking vessel. Still, going on board was exciting; I had never been on an oceangoing ship before. As the *Lavaca* left the harbor I stood on deck with T, feeling sentimental and a little scared as we left the familiar places—past the moored carriers, past North Island, where F6F's were taking off, and a P-boat was drifting down to a landing, past Point Loma, where I had led my flight through the antiaircraft range, past the offshore islands, where we had almost sunk the submarine. In open water outside the harbor the ship joined a convoy, and began to pitch and roll. Gun crews uncovered their guns and test-fired them. Off our beam destroyers slid by, covering the perimeter of the convoy. The war was still a long way off, but we were entering its atmosphere.

Hawaii would be the first strange place, the edge of a world that was not like anything back home. No one I knew had ever been there, except maybe a few Marines, and it existed in my imagination as a mixture of myths. The beach at Waikiki was a part of the romantic mythology of Minneapolis, a place taken out of a song, like Paris in the spring—it was all leis and hula girls and ukuleles. But Pearl Harbor was a part of that mythology, too; it was the stab in the back, the day that would live in infamy, columns of black smoke and diving planes. I couldn't put the two together into one place.

We hung around on deck all morning, the last day out, waiting for signs. First came patrol planes, like the first birds, signifying land ahead, and then picket boats, circling around us suspiciously. Then tugs pulled the antisubmarine nets open, and we entered the roadstead. Somebody on the deck recognized Diamond Head, and for a moment the mood was that of a cruise ship. We were seeing the sights, but as we steamed on we could see the inner harbor ahead, where the superstructures of the sunken ships still thrust up out of the water, with their trapped dead below, and our holiday mood faded. We moved slowly in past the wrecks, and I thought of the dead men's bones, down there in the sunken hulls, so many of them, all white and fleshless now. We had reached the real edge of the war.

"Come on," Rock said. "We've got one day to spend in this town. Let's spend it." And we did, the way any tourist would. We went to the Royal Hawaiian Hotel at Waikiki, because we had heard of it, and had a drink. We swam on the beach (it was surprisingly stony), watched a couple of surfboard riders (and speculated as to why they weren't in the army), and went back into Honolulu. For a famous city it had a disappointingly small-town look ("nothin' but Amarillo with a beach," Rock said); the streets were narrow and crowded, and the buildings were low and temporary looking, as though they might have all been built to last only for the duration of the war, or were a set for a war movie. We couldn't think of anything to do there. I found one bookstore—not a very good one—and after a good deal of deliberation I bought a book to last me for a while, *War and Peace*.

For lunch we chose the most Hawaiian-looking restaurant we could find, a place that was all bamboo and palm leaves, with a sort of a hut at one end of the room, where a band in flowered shirts played Hawaiian guitars. "Mainland rum or island whiskey?" the waiter asked. Those were the only options, and we chose the island whiskey— what was the point of being in the islands if you didn't share their customs? It was made from pineapples, the waiter said, and one swallow sent a pain through my head that was like being shot, a sort of instant hangover.

Honolulu, like its whiskey, was a failure. Perhaps no place could have been exciting enough just then, or at least no place that wasn't in the middle of war—London or Paris, maybe, or Berlin. But Honolulu on the last day of February in 1945 was only another crowded Navy town, much like Pensacola or San Diego, full of sunlight and sailors and bad liquor. We took our island hangovers back to the Marine base at Ewa, and lay around the pool there and waited to move out. At the pool side there wasn't much difference between being where we were and waiting on some other base. It was just another station where nothing was happening.

The flight from Honolulu to Ulithi atoll in the Western Carolines took three days—three days of almost total emptiness, empty air around us and the vacant sea below. I began to get a sense of the enormous expanse of the Pacific. We sat in bucket seats along the sides of the Navy transport plane, with our feet on the cargo that was stowed down the middle, and tried to read or sleep, or talked about where we were going. It took four hours to reach the first crumb of land—Johnston Island, a landing strip and a couple of buildings and nothing else, not even a tree to shelter you from the baking sun, and all around, stretching to the horizon, the empty, featureless, blinding sea. We ate a hasty lunch there, and were off again for seven more hours' flying to the next island, Majuro. It was night by then, and we landed in moonlight.

Majuro was a perfect coral atoll, a serene lagoon circled by a ring of islands set with palm trees. When we had carried our gear to the Transient Officers' Quarters we went to the officers' club and got cans of beer and took them out onto the beach. The moon was rising across the lagoon, making a bright track on the water, and the palm trees on the far islands were black silhouettes. It was a scene that demanded sentiment, and I knew that I should have feelings about it, sad romantic yearnings for the far-off beloved, something like that. But how could I have any real response to a tropical island in the moonlight? It was too damn much, too like a movie with Dorothy Lamour; and I could only feel the way I did in movies like that—charmed, but disbelieving. We all sat a little uncomfortably, looking at the moon on the water, overwhelmed by the actual existence of romance, drinking our beer. Then we went in to the mess hall to supper.

On the wall where the chow line formed was a bulletin board, and the first notice that caught my eye was a report of a court-martial: Seaman Second Class Somebody-or-Other had been found guilty of sodomy. How, I wondered, could there only be one sodomist. And which one was he? His sad crime made more sense than the moonlight and the palm trees, and I felt a little sorry for him, out there in that empty beauty in the middle of nothing.

In the morning we moved on again, first to Kwajalein and then to Eniwetok. Of these islands, touched only for an hour or so while we refueled, two impressions remain—of the litter that war leaves, and of the sun. Both islands had been bitterly fought over, and both were very small. There seemed to be nothing left on the surface of either except ruined block-houses, burnt-out planes, and a few splintered trees, and around the edges a ring of wrecked landing craft left to rust in the surf. They were violated places, torn up and left to bleed in the sun. You felt the sun always, not hot but burning, and the light—pure white, colorless, intense, pouring down from the sky and reflected up from the coral sand, from the heat-dazzled runways, from the sea. Under that sun you felt naked and exposed; there was no shade to escape into on those ravaged islands.

In the afternoon we flew on, to Guam, which was bigger, less distinct, and less memorable. There was a club there, and we all got drunk, and I fell and cut my hand—

a coral cut that instantly became infected, and made my whole hand angry red by the next morning. Christ, I thought, I'm poisoned; they'll cut my whole arm off, I'll never fly again; and I felt the old anxiety, the fear and rage at being left behind when the Test came. But it healed all right in a couple of days. By then we had flown the last leg of our journey, a short hop south from Guam to Ulithi. From San Diego we had come six thousand miles. All that way to find a war to fight in.

Ulithi is said to be the best anchorage in its part of the Pacific. It can shelter a thousand ships in its vast lagoon, and there were nearly that many when we got there, early in March, just before the fleet left for the attack on Okinawa. It was the ships that I saw first—black dots and dashes scattered densely over the surface of the sea, so many, over such an area, that the distant ones faded into the horizon's haze. As we flew closer, the near islands of the atoll became visible, first as arcs of a thin broken circle that enclosed the ships, then as narrow strips of bright sand and palm trees. They looked less substantial than the dark fleet that they protected. This ring of fragile islands, set in the vast Pacific emptiness, was land, a habitation for men, the sight that sailors thirst for. But the sea diminished it, and made the earth seem trivial. Out here the ocean distances commanded space, and the atoll was a meager refuge, a dot on the vast surface, something you could miss, or lose.

It was hard to see how any of these islands could hold an airfield large enough for our transport to land on; but the plane was banking and settling, the wheels dropped, and we were sinking toward water and then, when it seemed we would touch the surface of the lagoon, a strip of white coral sand slipped under our wheels, and we were rolling to a stop. On either side of the plane there were palm trees, and as the plane turned to taxi back I could see that we were at the water's edge—the strip used up the whole length of the island, and if you overshot, you swam. The plane stopped at a Quonset hut beside the strip, and the pilot shut down the engines. We climbed out into the white sunlight, and stood gawking and uncertain, like immigrants in a strange country.

And it was strange—it was a new world, unfamiliar in every particular, with an unexplained code of behavior, full of puzzles and mysteries. Where would we live? Where did you go to the toilet? What were those white canvas bags, hanging like udders from the wooden frames? Could you eat the coconuts? Were there natives? It was like my first day at Boy Scout camp—a mixture of excitement, shyness, and anxiety. The possible ways of doing something wrong seemed infinite.

Back among the trees, half-hidden in shadow, I could see tents—big ones for storage, and smaller ones for the men—and a couple of Quonset huts, and men moving about among them wearing shorts and naked to the waist. Taxiways just wide enough for a plane had been cut back into the trees (was that a jungle, I wondered?), and in revetments along the sides Corsairs and F6F nightfighters and TBM's were parked, some with the cowlings off, and mechanics working on them. An engine coughed to life, and the noise rose slowly to a full-throttled scream, like a bandsaw going through a log, and then dropped suddenly to a guttural mutter that was like silence.

The Adjutant came out of a tent, took our orders, and shook hands all around. "Officers' Country is over there," he said, "across the strip. Find a tent with an empty cot, and just move in."

Opposite us, in a stand of palm trees between the runway and the beach, I could see pyramidal tents scattered, half hidden among the trees. They were raised on pilings, and had screened sides that were open to the wind, and they looked cool and separate and private, like summer cottages by a lake, back home. I could see no human figures among them; nothing moved except the shadows of the palms on the tent roofs; and there were no sounds.

I rode across in a jeep with Rock and T, and we found a tent that looked mostly empty, and lugged our gear in. A very tanned young man was dozing on a cot at the far side. He was wearing only shorts—cut off, very carelessly, from a pair of khaki pants—and sandals that had once been high-top field shoes. He gave us a languid greeting. "You must be the new guys. Now maybe we can go home." His name, he said, was Telikoff, but we could call him Telly. Then he dozed off again.

In front of the tent was one of those frames with the dangling udders. It was a lister bag, a canvas sack with a tap at the bottom, full of water that oozed enough through the fabric to evaporate and keep the contents cool. Further on was a frame privy, clean and screened, and with a good view of the strip, and next to it a makeshift but workable shower. The building at the end of the area was the Officers' Club, where we would eat our meals and do our drinking. It was made of rough stained boards, and had a wide veranda on the ocean side, hanging out over the beach; it might have been a Minnesota hunting lodge, or the clubhouse of a small-town country club.

Officers' Country was a cool, quiet, shadowy place. The earth under the trees was soft sand, scattered with fallen coconuts, and bare of any undergrowth. A kind breeze blew from the sea, and rustled the stiff leaves of the palms.

It would be easy to sleep all day here, like Telly. Only the airstrip was a violent brightness; when we came onto it from the shadows under the trees, it was like entering a noisy room. The real activities of the island would be conducted out there, in the insistent sunlight, but back here, in the shadows, it was lotus-land.

Ulithi was an unreal world that never became familiar or habitual. The sun was always warm, and the breeze was always an ocean breeze. Wherever the island came to an end there was a spotless coral beach, with a lazy surf breaking. Wherever you stood on the island, and whatever direction you looked, the sea was always in the background, at eye level because the island was so low, a winking blueness behind everything. On the sand among the tents, coconuts lay waiting to be opened and eaten and drunk from. It was like Eden. And the life we lived was as easy and as pleasant as it should have been in such a place. After a day's flying—never very demanding—you could swim, shower, and go to the club for a cold beer. After supper you could sit on the veranda and drink and watch the tropical night come suddenly out of daylight, without any dusk at all, and then drift off to bed. The next day would be the same—from tent to mess, to ready room, and back at the end to the club, the veranda, and bed.

We were on an island called Falalop, a triangle three thousand feet long on its longest side. It would have been easy to walk around it in half an hour, but I never did. I stayed in Officers' Country, on the long side of the triangle, and never entered the country on the other side of the runway except to fly. Partly I felt that that was the enlisted men's world, and private to them, as our side was to us. The landing strip ran between us like a class barrier, as fundamental a reality of the island as the sea around us.

But part of my reluctance to explore came, I think, from a feeling that my presence on the island was temporary, and that it would somehow be wrong to become too familiar with it, to try to settle in here.

So I only walked along the beach a little way, up past the club, to where the only native building on the island stood. It was an open-sided thatched house, not much more than a frame of coconut logs, empty now, but with a waiting dignity. Out of that house the handful of natives must have thronged to gape at the United States Army, storming ashore in force from landing craft to capture the island the year before. The Army had expected resistance, but there were only the natives. And now they were gone, sent away, for our convenience, to other islands. They had not left many evidences of their lives behind them—their lives were not the kind that mark the earth with signatures—only this house with the steady, gentle wind blowing through it, on the beach beyond Officers' Country.

I saw those people only once, on a reconnaissance flight to Fais and Sorel, the islands south and east of Ulithi to which they had been exiled. "Just go down there," the Operations Officer said, "and look around. You won't see anything, nobody ever does. But it's part of the job." I didn't know what I was supposed to be looking for; but I flew out, found the two tiny islands, and flew up and down their beaches for a while, looking in at the thatched huts under the trees, and at the people who came shyly down to the water's edge to stare as I rumbled past. I couldn't see anything that looked threatening. In the water offshore an outrigger canoe bobbed, and two men seemed to be fishing. I flew over, low, and looked back to see them rising from the floor of the canoe. Could I make them jump out? I wondered. I made another pass, lower, and another, lower still, down on the waves this time, and when I pulled up and banked, I could see two heads in the water. I felt suddenly awful, like a bully or a cop, and I flew over at a safe altitude and waggled my wings to say that I hadn't meant it, that I was sorry. Then I went back to Ulithi, to the squadron life.

The squadron we had joined was VMTB-232, an outfit that called itself, when anyone thought of it, the Flying Red Devils. It was one of the old Marine squadrons. It went back to Bombing Squadron Two in the twenties, and it had a traditional pride in itself, like an old regiment that remembers its heroic days. The squadron had been at Ewa when the Japanese attacked Pearl Harbor, and a detachment of its enlisted men had fought in the defense of Wake Island. It had had a tour of duty in SBD's at Guadalcanal, and had gone back to the Solomons in 1943 to fly strikes on Rabaul, to sink ships (and lose planes and pilots), and to go on wild shore leaves in Sydney.

By the time we reached Ulithi, half of the squadron there had departed, as the forward echelon for a move to an unspecified new base—somewhere nearer Japan, we were told, somewhere where a real war was going on, or about to start. The half that remained behind was waiting, for us and for the orders to move. In the meantime, they flew milk-runs.

The squadron's assignment was simple—to provide a dawn-to-dusk antisubmarine patrol around the anchorage; to bomb Yap, a by-passed island to the west, often enough to keep its airstrips neutralized; and to fly reconnaissance flights over the other islands of the group. These were all boring, minor-league jobs, and the old pilots disliked them. And, besides, the men who had been out for a year or more had had enough; they had lost interest in the war.

They were tired and undisciplined and hard-drinking, and they had gotten careless in the air. They had lost three planes since they came to Ulithi, all of them in unnecessary accidents. Two pilots had sunk a midget submarine together, and somebody had bombed and killed a whale (which looks rather like a submarine submerged), and that was the sum of their action. You could feel the boredom and lethargy all around you. You could see it in the way the old pilots dressed—like Telly, with his cutoff shorts and his sandals—and in the way they lounged from their cots to the flight line, from the flight line to the mess, and back to their cots. They seemed to sleep for astonishing portions of every day, and yet when I got to the bar at the end of the afternoon they were always there, already half-drunk and singing.

They sang songs we hadn't heard before, songs brought up from other islands, other club-bars, or from Sydney; and Joe added them to his repertoire, and was very contented, singing and keeping time with a sloshing can of beer. If it was a slow song he would make it sound like a hymn, or a choral work for a hundred voices; it didn't matter how dirty it was, it came out like the songs we had all sung in Sunday school. "I love to see Mary make water," he would sing, with tender yearning in his voice:

> She can pee such a beautiful stree-ee-ee-eam.
> She can pee for a mile and a quarter *(long pause)*
> And you can't see her ass for the steam!

Rock told him he would have made a great Texas evangelist, singing and drinking the way he did.

The squadron doctor was usually there, drinking steadily but without apparent effect, and recalling difficult operations that he had performed back in Denver. He was a surgeon whose greatest glories were the incisions he had made and the organs he had removed. On Ulithi he got nothing in his sick bay except athlete's foot and coral cuts to treat, and he had gotten so bored and so hungry for surgery that one night, after a couple of drinks, he circumcised himself. Or so the story went. Harry, the squadron's lover, saw an opportunity to settle a question that had been bothering him. "Listen, doc," he began nervously one evening, sitting on the club veranda, "listen, how many orgasms has a guy got in his life? I mean, a healthy guy, well, a kind of stud, you might say." Doc had a pull at his beer, and was studiously silent for a minute, as though he was doing a multiplication problem in his head. "Well, now, Harry," he said at last, "it all depends, but I guess maybe ten thousand might be possible." Harry rose unsteadily to his feet and threw his arm melodramatically across his forehead. "My God," he muttered, "I'm finished." He lurched off toward the bar. The doctor went on drinking; he seemed as bored by Harry as he was by athlete's foot.

Here and there, an officer had adjusted himself to boredom in an individual way. In the tent next to ours a guy who had been out for a year passed the time by writing pornographic novels. He didn't aim to have them published; there was no commercial motive at all. It was just a hobby, like Sunday painting. He would lend one to you if you asked, and would lovingly describe the plot-line to see that you got one to your tastes. He thought I'd like *Two Blondes in One Bed*. "There's this guy who's married to this gorgeous blonde," he said, "and he makes her bring him his dinner stark naked. Well, she meets another blonde who looks just like her, and they decide. . . . "

By the end of the story he had worked in sadism, lesbianism, and transvestism, as well as a great deal of ordinary screwing. ''You'll like it,'' he beamed, ''it's one of my best.''

Clearly we had joined a collection of odd characters, but no one could call them a combat-ready squadron. This fact was made clear to me on the second day I was on the island. After breakfast the new pilots all reported to the ready room—a Quonset hut on the other side of the strip—for flying assignments and an introductory lecture by the Operations Officer. As we hung around outside the hut, waiting for the lecture to begin, a TBM from the day's first antisubmarine patrol landed and rolled to a stop just in front of us. The pilot reached for the lever that would raise his flaps and got the wheel lever instead. Slowly the long legs of the landing gear spread, and the plane settled, gently and carefully, like a fat lady sitting on a small chair, until the wheels had disappeared into the wing wells, and the plane rested on its belly on the runway. The propellers of the slowly idling engine dug into the coral surface and stopped, and the plane leaned slightly on one wing-tip, as though to be more comfortable in its humiliation. The pilot in the cockpit did not move, except to clutch his head in his gloved hands. Then the crash horn began to sound, equipment—a fire engine and a crane—appeared on the runway, and the pilot climbed down, and came toward where we were standing in the ready room door.

''This is Captain Childers,'' the Operations Officer said to me. ''You'll be flying wing on him.''

''Cain't understand how it happened,'' Childers said. He went on into the hut.

Billy Childers was a regular Marine from backwoods Mississippi who had been an enlisted pilot before the war.

When the war began, he was given a temporary commission, and he had risen, in the automatic way of wartime promotions, to the rank of temporary Captain. He was a tall, bony man, with a face that was at once weather-beaten and pale—I never understood how that could be true, but it was—and his eyes, which were always moving, were so light-colored that they seemed to have no pupils. (T, who flew on his other wing, said he had eyes like Little Orphan Annie.) Billy seemed to live at the edge of the squadron's life. He didn't drink beer at the club, or at least I don't remember him there, and he was never a part of the talk and the horseplay in the ready room. Maybe, I thought, that was because he was older; or maybe his years as an enlisted man had made him suspicious of officers. Or maybe, I added nervously, the other pilots mistrusted him. Maybe that dumb stationary accident of his was typical of the way he handled airplanes. And I was to fly wing on him, in combat.

To make this ragged gathering of misfits ready for combat, the Marine Corps had sent most of the old squadron home and had brought in a new CO. We called him simply The Major. Like the fierce Colonel at El Toro, he was a Regular and an Academy graduate (every other pilot in the squadron was a Reservist except Billy Childers). He had been a tank officer—in Samoa, as I remember—had gone through flight training, and was taking his first command. He seemed, to the rest of us, rigid, aloof, and impersonal, a guy who knew what he wanted and would quietly annihilate anyone who didn't cooperate. He started issuing orders on the day he arrived. The uniform of the day would be issue khaki, with fore-and-aft cap; the cut-off shorts and the baseball caps disappeared at once. All officers would appear at meals clean-shaven and in the proper uniform: goatees went, sandals went. Pilots would fulfill the squadron's combat assignment: strikes began to take off daily for Yap, reconnaissance flights to Fais and Sorel went regularly, antisubmarine hops left before dawn and landed after dusk. The pilots grumbled—you always got chicken shit like this, they said, when a Regular took over—but they began to look like officers and to fly like a squadron.

In the air the change came mainly from the new replacements. We were still held in the discipline of our stateside flying, and eager to show the old hands that we were as good as they were (secretly we thought we were better). We made our formation-flying even tighter, and our division landing approaches steeper, faster, and—in the language we used—"harier," dropping planes on alternate sides of the runway so closely spaced that a whole flight of six would be landed and rolling before the flight leader turned off. On a three-thousand-foot strip this took a good deal of skill and some nerve. Navy pilots, in from the carriers in the lagoon to touch earth and drink our beer, would come out of the club, beer cans in hand, to watch the squadron land. "It isn't so much a landing pattern," one of them said, "it's more a controlled group-crash." They regarded us as crazy and dangerous, but that was a kind of admiration. It was better, anyway, than being patronized.

Plane-watching is always fascinating for pilots. We would rather drink facing the strip, if there was anything doing, than face the other way, where there was only sun and water. If somebody was in trouble, all the better—that was like reading about a good accident in *BuAerNews*. One stormy day, when the wind was blowing hard at ninety degrees to the runway, instead of straight down the length as it did in fine weather, I saw Tyrone Power make five passes in an R5C before he got it down safely. Every pilot on the island seemed to know that a movie star was at the controls, and they came out in the rain to watch him and to take pleasure in his troubles. He was being a good and careful pilot, making a cautious approach, applying power when he felt the wind drifting him into the palms, and going around to try again. A strip like Ulithi's didn't allow for carelessness. It really didn't allow for a crosswind, certainly not in a lumbering transport that had a weather-vane tail and not enough power. But he was Tyrone Power, the guy who had stolen our commissioning ceremony, someone who existed in the world outside. And who were we?

The Major believed in flying—any kind of flying was better for a pilot, he said, than sitting on his ass in the ready room, or lying around in his sack getting fat. We began a daily weather hop, which took off before dawn and reported the weather up to twenty thousand feet. And we took over the island mail flight. It wasn't ordinary mail, not the letters from home that came in by transport plane from Pearl Harbor, but the official mail—pouches marked SECRET that were carried around the islands of the atoll by an official Navy messenger. He traveled his daily circuit in a light observation plane, and somebody, the Operations Officer explained to me, had to fly it.

The mail plane was a sort of overgrown Cub, with a high, broad wing and flaps as big as barn doors—the sort of plane that the Army had flown near us back in CPT in Texas. It could take off and land at 35 mph, which was a good thing, since the landing strips on the other little islands of the atoll were sometimes only 300 feet long. I tried out the plane a couple of times on the main strip at

Falalop, and as near as I could judge I got it down inside 300 feet. It didn't seem too difficult. So I picked up the messenger, a Navy Lieutenant with glasses and a nervous CPA's face, and took off for Mogmog, the next island. It seemed only fair to prepare my passenger for what was coming. I turned around in my seat and said, as reassuringly as I could, "I've never landed here before, but it'll be all right. If other guys can do it, why can't I?" He said nothing, just sat there clutching his official pouch and looking down at the waves below.

The trick was to drop full flaps, get low and slow, and drag around to the end of the strip as though you were landing on a carrier. As soon as you were within gliding distance of the strip, but before you were actually above it, you cut the throttle and held the airspeed steady while you settled—if you had judged everything correctly—to a three-point landing on the first ten feet of land. Then you got on the brakes to stop the plane's roll before you reached the water at the other end of the strip.

Mogmog was fine. We stopped, my passenger surrendered his pouch and got another just like it, and we took off for the next spot of land. There the strip was even shorter, and I tried to lower the flying speed a knot or two on the approach. We touched down nicely, very close to the end, and I tromped down hard on the brakes—and there weren't any. Something had happened to the brake lines on that last landing. I fishtailed the rudder to lose speed, but we were still rolling briskly along when we ran out of runway. I did the only thing I could do—I gave the engine a burst of power and held full left rudder. The tail swung around with a rush, the right wing dipped but didn't touch, and we were stopped. But there had been a sinister thump as we swung, and I climbed down to see what had happened. Just at the edge of the runway a palm log lay, with a rough end sticking out on the runway. The tail had hit it, just below the stabilizer, and the log had torn into the fabric covering. Christ, I thought, another tail. But at least there was no Colonel watching this time, only a very old native chief, the only native left on the atoll. He drifted up from nowhere, wearing a sort of a sarong, and stood looking sadly at the damage. His look was kind and sympathetic, as though he knew how I must feel—I had punctured my canoe. I shook his hand warmly, and he smiled a wide brown smile. Together we detached the airplane from the palm log. Then I climbed back into the plane. The Navy messenger was sitting still, as I had left him, his pouch in his lap, his gold-rimmed spectacles shining. He had neither spoken nor moved during the incident, but he looked at me as a condemned man might look at his executioner. I could see what he was thinking: Why me? and What a way to die! We flew silently back to Falalop, and I landed, carefully keeping the tail up as long as I could, in case it fell off when I touched it down. I reported to the Operations Officer that I didn't seem to have the hang of the mail plane. The messenger at my elbow agreed that this did seem to be true. The next day he had a new pilot, and I was back in a TBM.

From this time on my logbook customarily lists, under "Passengers," the same two names for every flight—Edwards and Campbell. They weren't passengers; they were my crew, though much of the time they did no more than just ride along. Edwards was a thin-faced, sardonic Texan, intelligent and capable, with that strong sense of self-preservation and self-interest that an intelligent enlisted man has, especially if he's a Reservist. It wasn't his war, and it wasn't his Marine Corps. He did his job well when it needed doing, but he did it for Edwards, not for glory. He was my radio- and radar-man. He rode in the belly of the plane, aft, in a dark cylindrical space called the tunnel, with his electronic gear around him. At the back end of the tunnel, under the tail, a thirty-caliber machine gun, the stinger, was mounted, and Edwards was also the tail gunner. Campbell was quieter and less distinct—dark, from Pittsburgh, very young-looking (though none of us was over twenty). He was turret gunner, and rode in a glass bowl on the backbone of the plane, with a fifty-caliber machine gun.

These two were my constant companions all the time I flew in the Pacific, but I have almost no memories of either. They rode with me on every flight, but they were back there in the guts of the plane, out of sight, two people I was responsible for, but didn't really need, or not very often. Flying in the same plane with them was not at all the bond that flying beside other pilots was. The pilots were my friends, but the crew was just a responsibility, like relatives or debts. On the ground we separated at once, to our segregated quarters, two areas that were as remote and isolated from each other as two countries that have cut off diplomatic relations. I never saw where my crew lived, and they never came to my tent. We never ate a single meal together. We never discussed any human problem. They simply rode at my back, prepared to fight off the attacking planes that never came, bored, reading their comic books, I suppose—though I realize now that I don't even know what they did read.

The first flight that Edwards and Campbell flew with me was a bombing attack. ''Strike on Yap,'' my logbook reads, ''pier and shore installations—strafing—4 × 500.''

Yap, a hundred miles west of Ulithi, had been bypassed when Ulithi was taken. It was of no strategic importance, except for its airstrip, which was pitted and broken by many bombings; but it was still occupied by a Japanese garrison. Looking at aerial photographs of Yap, our intelligence officers had persuaded themselves that in an inlet there might be facilities for docking submarines. Our planes were loaded with 500-pound bombs, and we took off to destroy the dock and to strafe whatever we saw.

I flew on Billy's wing out over the fleet, and beyond, until Ulithi was lost behind us, and there was nothing in sight but water and the empty air. Without visual references, we seemed to hang motionless above the sea, which seemed motionless too, while the minutes passed. Then an island appeared, first a low darkness on the horizon, then a green mass of palm trees. We circled over it, looking for the target, and the greenness became palm trees, each one a green asterisk on a lighter ground. The island had been bombed again and again, and in among the trees where bombs had fallen there were spots of exposed white sand, like pockmarks on dark skin. The airstrip was full of craters, and looked abandoned and desolate, a place where planes had once flown. Along the sides were the remains of wrecked and burnt-out planes, and one or two that seemed to be dummies, knocked together to tempt strafing planes down where the waiting guns could find them.

Nothing moved below us. Nothing suggested any life at all there. I saw no installations, no people, not a hut or a kitchen garden. The island seemed uninhabited and forlorn. We flew lower, across the inlet that Intelligence had marked. I thought I saw a fence strung across it—a few strands of barbed wire, perhaps—but I could see nothing else. We circled again and made our bombing runs. As I dropped my bombs I could hear the hard rattle of Campbell's gun, and the high, tinny popping of Edward's thirty-caliber. What the hell were they shooting at, I wondered. Just shooting, because they were in combat now.

I pulled away from the island and joined the formation. That was my first attack on the enemy, and I felt sour disappointment. Was that all there was to combat? No antiaircraft shells bursting, no fierce defenders at their guns, nothing exploding, no columns of smoke visible for miles. I had expected flame and ruin, but even our own bombs had gone off squashily, blowing up mud and water, destroying nothing (except maybe a barbed-wire fence). I didn't feel any different; I hadn't been initiated into manhood; I hadn't even seen the enemy. I flew disconsolately back to Ulithi.

The enemy was there, though; there were both men and guns on Yap. They bided their time and only took the easy shots, but they were there. The following week they shot a wing off a strafing plane, and it crashed and burned near the other wrecks along the ruined airstrip. The pilot who was killed had been Torchy's lover, back in Laguna. I though of him as her seducer; but then I had liked her on that wet night in November when T and I met her in the USO, and I didn't like him.

Even after that first death in action, Ulithi seemed a pastoral, innocent place, a long way from the real war. American troops were fighting in the Philippines, and the Marines were just cleaning up in Iwo, but we were thousands of miles from either battle, with only a bypassed island for an enemy. We went on living our simple life in our open tents, under the palms that dropped their nuts quietly, with a muffled swish and thud, through leaves to the sandy earth. We swam from the beach behind Officers' Country. Waves broke on a reef offshore in a fine show of foam, but within the reef the water was calm and clear, and the sand was clean and free of any flotsam. I suppose there was no place for anything to float from, out there in the empty ocean. I always felt when I swam there that no one had ever gone swimming on that beach before; it was sort of a Robinson Crusoe feeling, of being outside human existence, and alone.

Although it was February, the sun was hot, and our bodies grew tanned and our hair bleached, and our khaki shirts and trousers turned white in the sun. Sometimes we swam naked, and once Rock took a naked sunbath, fell asleep, and burned his buttocks so severely that he had to spend three days lying facedown and naked on his cot. His bottom turned scarlet and swelled so tight that if you flipped it with your finger it thumped like a drum. The doctor came round to look at the damage, but he couldn't find anything to operate on. "It could have been worse," he said as he left. "You could have been sleeping on your back."

Out in the lagoon the warships gathered and waited, but as we flew over them, coming and going on our solitary patrols, they did not look like menacing machines designed to burn and drown men, but like delicate abstractions—slender, tapered shapes at rest on the smooth bright water, part of the static pattern of our lives. And so when the air-raid sirens began to howl one evening in the early dark, we took it for a drill. After all, the nearest Japanese planes were away off in the Philippines, and there weren't many of them left even there. As the island lights went out, we left the club and gathered curiously at the lagoon-end of the landing strip, and watched the fleet black out—a ship here, a ship there, one or two of the big ones delaying, and then suddenly blinking out, until at last the whole lagoon was dark. Not a very successful drill, I thought; it had been far too slow.

And then, astonishingly, antiaircraft guns began to fire, and tracers sprayed up into the darkness, as though the lights that had burned across the waters of the lagoon were being hurled into the sky. I began to feel exposed, standing there on the runway while the guns fired; but no one else moved, so I didn't. Across the lagoon a plane screamed into a dive, higher and higher pitched, and there was a flash and an explosion, and an instant later another explosion in what seemed the center of the moored ships. Then darkness and silence, until the all-clear sounded, and lights began to come on in the harbor again.

It had been a kamikaze raid. The Japanese planes had flown all the way from the main islands, touching at the Philippines. They had planned to refuel at Yap, and then fly on to attack the fleet at Ulithi; but bad navigation, bad weather, bad luck, whatever it was, had delayed them, and sent some planes back. Others had crash-landed on the Yap beach. Only three reached Ulithi. One was shot down; one crashed into the deck of the carrier *Randolph*, where the crew was crowded into the hangar deck watching a movie; and one, taking an island for a large ship, dove on Mogmog and blew up a kitchen.

The whole lasted perhaps fifteen minutes. We were excited by it—perhaps *entertained* is a more precise word—it was a spectacle, like a *son et lumière*, with noise, light, explosions. We didn't know what was happening to human lives while we watched, but even if we had, I wonder if it would have mattered. We were a mile or so from the

Randolph, and perhaps a mile is too far to project the imagination to another man's death. We took it as a sign that the war was still with us, that we still had an enemy, and went to bed heartened by the incident.

Because the *Randolph* was damaged, her planes were catapulted and flown to Falalop to wait while repairs were done on the ship. The *Randolph* had just come back from a raid on Japan, where her planes had flown strikes against Tokyo, and the pilots were inclined to strut a little. They had bombed Tokyo, we bombed Yap. We couldn't blame them for feeling superior, but we didn't like it, and a couple of fights blew up in the club bar, and I had to restrain Joe. To amuse themselves, the Navy squadron flew a strike on Yap, and lost two planes to the invisible antiaircraft fire there. After that they were more restrained in the club, and we got on better.

March passed. We flew our desultory strikes, and our interminable antisubmarine patrols. Ulithi was a natural target for subs, and every day, all day, our planes flew out from the atoll on triangular tracks, watching by eye and by radar for enemy vessels. It was different, flying over water there, from what it had been at Pensacola or at Santa Barbara. At those bases you couldn't really get lost, or not for long; there was always a direction to fly that would take you back to land. But when the land is an island three thousand feet long, in the middle of the world's largest ocean, no course is sure. Even in the best weather Ulithi was hard to see (it was maybe ten feet out of the water at its highest point); and in the worst weather it was impossible. I would work out my navigation, fly out along the charted track, turn at the proper time, fly, turn again, and then at the predicted moment I would look round for home. Occasionally I missed, dropped down through cloud cover where the island should have been, and found the ocean empty, the island anywhere but there. Then I'd turn to Edwards for help—"Find me a course, for Christ sake!"—and Edwards would use his radar, offer a heading, and lead us home.

On a low, overcast day, like the day after Wally died, we heard that a carrier pilot had been lost near Ulithi, and I flew once more in a ritual search, this time alone. The clouds hung in a solid layer that seemed to slope down at the horizon into the sea, like an inverted saucer, so that my plane was suspended in a shallow wafer of space between the gray above and the gray below, a space entirely one color, and without a landmark or a point of reference. As I flew the set search-pattern the plane seemed not to move at all, everything in sight remained the same. It was an experience of total, gray isolation, in a space without life or identity or particularity, like some extreme psychological state—looking for a dead man in a dead space, without any hope of finding him, and in the process losing contact with, almost losing belief in, the reality of any solid object. The thought of being lost at sea became a new nightmare, the worst form of dying.

Late in March the orders came. We would be the first land-based bomber squadron in the attack on Okinawa. The forward echelon was already there, lying offshore with the invasion fleet, and would go ashore on D-plus-five. Those of us at Ulithi would fly the squadron's planes to join them, and begin combat operations. No one had heard of Okinawa. Intelligence knew nothing about it except that the natives were called Hairy Anus (many obscene jokes) and that the island was infested with poisonous snakes. We all drew combat boots, the kind with leather puttees attached. We had shots for every known disease, and were feverish, or fainted, and couldn't raise our arms. Then we packed up the squadron and waited.

The battle of Okinawa began on Easter Sunday, April 1st. We heard about it at Ulithi, standing around outside the ready room, where a loudspeaker had been hung on a palm tree. Tokyo Rose told us that the assault forces had landed, but had been repulsed; many ships had been sunk. On the second day she addressed our squadron specifically; she knew that 232 was coming, she said, but they would be ready for us. I felt ridiculously melodramatic, standing there being threatened on the radio; it was like stumbling onto the set of a B-grade spy movie, where an Oriental hisses, "Yankee dog, you die!" But I also felt a bit important—at least in Tokyo they had heard of us. It made up a little for not having bombed Tokyo with the Navy.

We were eager to move—D-plus-five was only three days away—but there were delays. The attack, we were told, was going well, but the weather was bad, the sea was too rough to land enough aviation gasoline to supply us. Finally, on the fifth, we left. It was the first time that I had seen all of the squadron's planes in the air together, and as we gathered into formation I felt a strong emotion that I couldn't define—Was it pride? Affection?—for that pattern of planes. It was *my* squadron, I belonged to it, I was in my place, and we were headed for combat. It isn't a surprising emotion. Men have always felt pride when they could for their military units, their regiment, their ship. But I hadn't felt it until then. Looking across from my plane I could identify some of my friends in the others, even at a distance, by the way they sat, the style of their flying. There was T, small, crouched forward, his head cocked, as though he was listening (to Louis Armstrong, maybe); Joe beyond him, very tall, very straight in the cockpit; Rock, solid-looking, like his name. The planes didn't look clumsy, but beautiful and intent, flying toward the war.

Chapter 8

We flew into Saipan on the fifth of April—the day on which, if the battle plan had been working, we would have landed at Okinawa. We knew that storms were battering the Okinawa beaches and delaying the landing of supplies, but there was another kind of delay that we didn't know about. The Japanese were sending suicide planes against the fleet, hundreds of them in those first days, and were sinking ships; and the constant raids, even when they weren't successful, kept ships' crews at their battle stations and interrupted unloading operations. Back in Saipan we weren't told about the kamikazes, and we expected to take off in a day or two, as soon as the weather cleared. All we had to do was to kill a little time.

Time died hard on Saipan. We lived together in a hot, crowded Quonset hut on a bare hill by the airstrip, and much of the time those first days we just hung around the hut, lying on our cots, reading if we could find anything to read, waiting for our orders, afraid to leave in case they came. It was like Miramar, in a way, but worse. At Miramar we were at the gateway to the whole Pacific war, and surrounded by men who had been there; there was excitement in the air, but no anxiety—we were all going to get there, to the war. But at Saipan we were isolated and immobilized, and raw with impatience to move on to the particular war that was waiting for us, like a birthday party that we'd been invited to, and would miss if we didn't hurry.

I had only one book with me—the *War and Peace* that I'd bought back in Honolulu—and I tried to read it; but I couldn't keep all those Russian names straight, and after a while I'd give up, wander outside, and just look around. Not that there was much to look at. Saipan itself was just one long, treeless hill, a hog's back that ran the length of the island, north and south, with a meager flatland around the edge, like a narrow brim on a hat. In the distance I could see Tinian, the nearest island, a rocky hill like Saipan, thrusting up out of the sea. Steve Bakos' squadron was stationed there, flying antisubmarine patrols. I thought how much I'd like to see him again, but of course I couldn't leave Saipan because the orders might come. So I stood around, and if there was any flying going on I watched that, and then I went back into the hut and tried Tolstoy again.

A loudspeaker had been attached to the front of the hut, and at noon and six P.M. we could hear the news broadcasts from the island radio station. We listened for word of the battle of Okinawa, and were told that it was going well (but still we didn't move up). And it was there that I learned of the death of Franklin Roosevelt. I remember hearing the news, standing in the sun there, looking out across the sea toward Tinian, thinking The President is dead, and not feeling anything. I couldn't remember when he hadn't been the President. I had seen him once, in the thirties—it must have been during the 1936 presidential campaigning—driving down Nicollete Avenue in Minneapolis in an open car, smiling and waving. But he wasn't a person; he was an institution of government, like the Constitution or the Supreme Court. I was surprised, I think, that he had died—institutions don't die. But his death would change nothing out here, the war would go on, planes would fly. It was nothing to me.

I heard of another death at about that time. From Tinian word came that Steve Bakos had flown on a patrol and hadn't come back. Steve, the ugly, happy family man with the pretty wife, and a small child by now, the man for whom the war was only an interruption in a peaceable life, was lost in the sea (that terrible way to die). I tried to imagine what had happened—engine failure, perhaps, a water landing, and the long waiting to be found? Or something else? A fire? Or a navigational error that ended with a dead engine and a drop into darkness? No other details came across from his squadron; he was just dead, that was all.

Days passed, no orders came, and our restlessness got worse. No one had any duties, and there was no flying to do. We waited in that Quonset hut on the hill, and the time dragged by. During those empty, fretful days I learned a basic truth about military life: that it's only the *doing*—the fighting, or just the drilling and the routine—that makes it endurable. Freed from the discipline of flying, we found that it was the only discipline we had. We missed the flying, but not out of love alone; partly we were lost without the shape that it gave to our lives. When time is empty, it stops; and every hour is just the past hour over again, and just as meaningless.

Old Regulars will tell you that the thing to do when you hit a temporary Station is to dig in as though you might be there forever. After all, they say, the Navy might lose your records. We began to think that we had been misplaced, that in the official, bureaucratic Navy there was no 232, and that we would be found, to everyone's astonishment, still sitting on that goddamn hill when the war was over. So we looked around the place we were stuck in, for ways to pass the time.

There were, it seemed, only two things to do: you could go sightseeing or you could bar-hop among the officers' clubs around the island. Saipan had been in American hands for about six months when we arrived, and it had already been transformed into a sort of temporary Navy town—Pensacola without the Spanish architecture and the whores. Along the road that followed the west coast of the island a string of little camps had sprung up, each the headquarters of a naval unit, each with its docks and its supply dumps, its Post Exchange and its club. The whole stretch looked like a third-rate resort, a string of crummy bars along a beach road.

But there were signs of war, too. Below our hill, between the beach road and the sea, was the first military cemetery I had ever seen. We went swimming there, on the sandy beach where the graves ended. Behind us a vast space was symmetrically patterned with rows of regular markers that ran back out of sight over the hill. At one side were the graves of some Japanese soldiers, and I was surprised to find them there, treated so courteously. Why didn't I expect so small a gesture of magnanimity from my own countrymen? I suppose because back home the

Japanese were the yellow devils of propaganda, not men like ourselves who could die on a Saipan beach, and be buried like other men. Along the beach and out in the shallow water you could see the usual debris of a beach assault—the shattered masonry of the defenses, the rusting hulks of landing craft, the abandoned equipment. All that, out there in the slow surf, had made these regular, monotonous rows of identical graves.

To get beyond the Quonset and the beach, to go drinking in all those promising bars, and to see the rest of the island, we had to have transportation. There was a motor pool from which we were entitled to draw jeeps, when there were any; but there never were. The obvious thing to do was to steal one. Stealing was not, of course, called *stealing;* you called it *scrounging,* and nobody had any qualms about doing it. In a world where everything belonged to the government, nothing belonged to anybody, and we quickly lost our back-home sense of the inviolability of personal property. If an object was portable and no one was guarding it, it was as much yours as anybody else's. And there were lots of jeeps sitting around unguarded.

We agreed that it would be wise not to steal a jeep if it had four stars painted on it, or one that seemed to be attached to an important command. We tried instead to concentrate on chaplains and on the minor functionaries of lower-level units (Joe always said that a laundry officer was the ideal victim—nobody could have less influence than a laundry officer, not even a chaplain). And if we thought of it, and weren't too drunk, we took the jeeps we had borrowed back where we had found them.

One day, in a Catholic chaplain's jeep, we drove the length of the island, up the west beach road all the way to the northern tip. Along the beach we passed the ruins of the island's sugar factories. Sugar had been a major industry on Saipan before the invasion, but it was dead now, and the factories were clusters of roofless shells. It felt wrong to me, that the war should have passed through this place where something useful had been done. The other islands I had seen that had been fought over had been nothing to begin with—a few palm trees, a few natives, maybe, and a Japanese garrison—ideal empty spaces to fight for. But this island had been a real community, with roads and factories, little towns, docks. What I was feeling, I suppose, was that it was like home, or a possible home, a place that my imagination could populate and live in, and that the ruined buildings were wounds in a real landscape. We drove on, through fields now; but there were no crops, no natives (they had been driven together into compounds), no life. We only saw other Americans, moving about in their American trucks and jeeps, each in its cloud of dust, and American camps, and supply dumps, and ships unloading still more American supplies.

The steep backbone of the island was always on our right, a single long ridge of rock. Japanese soldiers were still hidden up there, emerging sometimes at night to snipe into some American camp and, so one story went, to watch the outdoor movies that every camp had. I felt a shiver that was not quite fear, or even anxiety—just a feeling that up there, among those bare rocks, there were men who would kill me if they could, and whom I would have to try to kill if I met them. I had never been on the same piece of earth with an enemy before.

To the north the island was less crowded and less Americanized, and you could still see here and there the remains of a farmer's house and the unmarred shapes of his fields. At the very northern point, where the rocky central escarpment broke into the sea, the ruin of a Japanese blockhouse stood in a field. We stopped the jeep and walked across to look at it. I climbed in through the ruined door, and scuffed my foot around in the rubble on the floor, hoping I'd find a souvenir there. In the dust was a Japanese shoe, the kind with a separate toe, like a mitten. It still had a foot in it.

Back at the airfield, Joe found a headquarters squadron that had a few fighter planes, but no pilots. The planes were old ones, castoffs from the fleet. (A headquarters squadron, being mainly an administrative unit, is the sort of place where such odds and ends are assigned, when no one can think of what else to do with them.) But now that the planes were there, and had been tinkered with, they had to be tested, and Joe and I volunteered as test pilots. Neither of us had ever flown a fighter, we had never even been close enough to one to look in the cockpit. But Joe was confident: "Planes are like women," he said, "you fly one, you've flown 'em all." I was sure he didn't know much about women—he was a very monogamous man—but he might be right about airplanes. And we were bored. So we lied to the Operations Officer of the headquarters squadron, and were assigned to fly a row of F6F's and F4F's.

Ordinarily when you fly a strange plane you first read the pilot's manual, a book that explains how everything works and where it is. You sit for a while in the cockpit with the book open and find the levers for wheels and flaps, and the switches, and figure out how to start the engine and turn on the radio. But we couldn't ask for a manual—that would have exposed our inexperience—and so we had to sit in the cockpits and figure out how to fly the planes just by looking and groping. I was still peering around, muttering to myself "Mags, wheels, flaps, radio," when Joe started his engine, waved cheerfully, and taxied his F6F onto the runway. I got mine started in a billow of smoke and followed him apprehensively. What was I doing here, in a fighter?

The F6F was a boring plane, efficient enough but without any character. Flying it was like driving the family car on a Sunday afternoon. Even Joe, who loved flying so much that he even liked Links, was unimpressed. We circled the field for an hour, as we were instructed to do—you were supposed to be within gliding distance on a test hop, in case the engine failed—and landed. Nothing had happened; it was like being alone with a girl you don't like.

But the F4F Wildcat was marvelous—very small (so small that it seemed you could reach out from the cockpit and touch both wing-tips), simple, maneuverable, and delicately responsive to the controls. After the TBM, which needed hydraulic boosters to be flown at all, and the humdrum F6F, the Wildcat was like a toy designed especially to please pilots. It did acrobatics as though it wanted to, and had been hoping you'd try one; and when you did, it flew you through the most intricate maneuver in a cooperative, friendly way.

Joe and I would take off, soberly and separately, and rendezvous high above the island, and chase tails, or dogfight, or just drift around, one flying wing on the other, looking down at the military busy-ness going on below us. On our second flight Joe slid up into formation on my wing flying upside down. He had found a manual, and had discovered that the Wildcat had a pressurized oil system and could fly inverted without the engine seizing up. He flew along, head down, roaring with laughter, as though he were playing a great joke on gravity. For a while I led him in gentle turns and climbs, and he stayed there in position, flying as well upside down as I did rightside up.

I felt so much at home in a Wildcat that I even ventured a Victory Roll, the fighter pilot's grandstand maneuver. Approaching the field for a landing, I dived toward the runway, building up speed, and pulled up in a slanting slow-roll to the left. Beneath me as I rolled, five or six hundred feet below, I could see some of the squadron playing softball on a field behind the Quonset hut. Then the plane was rolling out, scooping a little, but safe; and I swung around into the downwind leg, and swept in to a landing. I was scared when I entered the roll—I remember thinking, This is the kind of dumb showing off that gets guys killed—and I was even more scared afterward, when I thought about it. Still, I was glad I had tried it, even though T said that it didn't look so hot from second base.

Saipan was a good place to fly. After the insignificance of Ulithi, the island had a secure solidity; it looked like the kind of island that you might lose and find again. And the flying we did in those old Wildcats was good, too—free and spontaneous. I remember those bright days as I do some in flight school, as days that held the true feeling of flight, the way it ought to be—two friends, easy in the air and with each other, just fooling around.

But we couldn't spend all our time testing those few tired planes. In the evenings we couldn't go sight-seeing either; there was nothing to do but party. It was easier to steal a jeep at night—chaplains didn't seem to do much after supper—and the clubs were livelier then. Sometimes you could even see a woman in one, a Navy nurse or a Red Cross girl; and though it never seemed worthwhile to enter into competition for such a rarity, it was pleasant to look at them. Joe, I noticed, censored his songs when there was a woman at the bar, even though some of them looked as though they could match him, obscenity for obscenity, and win.

One of the pilots in the squadron—a guy who fancied himself a great lover—went courting. Somewhere on the island he found a Red Cross hut, one of those places where you can get free coffee and writing paper from a girl in uniform, and stare at her breasts under the starched cotton. He met a girl there who was willing to have a date with him in a couple of days, and we heard all about his worries and preparations. He would lie on his cot at night in the Quonset hut and worry out loud to his friend in the next cot. "Christ," he would say, "what if we get our orders tomorrow? What if we have to leave before I get a chance to fuck her? I should have made the date for tonight." And "Should I get a new rubber? How long are rubbers good for? This one might be no good." And he would remove from his wallet a dirty little envelope, take out the Trojan inside and unroll it, and hold it dangling before his eyes, examining it for flaws. Or he'd review his strategy, how he wouldn't move in too fast, would talk first, maybe even dance, be a nice guy even if she *was* ugly, and then. . . .

It was a relief when the night of the date came. At least we wouldn't hear any more plans when we were trying to sleep. The cocksman came back late, slapping the screen door open and stumbling in the dark among the rows of sleeping men. He sat on the edge of his cot, shook his friend by the shoulder, and launched at once into an account of the evening—first the preliminaries, how he had gotten her drunk at a club, had danced, and at last had driven her to a secluded beach in her jeep. He had put his arm around her, made a few speeches, and kissed her. "And do you know what she said? Right then, when I'd just kissed her once? She said, 'Why honey, it's lucky I wore my diaphragm tonight!' What do you think? She must be some kind of tramp, a girl who'd say a thing like that." And then the guilt began: "I shouldn't have done it, should I? I mean, I'm married. What would my wife think?" Sleepers woke, cursed him and his date and his fucking wife, but he seemed not to hear them. He was alone with his libido and his guilt.

We had been on the island for more than a week, and had exhausted the nearby clubs. One night we set out, six or eight of us in one borrowed jeep, to look for a P-boat base somewhere on the northern end of the island, where the club was said to be especially fine and private. After some time and a lot of drinks on the way, we found it, and it was as good a place as we'd heard it was—well-designed, even landscaped, with a garden and a view of the bay, and a vast supply of liquor. Rock said it reminded him of the country club back in San Antonio. I thought it was more like some place in the movies, the Riviera, maybe. It even had gambling machines, one-armed bandits lined up along one whole wall. We felt very pleased with ourselves for having found it, and we all had a drink to congratulate ourselves. Joe sang his version of "Casey Jones":

He was found in the wreck with his hand on the throttle,
And his airspeed reading forty knots.
They searched all day for the poor pilot's body,
But all they could find were spots.
Hundreds and hundreds of spots.

And we sang the chorus:

> Ten thousand dollars going home to the folks.
> Ten thousand dollars going home to the folks.
> Oh won't they be delighted!
> Won't they be excited!
> Think of all the things that they can buy!

The officers of the P–boat squadron didn't join in and didn't seem pleased to have us in their club. Gradually they drifted off, until we were the only customers. We drank beer, and when each can was empty the drinker bent it in half and put it on the table. It wasn't so easy, in those days, to bend a can with one hand; it was a modest feat of strength, that's why you did it. Another test.

The pile of bent cans grew, covered the table, and spilled clanking to the floor. Between beers we began to play the slot machines, but without much luck. Joe in particular lost steadily, and badly; he seemed to think the machines were part of a Navy plot against him, or perhaps against the entire Marine Corps. The machines would never pay off for him, he was being robbed, the whole place was a trap for the gullible. I thought we'd better leave, and I began to shove people out the door, toward our chaplain's jeep. But it was gone; somebody had stolen it. We stumbled about in the darkness, muttering and complaining: "Steal a man's jeep, goddamn Navy bastards. . . ." There was only one jeep in the lot, and we climbed aboard it. Joe was still in the club, but in a minute he appeared, staggering, his arms wrapped in a bear hug around a slot machine. He had decided to take it with him; it was what they deserved, fucking Navy. It was no use arguing with him; we tried to make the machine inconspicuous in the back seat, and set off for the Station gate. The guard there was unfriendly and full of questions. Why were we driving the CO's personal jeep? Where had we come from? Where were we going? And eventually, he asked, what was that in the back? We were in trouble.

The Major summoned us all the next morning, and he was not happy. He had been on the carpet before an Admiral. Why shouldn't his officers be court-martialed? What did they think this was, a goddamn house party? You goddamn Marines think you own the Navy, well, he'd show . . . and so forth. You couldn't blame the Major for being sore. But he had defended us—we were restless, eager to get to war, a good combat squadron, morale was high, spirits were volatile. He had managed to delay the formal hearing, but if we hung around much longer we'd have to go before the court. He was to have another meeting with the Admiral the next day.

We followed the Major's negotiations with nervous interest, and discussed our prospects over the piled-up bent beer cans in various Navy clubs. Kelleher, the philosophical knuckle-baller, was gloomy: "We haven't got a chance," he said. "No more than a fart in a windstorm." But after all, Joe remarked, looking on the bright side, What could they do to us? Send us overseas? We went on drinking; we even stole a jeep or two to show each other that we were not downhearted. But the party spirit had gone flat, like last night's beer. Nobody wanted to be drunk any more. We wanted to move; our battle was already being fought, had been for two weeks now, and we weren't in it. We were afraid it might end before we got there, that the war would be over and we'd still be sitting on Saipan, drinking and getting court-martialed.

Then the orders came, and in a day we were off. We had stayed on Saipan for fourteen days, had been drunk and disorderly almost every night, and had left behind us a large number of misplaced jeeps, some angry Navy officers, and, on the Admiral's desk, court-martial papers that would never be served.

Chapter 9

Iwo Jima was an island so dead an uninhabitable that it seemed wrong to call it an island: it was a blasted, charred heap of sand, as littered and abandoned as a public beach after the Fourth of July. Except that this beach was black— a coarse volcanic sand that grated like cinders under the feet, on which nothing would grow. When we landed there, on April 19, the battle was over, the airstrips had been repaired, and fighter squadrons were flying from them to cover B-29's on raids to the Japanese mainland. But enemy troops were still alive in the caves and tunnels at the north end of the island, and emerged sometimes at night to hurl suicidal attacks on planes and guns, and on the tents of sleeping men. The night before we landed, a single Japanese soldier had run through the company street of a fighter squadron, tossing hand grenades into the tents until he was shot by sentries. One pilot had been killed, others were wounded. It was an unpleasant feeling, to be walking about, eating and sleeping there, while in their tunnels underground the enemy, like hunted nocturnal animals, waited for night. The squadron stayed at Iwo for three days while we waited for a storm to end. These days were as dead and empty as the island—fearful days, everything unnatural, even the ways men died, blown up at random in the night, or burned out of holes in the ground, or buried alive. I was relieved to take off for Okinawa; I didn't think I could have fought my war on Iwo.

We approached Okinawa through gray, broken clouds beneath a high overcast. The sea was gray, too, and empty at first; then I saw one picket ship, them more and more ships, all kinds of ships, and then the dark bulk of the island. It was the first place I had seen where a war was actually going on, and I looked down when I could as our flight swung round the southern end of the island, staying well out to sea, because it was the end that the Japanese held. I could see nothing very clearly, only wooded hills across which artillery smoke drifted like low clouds, but I knew that it was enemy earth down there. There could be nothing familiar about it.

We flew past the island, and over the fleet, where there was more drifting smoke from the guns of battleships and cruisers, and then turned back toward the island and began our landing approach. As we descended and crossed the beach, I saw the part of the island that American troops controlled, and familiarity returned. It looked more like a construction site or a highway project back home than like a battlefield—slashes of raw earth everywhere, bulldozers, steamrollers, cities of tents and temporary buildings, heaps of supplies. Seabees were building roads and airstrips, and the scene was full of American energy and bustle. It was only when we had landed and I was standing uncertainly on the flight line waiting for orders that I became aware of the presence of war—a distant rumbling, like a trolley-car passing late at night, that was the sound of guns.

Trucks took us and our gear to the squadron's area on a low hill near the strip, and I found a tent and moved in with Rock and Joe and T and Bergie. Officers' Country was the top of a rise in what had been a wheat field, and the tent stood in the spring crop of young wheat; under my cot the grain was still growing. I threw the parachute bag that held all my possessions down on my cot and went out to look around. At the end of the officers' street—only a dirt path between the rows of tents—and on either side behind the tents, the ground fell away sharply into narrow little valleys, gullies almost. The officers' toilet had been built in the valley behind our tent, and I walked down that way, past the toilet and on up the valley. In a hundred yards or so it came to an abrupt end, and there, set into the steep hillside, were fan-shaped walls of masonry that I knew must be tombs—each with a terrace in front, and a low, narrow entrance to the vault. I was a little afraid, alone there among the tombs—there might be a leftover Jap alive in one of them, or a booby trap—but I went nearer. The tombs had been broken open, and shattered funeral urns and bits of bone were scattered about. No doubt some Marine had hoped there would be something worth taking there; but these were poor people, and they had buried nothing but their dead. I crept inside one of the tombs and found in the stooping darkness only dust and fragments and dry, dead air. It didn't even feel like a special place, the way cemeteries back home did; war had robbed it of its reverence.

From our hill we could see the whole of Kadena air-field—fifteen hundred feet of runway, with a bright yellow bulldozer parked across one end to encourage short landing runs, and a makeshift tower. Taxiways led from the runway to banked revetments where the planes were parked, and a dirt road ran up the hill to the squadron camp. On the far side of the field was a gravel pit, from which all day trucks carried gravel to build more taxiways, and an extension of the runway, down beyond the parked bulldozer. To the north was Yontan, once the principal Japanese airfield and now a Marine base, spread out across the top of a low plateau a couple of miles away; to the south, three or four miles off, we could see the hills where the Marines and the Army were attacking the main Japanese defensive line. We could stand at our tent doorway and watch the battleships that lay just offshore shelling Shuri Castle, the Japanese strong point, and could even see the shells arcing through the air, changing color from white to red as they cooled.

But before we could watch the war we had to build foxholes, to hide in when the war came too close for watching. There are no conventions in foxhole design; you dig according to your energies, and cover according to the materials at hand. Down in the valley by the tombs Joe and Bergie had found a rusting pile of railroad tracks, and we used them for our roof-beams. The hole we dug was U-shaped, with the longest section at the base. We laid the lengths of track across the long part, and covered them with sandbags to make a cave, for which the two ends of the U were entrances, opening at the two back corners of our tent. We figured we would be up from a sound sleep and into the hole in under one minute. My cot was nearest to one entrance, and to make my own retreat even faster I placed a pair of rubber boots, with my pants stuck over them fireman style, beside my cot. I was going to be the first man in the hole every time.

But when the first air raid came, late in the night, I woke slowly and confusedly, and I was still trying to get my legs through the mosquito netting and into my boots when Rock shot past me, fully clothed, with a flashlight in his hand and his .38 revolver strapped across his chest, and plunged into the foxhole entrance. I had just managed to stand up in the boots, and was pulling up my pants when the sound of six rapid revolver shots burst from the hole, accompanied by dazzling flashes of light. Rock had fired all six of the tracer bullets in his gun.

"Christ," Joe yelled, "there's a Jap in the foxhole!" He began groping for his own .38. I sat back down again. It looked as though it might be safer to stay in bed. Down on the runway the air-raid siren was still wailing, up and down. Rock appeared in the foxhole entrance, and when I shone my flashlight on him he blinked and looked dazed.

"It was a rat," he said. "Big as a shoat. Right there in the corner, just starin' at me. I got him, but them tracers will blind a man." He stood, filling the entrance, squinching up his eyes, trying to get his vision back.

"Either get in or get out, for God's sake," Joe said. "There's an air raid on, and you're standing there blocking the whole goddamn hole!" Rock drew back in, and we tumbled after him. But when we had flashed our lights around the hole, there was no dead rat there, only a bit of the corner crumbled where the bullets had hit, and the smell of burning.

"I be damned," Rock said. "I don't see how I could of missed him."

"Next time there's a raid," Bergie said, "you leave that gun in your sack. I know you're not going to shoot a rat, and you probably couldn't hit a Jap, but you might just hit one of us."

That was the only time any of us ever fired a pistol, though we all went on carrying them when we flew.

At that time, early in the battle, the Japanese were sending desperate waves of planes down from the main islands, and we spent a good deal of our time hiding. The sirens would wail, we would throw ourselves into the hole, and then if the guns around us didn't begin to fire we'd peer out, cautiously at first, and then more boldly, and finally climb onto the roof for a better view. The air raids became a spectacular show, and the roof of our foxhole was our box seat. From there, one night, I saw a Japanese bomber (the twin-engine type called a Betty) fly the length of the island along the west side, held in the searchlights all the time, and in a network of tracers and exploding shells, and when he was over the fleet, at the point of fiercest fire, do a perfect, insolent slow-roll and fly on out of range. It was a beautiful gesture, the pilot up there with his lost war, showing his skill, being a pilot still.

Once a raid came suddenly in the twilight and caught me sitting contemplatively in the officers' head, down in the little valley behind the tents. There was nothing to do, no point in running up to the foxhole; I simply sat there with my pants around my ankles, and went about my business. It was very quiet, and then, with a sudden ripping sound, a Japanese fighter swept over the trees by the mess hall, very low. I could see the blinking of his machine guns as he rushed toward me and then swung toward the parked planes on the field. Then he was gone. Not a single gun had fired at him. I had the feeling that no one had even seen him but me. I pulled up my pants and walked up the valley to the tent. Only then did I think how embarrassing it would have been to die down there, on the toilet, with my pants down.

As time passed and the Japanese expended their experienced pilots and their best planes, they began to send beginners, in anything that would fly. One night we saw, caught in an intersection of searchlights, a biplane, a trainer much like the Yellow Perils of our primary training. The lights, like long clutching fingers, held it almost motionless in the center of brightness. No guns seemed to be firing at it, there were no explosions of shells, no tracers, only the fragile plane alone in the light. Then it began to spin, slowly, never picking up much speed, down out of the lights into the darkness beyond Naha. Some kid, not used to night-flying, had been dazzled by the lights and had spun in. It wasn't a kill, it wasn't a credit to anybody—just a flight accident, the kind we used to read about in *BuAerNews*. *Poor bastard,* I thought, remembering my own night flights, *so scared, so unready for war, and now so dead.*

Our own losses began too, almost at once, though they were less spectacular than the deaths of the Japanese pilots. I had been on the island only three days when a pilot named Fox died. He was one of the old hands of the squadron, who had left Ulithi with the forward echelon before we arrived, so I hardly knew him. He didn't even have a first name for us yet, and when Joe came into the tent to tell me about it he said simply, "Fox is down."

Fox had been flying an artillery spotter around over the front lines. It was a job that we all did, but that nobody liked—flying back and forth across the island, low and not too fast, while the spotter looked for gun flashes and radioed their locations to his own guns. It was at once boring and dangerous. The air was full of shells, the Japanese gunners were accurate at low altitudes, and yet there was nothing to see, and nothing to do except drive, like a chauffeur. Shuri Castle was down there, at the center of the front, and two armies were struggling for it, but you didn't notice it. You only saw guns winking, tanks breathing flames like dragons, maybe a patrol running across a field, but nothing more, nothing that looked like a big war.

That's what Fox was doing when his plane was hit. An Army artillery captain saw it happen and wrote a report. The plane was flying at about 250 feet, he said, when it was hit—by a "high trajectory shell," so it must have been one of our own mortars, lobbing shells over the line, maybe a mortar that the Captain commanded. The plane crashed on our side of the front, and the Captain got to the wreck within ten minutes of the crash. There was, he said, no sign of life in the area.

Three days later Bergie took off on the same kind of flight and simply disappeared. This time there was no eyewitness, and though later a rumor reached us that a plane had been hit by mortar fire that day, it was never verified, and no wreck was found. Our friend Bergie—the church-in-the-wildwood tenor, the gentle husband, the "father" of our Santa Barbara family—had simply vanished from our lives. There was no body, no grave, and no funeral, no one, it seemed, to mourn for. T and Joe and I put his possessions together—there was almost nothing worth saving—and gave them to the Adjutant to send home, and took his cot apart and moved it out of the tent. For a while there was a patch of dead wheat where the cot had been; but gradually it was worn away, until it was like the rest of the tent floor.

When you have flown from an airfield for a while, the landscape around it become as familiar as a neighborhood. You know where you are by the pond there, the hill over there, the highway, the smoke of the town. But at first it is strange, and no feature is yet a landmark. At Kadena the land was even more alien. It was a foreign place, with tiny fields and tombs, but with no railroads or water towers or highways; and it was a battlefield, devastated and smoking. In the island's principal town, Naha, there was only one wall standing—not a single entire building, just that one white wall (it looked as though it might have been a public building, perhaps a school), rising uselessly from the ruins. All the villages had been destroyed, and the people who lived in them killed or driven into camps. The only signs of human life that you saw from the air were military signs—the supply dumps along the beaches, the airfields, and the columns of trucks creeping along dirt roads toward the front.

I still had this sense of an unknown landscape below me when I flew my first strike at Okinawa. Our target, we were told, was a set of torpedo launchers, thought to be hidden on the eastern shore of the island. We flew there and circled in formation, in over the beach, out over the anchored fleet, and back again to the shore. Pine trees grew to the edge of the water there, and it looked quiet and pleasant, the sort of place where you might stop for a swim or have a picnic. It would also have been a good place from which to launch torpedoes against the motionless ships in the bay, but we couldn't find any launchers.

From my position as wingman in the rear section, I couldn't even look for them; I had to watch for planes ahead of me, and I had only a vague sense of where we were—now over water, now over land. As we turned in over the beach for maybe the tenth time I looked along my port wing toward my section leader, watching him, working to hold my position, and there on the wing surface, a few feet out from where I sat, a row of holes appeared, suddenly and almost unobtrusively. We flew on, I kept my position in the flight, we swung once more out over the bay; the holes seemed to have nothing to do with anything. I had been hit, that was all. Not as dramatic as losing your virginity, not even like a first drink; just four or five holes the size of quarters in the smooth dark metal.

We gave up looking for the rocket launchers and turned across the island toward Naha, where the Japanese still held the bombed and shattered airfield. We had to do something with our bombs, so we would attack the gun-emplacements there. The air over Naha was full of Navy planes and confusion. It seemed as though all the failed strikes for that morning had come to the same place to unload. We circled, waiting for an opening in the traffic, and then swung into attack formation. The flight leader peeled off and dived, and when my turn came I followed, trying to remember all the things I should do: bombsight on, bomb bays open, bombs armed, machine guns armed (don't forget to fire them!). I could see the other planes of the flight spread out in a loose diagonal below me and to the left. Some AA fire was rising from somewhere on the field, spotting the sunshine with little clouds of smoke; but in the flurry of my preparations I couldn't see the guns.

Bombs began to explode, scattered randomly over the field. I was nearly at the point where I had to drop, and I hadn't found anything to drop on, hadn't even had time to look for a target. Then, in the right angle where two run-ways crossed, I saw the gun emplacement, with tracers rising out of it like roman candles. But it was too late, I couldn't turn, the altimeter read 2,000 feet, then 1,500 feet, I had to pull out. I dropped my bombs—just threw them away like rubbish, something to be got rid of—and pulled out and to the right, across the beach and out over the fleet, and joined up with the rest of the flight. Two years' training, I thought gloomily, for this—this aimless attack on nothing. I had come at last to the Big Test, the moment of action in the real war, but somehow I had missed it, or it had missed me.

This sense of the aimlessness of the war never quite left me, though later strikes were sometimes more comprehensible, as the squadron found its special mission. We began to fly attacks in support of the infantry—low-level precision bombing of enemy positions just in advance of our troops. We'd circle over the lines, and a controller on the ground would give us our target: "Do you see a hill with a road running up it? We're marking it with blue smoke. There's a gun in a cave at the top, to the left of the road." The strike leader would find the target, drop on it, and we'd drop on his explosion. The system worked pretty well, though one hill with a road up it looked very much like another, and the Japanese sometimes confused things by firing blue smoke back into our own lines, so that occasionally we dropped on the wrong troops, and an angry complaint would come to us from an infantry commander. But our own soldiers were not much more real to us than the enemy. If they were in the Army they were called Doggies, which was short for Dog-faces, and Marines despised them, along with their commanders. (Marines taught Okinawan children to stand by the road when Army units passed, shouting "General MacArthur eats shit!" They thought it meant "Give me a cigarette.") Even our own Marine infantrymen were a different species, called Gravel-crunchers or Crunchies—remote allies, at best. And anyway, they were all down there on the ground, invisible except when they did something spectacular, like attacking with flamethrowers or tanks; and we were up here, separated from them by the supporting air.

After each strike there was a debriefing session with the squadron intelligence officer. You gathered around his desk and told him, one at a time, what you thought you had seen and what you might have hit, and he turned it all into extravagant claims of destruction and pinpoint accuracy, and put it in the squadron war diary. If anything had really been achieved, he sent a news item back to Washington, which sent it to your hometown paper, which might run it, especially if it was a small town, maybe even with your picture; and then the cuttings would come back, from McComb, Mississippi, or Albany, Minnesota, and we'd sit around with some beers and the mail and laugh about what the folks back home thought we were doing. Once the intelligence officer sent the same item out for every pilot in the squadron, about what a great job we were doing, and mine got to a brewery in Chicago that had a Hero of the Week award. My name was mentioned on the radio, and my father got a certificate suitable for framing. He was very proud of the certificate, but he wouldn't frame it because it came from a brewery.

Slowly life at Kadena began to take shape, and our squadron camp became a sort of village. The road down the hill to the strip was our main street, and along it a village life moved. At the top on one side of the road was Officers' Country, and on the other side the squadron mess hall. Downhill from the mess hall were the enlisted men's quarters, rows of tents like the officers' but closer together, and with more men in each tent. A Quonset hut across the road was the Operations office and also the village post office, a place you could just drop in to when you were passing by, to talk and listen to the latest rumors.

A little farther down, two tents together were the offices of the Commanding Officer and the Adjutant, a sort of town hall. At the bottom of the road, beside the strip, were the squadron shops: tents for armament, for radio and radar, and for the quartermaster's supplies. On an ordinary day men moved up and down the street or stopped in little groups to talk and laugh, jeeps threaded among them, and from below the sounds of men working drifted up—the clanking and hammering, and the rise and fall of engines being tested.

It was an odd community—a village with no women or children, in which only one business was conducted—but it had a wholeness, and it felt familiar and comfortable and not, like the rest of the island, exotic and foreign. Everything you wanted (except women, children, and peace) you could get there: clothes at the quartermaster's store, food at the mess hall, your mail at Operations. The Red Cross tent down by the strip provided tobacco and writing paper, and sometimes a brown rocklike substance called Tropical Chocolate, which would not melt, and had to be pulverized between the teeth. Back of the tents in Officers' Country there was a tub for washing clothes, and a shower-bath made from an oil drum; you could build a fire under it and have a hot shower, if you wanted one.

There was even a village movie theater on the hillside behind Operations. It was primitive and uncomfortable—you sat on cartridge cases in the open air—but it completed village life, and made it more like life back home. A movie began every night as soon as it was dark enough, just about when the first nightfighters took off. It usually began with a newsreel, edited to give an encouraging view of the war, and a short, which always seemed to be Lawrence Tibbett singing "The Road to Mandaly," and then the feature film. Most nights we didn't get through the whole program, though; the feature would start, and then the air-raid sirens would begin to wind up to a howl, and the screen would go blank and dark, and the ninety-millimeter gun on the hill behind Officers' Country would begin to fire. I saw the beginning of a Spencer Tracy-Katharine Hepburn movie five times, and never saw the end; they were together in a buggy, and he was courting her—and then the sirens would blow.

In the residential section of our village, domestic improvements continued. Joe and I walked up the road, away from the airfield, and found a ruined house that must have been an impressive place before it was shelled. It had a tiled roof, now mostly blown off, and many rooms. In one was a sort of toilet, apparently designed to save human excrement for fertilizer. In another stood an elaborately lacquered dresser. The drawers were all gone—perhaps the inhabitants had simply seized them and run off with the contents—but the frame remained, with flat surfaces where the drawers had been, which could be used as shelves. It was beautiful, even in its devastated form, and we carried it back to our tent. It looked a little odd there, on the dirt floor, stuffed with khaki pants and T-shirts, but it made us feel settled.

Rock built a floor lamp out of two-by-fours, with a helmet liner for a shade, and T constructed a primitive brazier out of a gasoline can. It was filled with broken roof tiles, and you doused the tiles with gasoline and lit them, and you could make coffee. Once T heated a can of soup on it, but neglected to open the can. It exploded and covered our cots, our mosquito nets, and the walls of our tent with Campbell's tomato. Liz sent me two photographs of herself, and I asked a maintenance man to make frames for them. He made them out of cockpit plexiglass, in two panels, hinged like a book, and painted them with blue airplane paint, like the TBM's on the line. I put them on top of the Japanese dresser—two pictures of the smiling, pretty girl who was my responsibility.

In the evenings junior officers took turns doing the dreariest of squadron jobs—censoring the letters that the enlisted men wrote. Most of the men were not very literate, and their letters home were composed of clumsy expressions of affection and preposterous lies about their military exploits. They knew that we censored their letters, and some of them resented it and played a game with us, trying to sneak information past us, to hint by some elaborate circumlocution where the squadron was and what it was doing. Our part of the game was to snip out whatever seemed too obvious, but never to report a man to the CO.

Sometimes their amorous feelings for their wives and sweethearts were expressed with a forthrightness that seemed pornographic to middle-class young men like us. We'd be sitting in the tent, each with a pile of letters to be censored, and someone would begin to laugh: "Hey, listen to this guy," and he'd read out some mechanic's fancy, addressed to his wife, of what he'd do to and with her when he got home. It was funny, and it was astonishing, that there were marriages in the world in which a man said *cunt* to his wife, and in which sexual relations were apparently conducted with such violent and inventive enthusiasm. Men like that mechanic made censoring an endurable and sometimes an educational activity.

For one pilot in the squadron it was different. In the tent opposite mine lived a gentle, priest-like Catholic boy named Feeney. He never spoke above a murmur, he didn't drink with us, and he lived in general the life of a seminarian. Feeney was a good pilot and a nice guy, and we all liked him, but he wasn't like the rest of us. Eventually, in the rotation of censorship duties, he came upon one of the pornographic mechanic's letters, and was horrified, so horrified that he summoned the man to his tent. We hovered outside and heard this interview:

Lt. Feeney: "Sergeant, you can't do this."

Sergeant: "Do what, sir?"

Lt. Feeney: "Write a letter like this to your wife."

Sergeant: "What about it, sir?"

Lt. Feeney (nervously): "Well, you say you're going to fuck her cross-eyed. That's no way to talk to your wife."

Sergeant: "Why not? She's my fucking wife, ain't she? Sir?" Feeney could find no answer for that one, and the Sergeant continued to embellish his descriptions of his return home with sexual fantasies.

The shock that Feeney felt we all shared. But still, we expected that sort of thing from the enlisted men. Yet it was surprising and upsetting when one of our own talked that way. I remember walking down the road to Operations one day with Jimmy and Sly. Sly was telling a long, boring story about something that had happened at El Toro, but I wasn't really listening. It was a sunny spring day, early May probably; and I could see that the low hills beyond the strip, where the fighting was still going on, were beginning to turn green, in spite of the war.

Jimmy seemed distracted, too, walking along, hands in pockets, scuffing his feet like the small boy he seemed to be; but Sly bored on relentlessly. "I remember, it was January. . . . No, it must have been December. Anyway, it was raining, and I was home fucking my wife. . . ." Jimmy stopped short on the road and turned. "Goddamn you, shut up!" His face was white with anger. "Don't ever talk that way about your wife, not in front of me,'' and he stalked away into Operations. Sly stared, and his mouth beneath the limp mustache gaped open, but he didn't say anything. I don't think he understood, even then, that though Marines did talk about women that way sometimes, a wife was different—even the wife of a man like Sly.

Air raids continued, but more sporadically now—a single plane at night, high in the lights, or a crackle of AA fire over the fleet. We woke in the dark, sometimes to the mournful howling of the sirens, sometimes to the cough of the ninety-millimeter behind the hill; and crowded, half asleep, into the open ends of the foxhole; and stood there, shoulder-deep in the earth, to see what was happening. We were standing that way one night in May when the darkness over Yontan lit up like a Fourth of July show. Bright fingers of searchlights probed and crossed the sky, and guns sprayed tracers into the dark. Guns in the fleet began to fire, too, and then our own guns at Kadena, and others, until it seemed that every battery on the island and in the anchorage was hurling a converging fire at Yontan. As we watched, the guns' trajectories gradually lowered, until they were firing nearly horizontally, a dense crisscross of fire that was almost solid.

Up from the net of fire a sudden ball of flame rose, and a moment later we heard the explosion, and then another and another. Something was burning, a plane probably, and other fires started and rose up, filling the sky with flames that were brighter than the tracers' tracks. What possible attack could be taking place there, a mile or two away? We could see nothing except the tracer fire and the flames, and we knew nothing except what we saw. The defensive fire seemed desperate and irrational—they must be firing into their own positions—as though the attacker were something monstrous and inhuman, that could not be fought in a customary way. Then the gunfire began to subside, and for a time there were only the tall flames, and scattered explosions, tardy-sounding after all that noise. And then the flames died, very slowly at first, and then they were gone, and the night was dark and silent.

The next day we heard the story. The Japanese had sent seven bombers, loaded with troops, in a suicide raid against Yontan. The planes were to crash-land on the runways, and the troops, armed with explosives, would leap out and destroy the aircraft parked on the field. Three of the bombers were shot down by nightfighters before they reached the island, but four got through and approached the field, coming in low over the trees in the darkness. The horizontal gunfire we saw had been directed at them, and three were shot down in the last seconds before they landed; the first flames we saw were those exploding planes.

Only one pilot managed to land and to get his load of troops out onto the runway. They ran among the parked planes, throwing grenades and firing machine guns, until they were killed by the rifle fire. When daylight came, the field at Yontan was scattered with smoking wreckage and bodies. Forty planes had been destroyed or damaged, seventy thousand gallons of aviation fuel had been burned, and two Marines had been killed. The control tower was flattened, and the runway was blocked by the burned-out Japanese plane. In the three crashed bombers, and scattered in ones and twos along the strip, were sixty-nine dead Japanese. No one could say how many of the burned planes had been hit by the Japanese raiders, and how many by the wild AA fire, or whose bullets had killed the two

Marines (they were in the tower, and were caught in the crossfire).

The raid had no effect on the progress of the war. How could it? We had more planes and more Marines; we could pile a field with wreckage, burn a gasoline dump, and go on fighting without an interruption. The men in those dark bombers must have known that, and the men who sent them certainly did. Yet the raid came. By happening at Yontan, up there on the next rise where we could watch the whole spectacular madness of it, it forced upon us the strangeness of the people we were fighting.

For in an air war you are not very conscious of your enemies as human beings. We attacked targets—a gun emplacement, a supply dump, a radar station—not men, and succeeded or failed in terms of the things we destroyed. I flew more than a hundred missions during the Okinawa campaign and never saw a single Japanese soldier on the ground. If I thought of the men down there at all, I thought of them as ordinary, like us—men who ran supply dumps and radar stations, and who manned their guns and shot at us when we attacked them; the rules of war, I thought, were the same. But the raid on Yontan was different; it wasn't something we could have done. It was not concerned, as our raids were, with destroying, but with dying. It seemed to me then that the true end of war for the men I was fighting against was not victory, but death. And spectacular death, fire and explosions, the body bursting in a terrible, self-destroying orgasm. One of the Japanese at Yontan had held a grenade in his belly and blown himself up.

Later that month I woke in the night to the sound of a shout and then a burst of automatic rifle fire. There were hurrying footsteps in the company street, and voices, and when I looked out people were running past with flashlights. I ran, too, in my rubber boots. At the end of the row of officers' tents, where the hill dropped off sharply, a sentry was posted; and it was his voice that I had heard, and his rifle. Someone had crept up the gully below and had begun to climb the hill toward him. He shouted once, as the regulations told him to, and then fired a whole magazine, point-blank.

The body lay at the bottom of the hill. It was the first dead man I had ever seen. After all that dying, the friends lost, the wrecked planes crumpled on the bombing target, this was the first time that actual and particular death had reached me. I went down the hall and pointed my flashlight at the body. It didn't look like a man who had just been alive. It didn't look like a man at all. The clothes seemed to have neither color nor shape, not to be clothes at all; it was a bundle of rags that lay at my feet, just rags without even the shape of a human being. Perhaps he wasn't even a Jap, only an Okinawan, hiding and hungry, not murderous but only desperate with hunger and fear. I felt revulsion at his deadness, so ugly, sprawled and defaced by the bullets that had killed him, but no fellow-feeling at all. He might have been a dead dog, hit by a car and thrown to the side of the road. We all turned away and left him there, and went back to bed.

The next morning T and I went to see Billy Childers in his tent, to talk about something to do with our section—the next strike, probably, or a problem of armament. When we came in, Billy rose from his cot, put his hand slowly into his pocket, and brought out a dirty handkerchief. Slowly, carefully, he unwrapped it, holding it on one palm while he turned back the handkerchief with the other. Then he looked up proudly. On his extended palm, on the handkerchief, lay the dead man's ear. "Got me a souvenir," Billy said.

That was the only dead man, but there were many deaths, and the images of those deaths come back like film clips. We are watching a move on the makeshift screen near the strip. A nightfighter pilot, approaching to land, mistakes the lights of a road for a row of landing lights and settles to a perfect three-point landing between the road and the strip, in the gravel pit. The plane explodes, and a sudden ball of fire rises into the night. The movie is stopped until the darkness settles again, and then continues. I sit in my plane on the taxiway at Yontan, waiting for clearance. A Corsair damaged in a fight approaches for an emergency landing; it levels off, stalls, a wing drops, and it flips over to crash beside the runway. From my foxhole I see Japanese planes hit; they blossom in flames; are shot to pieces, crash.

I remember a day in May—a warm, sunny, still day. I was lying naked in the sun, stretched out on a canvas cot reading not very attentively one of those odd-shaped, lengthwise paperbacks that the Army distributed to the troops. The day seemed peaceful, though the war was there, if you listened for it. A mile or so offshore, the *Missouri* was still shelling Shuri Castle, and the sound of the firing and the detonations of the shells reached me as a dull, monotonous rumble, like the sound of a factory making something heavy but uninteresting. But where I lay the earth was silently, soporifically hot, and I might have been on any beach back home, sunburned and sweating and thinking about nothing.

On a cot next to mine Rock was lying propped on his elbow; we were probably talking about girls, or the wild parties he'd known back at A&M. But at the sound of planes we stopped and watched a flight of Turkeys come rumbling over the field. They looked as they always did in the air, cumbersome and tired, as though they didn't like flying very much and weren't much good at it; but they were in good formation, a tight V of V's, trying to look as much like the fighters as their ungainly shapes would allow. They flew the length of the strip and began to peel off for landing, and as they did, I counted them. There were only eleven; one was missing.

I tried to remember who had gone on the strike and where they had gone, but I couldn't. None of my close friends, anyway. We watched the formation break into a stretched-out string of separate planes, watched the wheels and flaps come down as one by one they turned to touch down.

Then I saw the other one approaching from the south, flying low and slow. It passed over us, so close and so slow-moving that I could look up into the ragged hole that gaped in the belly of the plane, just aft of the wing. And I could see that the gunner's door, toward the tail, had been jettisoned; there was someone in the open doorway, motionless, facing out.

The plane made a slow circle of the airfield and once more headed down the strip. *The radio must be out*, I thought; *he's looking for a green light from the tower.* We could see the controller in the tower raise his signal light. The pilot began to rock his wings, slowly back and forth, to acknowledge the controller's signal.

Then, from the open door, something fell. Slowly, as though the sunlit air were bright water, it sank toward the earth, turning and turning, very slowly. It struck the airstrip near the tower and bounced, suddenly and surprisingly high. And as it bounced, it opened, and became a spread-eagled man, and fell again to the earth and lay, once more a lump, a something. The plane, as though relieved of an intolerable burden, circled more swiftly and prepared to land. On the strip near the tower there was a sudden flurry of jeeps, an ambulance, and men running, but there was no sound—I particularly remember that there was no sound—except for the quick bass roar as the pilot changed to low pitch for his landing.

The ambulance began to move slowly up the strip toward the sick bay, and the jeeps and men scattered as quickly as they had come. The strip was empty except for the plane rolling slowly and clumsily to a stop. Even the sky was empty, not a plane or even a cloud in sight.

The plane had been hit by groundfire, and a shell had exploded inside the fuselage, somewhere behind the wing. It had knocked out the radio, killed the turret gunner, and wounded the radio operator. The wounded man couldn't talk to the pilot with the radio out, and he could see the great hole in the fuselage, so he tried to bail out, but fainted in the doorway. When the plane tilted over the strip, he fell, and died. Of all the deaths in the squadron, his was the only one I actually saw.

It must have been about that time that Dick Whitfield got lost over clouds on an antisub patrol, and radioed in to Ground Control for a heading, but never reached the field. For a while he could be heard on the radio, reporting in, flying the heading and complaining that he hadn't reached the field yet. Then he faded out. Three or four days later we heard what had happened, how he had been given, not the correct heading to the base, but its reciprocal (an error that's easy to make if the plane is close overhead, as Dick's was). He had, on instruction, flown directly away from the field until his gas was almost gone.

Then through a hole in the clouds he saw an island and began an approach. But it looked unfamiliar, and after consulting his maps he concluded, correctly, that he was preparing to land on a Japanese-held island several hundred miles east of Okinawa. He turned round and flew back west until he ran out of gas. Then, with a dead engine, he began a descent through clouds, and skillfully made a smooth, power-off landing in the sea. It was early afternoon. He and his crew unloaded their survival gear—the two rafts that the TBM carried, Mae Wests, rations, everything—and had the rafts inflated and were aboard them before the plane sank. Then they rigged a sail and set out to sail home, or to survive until they were found.

That afternoon they heard a plane fly over, but it was out of sight in the overcast. Later another appeared, this time lower. It was Japanese. They lowered their blue sail and hid under it until the plane flew away. As night fell the wind rose and the sea became rough. Whitfield took down the sail and improvised sea anchors to hold the raft into the wind and keep it from capsizing. On the second day it was the same—the storm continued and planes passed high up in the overcast.

The weather improved on the third day, and the clouds lifted. They saw an American transport overhead and signaled with flares and mirrors, as the survival instructions directed, but got no response. Other planes passed, and finally someone in a flying boat saw their blinking mirror, and circled over the raft, wiggling its wings. It didn't land, though, but flew off toward where they imagined Okinawa must be; there was a Very Important Person aboard, and the pilot wouldn't chance a landing in that high sea. But he did radio the position of the raft, and in an hour or so another flying boat appeared.

That plane (now this is Dick's story) landed heavily into the waves and taxied to pick them up. Dick climbed aboard last—he had a feeling the officer in command was supposed to be the last to leave the ship—and with relief turned and stuck his sheath knife into the raft, and let it sink. "I wouldn't have done that, if I were you," the pilot said. "When we landed just now we sprung all the plates in the bow. We may sink." The plane didn't sink, but it couldn't take off in that sea, and so Whitfield and his crew were taxied the hundred miles home. It took twelve hours. They had been at sea for more than three days.

A message came from the taxiing plane that the rescue had been accomplished, and we began to prepare a welcome for him. We removed from his tent every object that was his—his clothes, his footlocker, his cot, every single possession. Then we waited. Days passed. Where was he? It turned out that he had been taken to a naval hospital for examination, which revealed that the three days in the raft had given him a case of the piles. A doctor (no doubt another rusty surgeon, like the one at Ulithi) operated at once, and when he found that his patient had not been circumcised, he performed that operation as well, "as long as I'm in the neighborhood," as he put it. Whitfield came out of anesthesia unable to lie either on his back or on his stomach; he felt, he said, a lesser man.

At last he returned to the squadron, where he was met with feigned embarrassment. "Gosh, Dick," Kelleher said, "who'd have thought you'd survive? We drank your whiskey at the wake. You'd have liked that wake." "Clothes?" another tentmate added. "Shit, they were worn out anyway. We couldn't even give 'em back to the quartermaster. Chaplain gave 'em to some gooks." "Letters? You don't mean those were *love* letters? I sent them to your mother."

Whitfield had been erased. He got quite upset about it, standing there in his tent looking at the bare place where his cot had been. He said he sort of knew now what being dead would be like, and it wasn't worth a shit. So we gave him back his possessions and put his cot together again for him, and then we drank all his whiskey, and after a while he felt better and told us the whole story, except about the circumcision. Rock said he didn't want to hear about cutting a piece of a man's cock off while he was drinking. Whitfield was unique—the only dead man who was ever restored to us alive—and the way we responded was cruel, but understandable. It was a chance to exorcise death by parodying it.

As the campaign continued, 232 began to fly more and more antisubmarine patrols; probably some of the Navy carrier squadrons had been withdrawn from the area. It was boring flying, and nobody ever saw anything. I generally took my mail and a cigar with me, and I would put the plane on automatic pilot, tune the radio to Shanghai if I could, and listen to music that was like the crashing of garbage-can lids while I read and smoked. Once I ran a tank dry while I was dozing along that way, and it took a while to get the engine started again, and Edwards and Campbell were quite annoyed. I suppose I had waked them up. Sometimes an air raid would come while I was on a patrol, and the radio would begin to sputter warnings and instructions—"Bandit in your section" or "Remain clear of fleet anchorage, where a kamikaze might be attacking"—and the air would be full of AA fire.

I saw an attack happen only once while I was flying. I was out over the water west of the island, patrolling, when Ground Control reported that a Japanese bomber had just dropped a Baka bomb and that it was in flight somewhere between me and the island. (*Baka* means stupid or crazy in Japanese. A Baka bomb was a tiny suicide plane, powered by a rocket engine and carrying in its nose an armed bomb. It had no landing gear, no armor or defensive armament, no radio, and almost no instruments. It was carried into attack position by a bomber and dropped. The pilot then fired his rocket and flew the bomb into the largest enemy ship he could see. In a revetment near Yontan there was a captured Baka—stubby-winged, fragile-looking, like a toy. It made me sick to look at it. A machine for killing pilots.)

Control said I was to continue my patrol and stay away from the island. But this time I turned and flew back, searching the sky. It was one of those warm, hazy spring days, when there is no horizon, just one curve of gray from the sea beneath you right round to the sky above. The island was an indistinct dark mass in the distance, and though I knew the fleet was off to my right, in the anchorage around Kerama Retto, I could only see a few of the closest ships, dark streaks on the gray water. The Baka appeared first as a dark line of smoke drawn diagonally downward across the grayness, from high on my left, descending toward the shrouded fleet on my right. Then I could see the little plane, looking like a model a child might make, moving very fast, nearly in front of me now, in a steep glide. Ahead of the plane AA shells from the ships below began to burst, silently, leaving small white puffs of smoke that hung against the darker haze like bits of cotton wool. I armed my guns, flipped on the gunsight, and began an intercepting turn, the kind of maneuver I had learned on gunnery sleeves in flight school. But a Baka is faster than a gunnery sleeve, and Turkeys are slow; my target fled past me as I turned, and disappeared into the haze and smoke over the fleet, leaving behind his scrawled trail, like a derisive message written on the air.

I felt foolish and let down. Of course you couldn't catch a Baka with a TBM; and why was I trying, anyway? Fighters chased their targets through friendly AA fire, and sometimes out again, but why behave like a fighter pilot? And especially *now,* at the end of a war that was already won. Yet, when the word about that Baka came, I turned. Perhaps the indoctrination had worked, after all, and I was like the third-string quarterback, running onto the field for his chance in the Big Game.

Ground Control for the antisub patrols was handled by our own pilots. Once every week or so you would have to spend a day in a dark, cavelike control room at Yontan, watching a radar scope and directing your friends around their patrol areas. That part of the job was dull, but the room itself was very exciting. This was where all the planes in the air over Okinawa and to the north were tracked, where enemy raids were first noted, and fighters sent against them. So that while the antisub controller's job was simply to see that his man wasn't shot down, he could watch the drama of fighter interception on the screen before him and follow the action on his earphones.

The visual part of this show was tense and dramatic. The intruding spot of light showed first on the rows of radar scopes before which the controllers sat. It was then transferred to a large transparent screen as a flourescent spot of crayon located on a map of the area. As the enemy plane flew on toward the island, the bright spots followed it, making a track on the screen, and our fighters left their own trails of light as they moved to an intersection; and then, if the controlling had been good, the intruder's trail stopped, and a circle on the screen marked the place where he had been shot down into the sea.

It should have been a silent show, but unfortunately the Navy had written dialogue for these occasions. There was a whole arch vocabulary for communicating a few simple facts: an enemy plane was a "bandit" or a "bogey"; altitude was given in "angels" instead of thousands of feet; and a kill was supposed to be reported in the laconic line "Splash one bogey." And of course you said Roger and Wilco and Over and Out all the time. It always seemed to me melodramatic and phony and unnecessary. Who were we supposed to be fooling, saying angels for altitude? And all that understatement, it was straight out of the movies—the influence of Gary Cooper and Bogart on American military procedures. The true line would have been, "Hey, you guys, I just shot a fucking Jap." But the script read, "Splash one bogey." Very phony.

It was while I was on my way to Ground Control duty that I suffered my only war wound. I was driving a squadron jeep, and I was late, and I drove along the empty Okinawa lane at pretty near top speed, which was probably around fifty in that jeep. The lane was narrow, and sunk between banks higher than my head, but there was no traffic, and I hurried along, not thinking about much, probably wishing I was in the air instead of down there in all that dust. A blind corner was coming up where another sunken lane crossed the one I was driving in, but my road was empty, the other one must be, too. I shot into the intersection. In from my left rumbled an amphibious landing craft—one of the kind that the Marines called Ducks. On land it was clumsy, like its namesake, but it was also tall and massive-looking as it bore down on me. I braked and swerved away, and the driver of the Duck braked and slammed into the back of my jeep, lifting it into the air, and tossing it head-first into a ditch. I gripped the steering wheel and hung on, like an unskilled rider on a mean horse, and I stayed in the seat; but my head snapped forward when I hit the ditch, and my forehead struck the screw-and-bar device that opens the windshield. I climbed out, feeling stunned but as far as I could tell unhurt, and scrambled up out of the ditch. There, looking down at me, was a frightened-looking pfc. "Oh my God," he moaned when he saw me, "I've killed an officer." I realized then that my forehead was cut and that blood was pouring down my face and onto my shirt.

The jeep wasn't damaged, only bent here and there where it didn't seem to matter; the Duck wasn't damaged, and the pfc wasn't hurt. And it was my fault. The important thing, then, was that the pfc shouldn't get into trouble. So we found a first-aid kit, put a patch on my head, and agreed that nothing had happened—neither of us had ever been there, there had been no accident. Then we hauled the jeep out of the ditch and I drove on.

At Yontan I went first to the sick bay. There was no doctor on duty—probably out circumcising somebody—and the corpsman was dubious about treating me. A flap of skin and flesh had been torn loose, and hung on my forehead like a small red tongue. It should be sewn up, but the doctor wasn't there, and the corpsman couldn't sew up a head. Finally he said, "Well, I can't sew it up, but I can cut it off." He took a huge pair of scissors, snipped off the flap, poured on Merthiolate, and bandaged me up. I went to the control room, thinking that when people asked me how I got the scar on my forehead, I could say, "I was hit on Okinawa."

In May we began to fly at night—solitary flights over

the Japanese lines that were meant to disturb the enemy's sleep and to prevent him from moving supplies. Any light—a truck's headlights, a fire, a lighted doorway—was to be fired on. It was the kind of flying that I hated, hovering around at a thousand feet, above invisible watchers, a target for any gun. And because I hated it, I did it; you could only evade what you weren't afraid of—that was understood.

The strip, with its rows of flickering flare-pots, was dark and unsubstantial-looking; but once I was in the air I could see lights all around—the fleet lit up for miles on both sides of the island, Yontan with its rotating beacon, the lights of camps, jeeps moving along the roads. It might have been California, or Memphis, or Pensacola. But the lights stopped suddenly in a ragged east-west line below Naha, and from there south the island was as black as a night sea. It was like an allegory—the good side full of light, and the evil side covered in darkness.

I flew out over the eastern bay, and south, and swung in toward the dark land. The observer riding with me began to scan the ground below us for gun flashes. I looked around for something to attack, somebody boiling a pot of tea or lighting his way to the toilet, but I could see nothing. To the north, across the lines, Army artillery was firing sporadically, lobbing mortar shells onto some Japanese position. It was one of those guns that had killed Bergie. Poor me. The island below remained black and inscrutable, a shadow over waiting men. I flew on, waiting, too. Nothing happened, there were no lights, no guns were fired, and I didn't drop a bomb or fire a single round. Then on my radio I heard my relief report himself airborne, and I turned back toward the lights, toward possible life.

Because Yontan had a beacon and electric landing lights, and Kadena had only flare-pots, we returned from these night flights to Yontan, and hung around there until dawn. There was a mess hall near the ready room that was open all night, like a highway diner, and the cook could do something with Spam and powdered eggs that made them taste reasonably good, at least after a night hop. So we hung around there, eating and drinking coffee, and listening to the stories of the night pilots as they came back. Sometimes the stories seemed a bit doubtful, the kind of yarn you'd spin for the intelligence officer. One pilot—not a guy I liked or trusted very much—claimed he had attacked twenty soldiers who were trying to launch a boat and had sunk the boat and killed all the soldiers. His description of the bodies floating in the water was very vivid, but it was hard to understand how he could have seen such detail at night, when I couldn't even see the ground. Kelleher told us how he had been in the air over the southern end of the island when an air raid began, and how every time he tried to come home and land his own AA guns started shooting at him. The Turkey had about four and a half or five hours of gas in it, but Kelleher stretched his to five and a half ("I could hear that engine sucking the last drops," he said, "like drinking a soda through a straw") before he was finally allowed to land.

Joe, the man things happened to, was hit by a shell on one of these night flights. It knocked out his hydraulic system, and he had to make a no-flaps, wheels-up landing in the dark. He did it perfectly, and the plane was repaired and flew again. Joe told the story, sitting there in the mess hall at three in the morning, eating Spam and eggs and laughing, as though it was a good joke on him. The next night the same thing happened to another pilot, but he wasn't the flier that Joe was, and though he survived, the plane was destroyed.

It was on one of those night-heckler hops that one of our pilots—his name was Fred Folino—shot a Jap plane down. He was down there at the southern end of the island, strafing up and down in the dark, when an air raid began. Control told him to clear the island at once and orbit to the southwest, but as he did he saw another plane ahead of him, its exhaust flames just visible in the darkness. He complained to Control: why was he being sent off the island into a boring orbit, when this other guy was allowed to stay here just flying around? You idiot, Control replied, that's the bandit.

By this time Fred was closing in on the plane and could see it more clearly. It was a float plane, with two pontoons, and it was flying straight and level at about his altitude, and on the same course. He slid into position astern, armed his guns, and turned on his gunsight. But then, he said, he couldn't see the Jap, he couldn't see anything but the bright bull's-eye of the gunsight. So he turned it off again and tried a burst in the dark. The tracers fell short. He added all the power he had, and slowly began to overtake the plane ahead, and when he thought he had gained some distance, he tried another little squirt, but he was still too far back. All this time the Jap didn't seem aware that he was being followed and shot at; he flew on on a straight course, Fred and his TBM grunting and straining behind.

At last, Fred said, he was sure he was close enough; the twin floats seemed to be sticking into his propeller. He took careful aim and squeezed the trigger. Nothing. He had run out of ammunition. But Fred was a calm man, and he considered what was left to him. He was carrying rockets, four on each wing, to be fired in pairs against ground targets. He armed them and fired the first two. They swished past the Jap, just below his wings, and now he knew he was being hunted, and he rolled into a diving turn. Fred followed, took a lead on his target, and squeezed off the second pair of rockets. There was a bright flash, and debris flew past his plane. He reported his achievement to Control. Control told him to get back on station where he belonged.

It was the only plane destroyed by a member of the squadron, and as far as I know the only one ever shot down at night with rockets. We were proud of old Fred, and of the little Jap flag that was painted on the fuselage of his plane the next day. It was something to show the fighter pilots.

Not all the action took place at night. Feeney, the gentle censor of enlisted obscenities, was attacked by a Japanese fighter plane one afternoon on a patrol. He told the story with a mild astonishment, as though it were an account of bad manners. "I was out on this ASP," he said, "just drifting along below the overcast, thinking about Boston, and letting my radar man do the looking—and all of a sudden there was this Irving making a head-on run at me!" ("Irving" was the American name for a kind of Jap fighter.)

"So you made a 180 and fired both fifties and shot him down, right?"

"Are you kidding? I pulled up into the overcast and began evasive maneuvers. At least I thought they were evasive, but the Jap kept finding me again. I couldn't see much—my engine was throwing oil—and my compass was swinging, so I wasn't too sure where I was going, but I just kept on twisting and turning and trying not to spin out, and the Jap kept coming back and losing me in the clouds again. Once he flew right over me, maybe twenty or thirty feet above, and never saw me. After a while he quit. I guess he was disgusted with me for not being more gung-ho.''

Two or three days later another ASP plane met a fighter, and wasn't fired on, and a few days after that a Tony made a head-on run on somebody else, and again didn't fire. Three interceptions in a row, and not a shot fired—it was very odd. The Japanese pilots seemed uncertain, as though they hadn't been told what to do if they met an American plane, or they had been given some other, quite different mission that was preoccupying them. I suppose most of them had been sent down to crash into ships and not to waste themselves on single aircraft. None of them ever shot at one of our planes, and except for Fred Folino's rocket shot, none of us ever hit any of them. "You'd think we were fighting in different wars," Feeney said wonderingly, "the way we just pass and nod to each other." And certainly it seemed that whoever our squadron was fighting—and I didn't usually have much feeling that we were fighting anybody in particular—we weren't fighting the Japanese air force.

The strain of combat flying began to tell on some pilots. One night-fighter pilot I knew had three consecutive engine failures (maybe he was hit by ground fire or by a Japanese plane, maybe the engine just stopped, I've forgotten) and had to land three times in the sea in the darkness. He didn't seem affected by these experiences—his conversation was normal, though he talked about water landings a good deal—but he began to paint things blue. Everything: his Mae West, his helmet, his flying suit, finally his tent—all blue. His CO concluded that the man needed a rest, and so he sent him back out of the action, but only as far as Saipan (we had been envying him a trip to Honolulu). In a week or so he was back with his squadron, supplied with a new helmet (biege) and a new Mae West (yellow). He seemed to be recovered—at least he went back to night-flying.

Nobody in our squadron seemed especially disturbed by the life we were leading, flying day and night and meeting Jap fighters; nobody went noticeably crazy, nobody painted anything blue. Still, someone must have thought that we were showing signs of weariness, and we were sent, a half-dozen at a time, to a rest camp farther north on the island, away from the fighting. The camp was nothing much—a few tents to sleep in, a small mess hall, and some cases of beer—but the setting was beautiful and restful— a pine grove on a rock promontory, looking over a small, untroubled bay. Pine woods always have a tidy feeling, of being empty and just swept, a feeling that I associate with Japanese orderliness and Japanese gardening and painting; and in that camp I felt as though we had been allowed into the best part of our enemy's world, a place that expressed his sense of beauty. Out in the center of the little bay there was a cluster of jutting rocks, and on the largest was a torii, one of those formal arches that you see outside Japanese temples. It was the only Japanese structure I ever saw on the island that was intact, and it seemed serene and eternal, out there on the rock, away from the war.

At the rest camp we got up when we felt like it, lay about reading and drinking, and in the afternoons climbed down the steep face of the promontory to swim and lounge on the rocks at the edge of the bay. Among the rocks and trees on the opposite promontory, a Japanese sniper was hiding, though our troops had long since passed him by and had gone on up the island. Sometimes while we were swimming he would lob a few rifle shots at us, just to show us that he was still resisting, I suppose, and to keep his courage up. We would hear the distant crack of his rifle, and a plunk where the bullet struck the water. I rather admired his lonely, stupid defiance over there.

It was obviously a good life up there at the camp, just what we needed, but it felt strange, and we were restless and ill at east. We weren't used to unscheduled time, and whole days without duties made us feel disoriented. And it was so quiet—there were no engine sounds, and we had been living with airplane engines for years, and got a feeling of security from hearing them in the night. Everything that was energetic in our lives—all the noise and the bustle—was absent in the pine-wood hush, and we were homesick for it. Three days was all we could stand, and we piled into the trucks that would take us back to Kadena like schoolboys at the end of term, headed for their vacation.

We went back to flying strikes, and I learned, one day, what I had not known before, that it is possible to feel pity for a machine. It was one of those on-the-island strikes, and we were loaded heavily: four five-hundred-pound bombs, eight rockets, full machine-gun ammunition. I taxied into position in my turn, ran up the engine, and released the brakes. The plane began to roll, ponderously at first; then as the speed increased the tail came up, the plane felt lighter on the stick, it was nearly flying. I reached for the wheel handle; I would pull up the wheels as I left the ground, a foot or two in the air. It was a way of showing off for the fighter pilots—like our landings, a foolish demonstration that we were hot pilots, too. I raised the handle, and the wheels began to fold up into the wings.

And the plane began to settle. The throttle had slipped back, the power had dropped, I was no longer flying. The plane touched the runway with a scream of offended metal, a blade of the propeller broke away and skittered across the runway, and we skidded to a stop, one wing down, in a cloud of dust. I sat in the cockpit, helpless with misery. I had busted another one. At this rate, I thought, I'll be a Japanese ace before the war is over. Then the crash truck was there, and I climbed out. Far down the runway I could see Edwards and Campbell still running; they must have jumped before the plane stopped sliding to have got that far. Then I realized that I had crashed with all those bombs and rockets, and I wanted to run, too. But it didn't seem right, after I'd wrecked that poor plane, to run away from it. I waited for a jeep and rode back to the squadron in wretched silence.

The CO dealt with my misdeed in what seemed then, and seems now, an exemplary way. He grounded me for a week and put me to work salvaging the wreck with a couple of mechanics. I tore up my knuckles taking off spark plugs, I covered myself with grease and oil, and I learned a good deal about how a TBM is put together. It was like sending a hit-and-run driver to work in a hospital. By the end of the week I was so sorry for that dead plane that I'd have given it a funeral if I could. I said as much to Kelleher. "Forget it," he said, "it's over. Never look up a dead horse's ass."

The rains began in late May. Clouds slid in from the China Sea, and lay low and motionless over the island, and the rain fell heavily and ceaselessly, day after day. I would wake at night and hear the rain droning on the tent roof, and wonder if it would ever stop, and fall back asleep to the dull sound of the rain, and wake to find that it was morning—dark, gray, and the rain still falling.

We lived in a world of water and mud. The company street ran first in rivulets, then streams, until it became a bog of gluey mud that sucked at your feet as you walked. Tent roofs sagged with the wet, and dripped where you touched them, and tent floors were slick with mud. Foxholes filled slowly, like bathtubs. We were always wet. Bedding never dried, and clothing never dried, so that night and day our bodies were always in contact with something damp and unpleasant to the touch. When we went out we wore suits of Navy rain gear—rubberized parkas and baggy pants that were clammy and cold, and high rubber boots; but the rain found entrances, streamed down our faces and necks, and in at our sleeves. Rain became the medium we lived in, a part of our air.

In the rain the airstrip looked like a dirt road to nowhere. Water stood in ponds on the runway, and the taxiways were rivers. Nothing was flying, no planes moved on the flight line, and no human beings were in sight. Our Turkeys sat in rows with their wings folded, like wet, melancholy birds. The air-raid sirens were silent—the Japs were grounded, too, and were not even sending suicide attacks against the fleet. It was as though man's gift for flight had been withdrawn from him, and he had been returned to earth and water, and to primeval mud.

The roads on the island quickly became impassable, slippery in the high places and flooded in the hollows. Every road to the front was jammed with stalled trucks, tanks, and jeeps, mile-long lines of them, motionless and abandoned. Only the shelling went on, very muted and distant in the rain, but audible, if you listened—the rumble of shells from the fleet, and the more staccato sound of the field artillery. Sometimes at night, even through the rain, you could see the flicker of shellfire along the southern horizon, like summer lightning.

As the rain continued and the roads remained clogged with mired vehicles, the troops in the line began to run short of supplies. Our squadron was given the task of delivering those supplies by parachute drops over the lines, and for nearly a month we delivered everything that reached the front lines: food, water, ammunition, medical supplies, even a telephone switchboard.

We would take off in the rain, splashing through puddles that threw sheets of water back over the cockpit, and climb to the base of the hanging clouds—five or six hundred feet, most days—and slide into a loose formation and head south, toward the lines. There a controller on the ground took over by radio and directed the flight toward the drop area, where a colored panel spread in a field or a smudge of colored smoke identified the exact place for the drop. As we rumbled along over the low hills, I looked down into what seemed the ruins of an ancient, peaceful world—tiny fields and old stone walls, deep, narrow lanes lined with gnarled old trees, a heap of stones where a house had been, all very close under our wings, everything clearly visible, even in the rain. I wondered where it ceased to be American-held, and became enemy territory, and what the Japs would do to me if I were shot down there.

When the flight leader had located the marker, the flight would string out into a long column and the leader would begin his pass. His bomb-bay doors would open, and as he passed over the marker the bundles of supplies would tumble out and behind him the parachutes would open— bright-colored, like flowers against the dark, wet earth, settling gently toward the ground—and more and more chutes as the other planes followed.

To drop supplies this way successfully you must fly over the target low and slow, and in a level straight line. If you fly too fast, the chute will split when it opens; if you aren't straight and level, it may entangle itself in the bomb bay. You must calculate the wind and correct for it, or you may deliver your supplies to the wrong army. You settle into your run, the marker ahead and just to one side. It slides under your nose, and you open the bomb bays and begin to count. You feel exposed, the plane maybe five hundred feet from a Japanese gun, the belly open, the airspeed dropping. It seems that a Jap with a good throwing arm could hit you with a rock. You wait, counting. Now! The weight drops free and the plane lifts, you throw the throttle forward, the plane surges, and you swing north, away from trouble, and head for home. It has all taken less than an hour.

The squadron flew nearly five hundred of those drops during that rainy stretch; my logbook says that I flew nine in the first five days of June. It was surely the most useful thing we did during the whole campaign.

While the rain fell, air raids ceased, but in their place we began to have shelling. One gun, hidden from the spotting planes during the good weather, could now be run out of its cave, fired for a few minutes, and hidden again before it could be located. The shelling could come at any time—in the night, while we were at lunch, or just as we taxied out to fly a parachute drop. There was no warning—just the first whuff of the distant gun, the descending shriek of the shell, and the explosion. Other shells would follow as the gunner worked his way around Kadena, aiming blind and changing direction slightly for each firing. We called him Pistol Pete, and his presence, down there in the hills in the rain, became a part of existence.

Pistol Pete caused two kinds of fear. One was the steady, subliminal fear that you felt when he wasn't shelling, the fear that soon, now—right now—as you crossed the road, exposed and helpless, the shriek would sound and the shell would fall, carrying your death. It was a terrible game that we all played. *Now!* (walking down the hill to the head). No, *now!* (sitting at dinner). No, *now!* Always the thought that at this very moment you might have finished all your living. The other kind was the fear that came while the shells were falling. It was deep and clutching, like a seizure. I sat in the foxhole with Rock during a shelling, and though he was a brave man he was shaking uncontrollably. None of us was surprised or shocked; we all felt the same, though it had not seized our bodies that way. And we were right to be frightened; before Pete was silenced he had wounded seven of our men.

The rain ended; it was June, summer weather, flying weather. The squadron grew restless. For two months we had been flying hard—two or three hops, some days—but they had been local, unspectacular flights—a strike against a cave or a hidden gun, supply drops, antisubmarine patrols. In one month we had flown a thousand combat missions and had dropped a hundred tons of supplies. We had delivered mail, sprayed the island with DDT, dropped propaganda leaflets behind the enemy lines. These had been useful services, and we might have argued that 232 was the most useful squadron on the island; but usefulness is only a military virtue among the upper echelons— generals cherish it, but second lieutenants don't. We had been raised on movies like *Dawn Patrol* and *Wings,* and for a year or more in flight school we had been handed the Navy's literature—all those glossy leaflets with titles like "Winning Your Wings of Gold." Military flying, these sources agreed, was bombing and shooting, sinking carriers and sending planes down in flames; it was daring, not utility, that counted. After all those services we wanted a bit more daring in our lives.

Down at the southern end of the island our strikes were less and less necessary as the Army and Marines tightened their ring around the last defenders. The Japanese fought on, but the battle was really over; they had no more guns, and their caves and tunnels were blasted and burned out one by one. Shuri Castle had fallen. There was nothing left but the killing, and the infantry could do that. We flew our last strike on the island against some trivial target on June 19th; Joe came back to assure the intelligence officer that he had got a direct hit on a three-hole privy. On the 21st Admiral Nimitz, commander of the combined attack forces, announced that organized resistance had ended and that the island was secure. We heard stories, afterward, of what those last days had been like for the defenders, and of how at the end the senior officers had ceremoniously committed suicide. But we didn't know enough about the defense to know that it had been brilliant and courageous. All I felt when I heard those stories was incomprehension: How could men behave like that, when they had lost?

We began to fly strikes against neighboring islands—to Mayako and Ishigaki, south of us toward Formosa, and north to Kikai Jima and Amami o Shima. This was more like what we had expected—the massed flotilla of attacking planes, rumbling in formation toward the invisible target, the high, nervous movements of the fighter cover, nothing else in sight but water and clouds. And then the island appears ahead, the planes slide into attack formation, the high-speed descent begins, the first plane peels off, and you really see the island for the first time, in your bombsight—a grove of trees on the right, an airstrip, a few buildings—and the tracers begin to rise lazily toward you, and little clouds of AA bursts hang in the air as you dive past, and you have dropped and are pulling away, over the trees toward the beach and safety.

They were classic, beautiful strikes, the feeling of planes and men relating in the intricate choreography of a strike formation, the gut-knotting climax, and the long, calm return. What memory returns to me is images. On a flight to Ishigaki I look out over the formation, the planes invisibly linked together, a squadron, and the weaving fighters above us, and I feel the sun warm on my cockpit canopy, and I am content to be there; and a later moment, an image not of contentment but of heightened life—diving, the plane bucking in the troubled air, and the tracers rising.

But that strike, though it offers me such images, was the grimmest one I flew on. We returned to Kadena to learn that the fighters had lost planes—five? ten? I have forgotten how many—and all to stupidity. Some of the Corsairs had carried bombs with proximity fuses. Once such bombs are armed (a wire is removed from the fuse) a small propeller on the nose begins to turn. When it has turned a certain number of revolutions, the bomb begins to send out radio impulses, and when they return, bounced back from some solid surface, the bomb explodes. If you arm the bomb as you attack, and drop it, its impulses will bounce back as it nears the ground, and it will explode in the air and scatter shrapnel; it is therefore useful against troops, parked planes and vehicles, and supplies. But these bombs had been rigged incorrectly, the arming wires had dropped out in flight, and the bombs began transmitting impulses too soon, before they were dropped. When those impulses returned, bounced from another plane, the bombs exploded, and plane after plane was blown from the sky. I saw none of this—the bomb-carrying Corsairs were either ahead or behind our formation—but we heard the story when we landed, and felt the rage that other pilots felt, that a fool of an armament officer, who never left the ground to get shot at, should have killed good men.

The beauty and the stupid deaths are both parts of the whole. I grieved for the dead men, and I hated the unnecessariness of their dying. But the images that the mind cherishes remain beautiful.

We flew a strike against Amami, and there I got the only certain direct hit on anything that I can remember—two bombs dropping precisely through the roof of a building, and quite effectively destroying it. But what was in the building? Radar equipment, we were told, and certainly there was an antenna near by; but it might have been a barn or an abandoned warehouse, or almost anything. It might have been a barracks; perhaps there were men in it, but I don't think so, and of course I want not to think so. Being a bombing pilot, I had never had to set out to kill anyone, or to think of human beings as my target. I discouraged my gunners from firing at random when we flew against little islands like Amami, which lay so peacefully in the summer sea, and looked as though it must be occupied by peaceful people—a few farmers, maybe, and a couple of radar men who kept a garden, and wrote haiku about loneliness.

Kikai, across a narrow strait from Amami, was more

military—it had a bombed-out airstrip, and the guns around the strip were manned by skillful gunners. Like the gunners back at Yap, they conserved their ammunition, only fired at sure targets, and never used tracers; so you never knew that you were being shot at until you felt the shots hitting your plane. We flew strikes against Kikai occasionally, bombing the strip just to keep it out of operation, but we were cautious there—get in, drop, and get out, away from the hidden guns.

As the strike targets were extended, our ambitions grew grander. Shipping was reported near the China coast. Why not a torpedo attack? After all, we had lugged torpedoes with us all the way from the far south, from somewhere before Ulithi (nobody in the squadron was sure exactly where we had acquired the damn things). It would be a long flight, very near the limit of our range, but it would be glorious—a chance to sink ships. But when the armament officer examined the torpedoes, he found that they were all dry, someone had drunk the fuel (they ran on alcohol). And before bombs could be substituted, the flight was cancelled; maybe the ships weren't really there, or maybe they were sunk by the Navy. They might even have been our own.

We returned to our bombing attacks against nearby islands. On one of these Joe took a bullet through his engine cowling that hit an oil line, and on the way home he gradually lost oil pressure until, as the flight crossed the eastern coast of the island, his engine stopped dead. Below him was a new airstrip, just being finished, and he glided down and made a fine dead stick landing there. He came back to Kadena later that day in a jeep, in very high spirits; he had spoiled the Colonel's Grand Opening, he said, and the Colonel was very pissed off. It had been arranged that the Colonel commanding our group would land the first plane on the new field the next day, thus officially opening it; but Joe had got there before him. Still, as Joe said, the Colonel would be the first to land a plane with its engine running.

The next day the squadron was told to prepare to leave Kadena. Henceforth we would operate out of Awase, the new field that Joe had just initiated. His forced landing seemed an appropriate beginning to a new kind of life.

Chapter 10

Moving from Kadena to Awase was like moving from the frontier to the suburbs. Kadena had been built in a hurry, while the war was being fought a mile or two away, and it had a hasty feeling, even after months of village life. The tents still had dirt floors, and every tent had its foxhole; the shower was still an oil drum, and officers and enlisted men still ate together in one mess tent. It was an agreeable kind of place, and I was happy there. But it was primitive—there was no denying that—and we moved to Awase with a sense of upward mobility.

Awase had been built like a real-estate development. Along the beach, at the edge of the eastern anchorage called Buckner Bay, ran the airstrip—new, hard-surfaced, and longer than we were used to. The Air Force had installed a P-51 squadron there, on the east side, by the water; we were to have the west side. Inland from the strip the land rose steeply in irregular, treeless hills. Roads had been built up into these hills, and the squadron quarters were scattered along the roads, like development houses. The roads even had development-sounding names—Roosevelt Road, Admiral Something Street, General Somebody Boulevard. They had been named, we were told, by the former congressman from Minnesota who commanded the base.

Our squadron area was high up, on a hilltop with a view of the field and the harbor. We had Quonset huts, tents with floors and screens, a mess hall with a separate officers' mess and an ice machine, electric lights, a hot-and-cold shower, even a laundry, staffed by flat-faced, gold-toothed, grinning native women. There were no fox-holes, and we didn't dig any; it would have been like digging a foxhole in Edina, or Great Neck. It was summer 1945, the island was secure; it was a time and a place to be soft. We lay in the sun, drank in the evenings, and flew uneventful antisub patrols and mail runs, and occasionally an unnecessary strike to neutralize an already bombed-out island. It was like summer vacation, when we were kids—the sun always shining and hot on the skin, nothing much to do, the rhythm of life slowed.

For the moment our war had ended, and we lived a pleasant, suspended life while we waited for it to begin again somewhere else. The next assault, we knew, would be against the home islands of Japan; and we had heard from someone in group headquarters, who had it from someone in the wing, that our squadron would be the first bombing squadron to be based on Kyushu, as it had been the first one on Okinawa. When I thought about what that would be like, I felt doomed, with a Japanese fatalism. I imagined the desperate defense of the homeland, the suicide attacks, the fierce concentrations of AA fire. The whole population would fight against us. In my imagination farmers attacked with pitchforks, crying "Banzai!" and geisha girls held grenades between their inscrutable thighs; every object was a booby-trap, and all the roads were mined. We would all be killed, I thought, by fanatics who had already lost their war. We would die a month or a week before it was all over; come all this way and die at the end of it, stupidly.

But now it was summer, and we lived a summer life. We wandered the hills above the camp, and found in the highest hill a tunnel, cut through the rock of the hill's core, that led to a chamber with gun ports overlooking the valley. Japanese defenders had crouched here with their weapons, scanning the valley, waiting for an attack that came another way. Looking through those slits in the rock was like looking through their eyes—you could imagine the expected battle, the machine-gun fire pouring down on troops as they toiled up the slope below. And you could imagine the lone despair of waiting, guarding those empty hillsides against an enemy who never came. Now the tunnel and the room at the end were empty too; only a sad dampness, the smell of cellars and funeral vaults, filled it. This one defensive post was the only sign around us that Japanese soldiers had lived here, that a war had been fought on this ground. All the other evidences had been erased, swallowed by the American suburb in which we lived and waited.

In our suburb the new mess hall with its officers' section and its ice machine was our country club; it was inevitable that we should have a Saturday night dance there. Women existed on the island; a few men had even seen them— nurses, mostly, in the hospitals that the war had filled. An invitation was sent, and on the Saturday night busloads of women appeared. They were of all sizes and shapes and ages, most of them rather plain-looking. I was surprised that after all these months away from women I still thought these plain; the myth of the Pacific war was that after a while even the natives turned white and became beautiful. A band began to play, drinks were poured, dancing began. I remember Sly engaged in an intricate bit of jitterbugging with a stout nurse—and how comical her sensible nursing shoes seemed in those steps.

But most of us just stood around, watching. Nobody competed for the women—there were far fewer of them than of us, but we seemed to sense who wanted them most, and the rest of us drifted away after a while, up the hill to the Quonset hut, and started a card game. I could hear the dance music through the open door, like the sound of peacetime, the sound of our world before the war. I remembered Spring Lake Casino at Lake Minnetonka, and how when you walked with your girl along the beach the music followed across the water, all those songs that seemed so tender then—"Green Eyes," "I'll Never Smile Again," "Perfidia." We sat there, in the hut, and down the hill the band played; but we didn't go back to the dance. Nobody wanted to fight for a dance with a plain stranger; nobody wanted to make love to one.

We had been away from women then for nearly a year, yet I felt no sexual need and neither, apparently, did anyone else. In all those months I could only remember two incidents that were explicitly sexual—the quiet man at Ulithi who wrote pornography, and the stud's guilty night with the Red Cross girl at Saipan. We were young men at the peak of our sexual powers, but those powers slept. The native Okinawan women—grinning, gold-toothed, perhaps obliging for all I know—were not looked upon as sexual partners at all (though there was a story around that some enlisted entrepreneur had established a makeshift brothel somewhere); and though the nurses had been at hand for months, no one had sought them out until the dance. Is it really true, then, that sex is a form of aggression like war, and that one form drives out the other? Were we living our sexual lives in the bombing and strafing? Or in the comradeship of the all-male, committed life of the squadron? I only know that for nearly a year we lived like monks—hard-drinking, obscene monks, but poor, obedient, and chaste.

Being Americans, with time on our hands, we set about to furnish and domesticate the camp, as we had done at Kadena, but this time in a more suburban way. The squadron's radar officer, our best scrounger, appeared one day with a truckload of plywood. He didn't particularly want plywood; nobody in the squadron wanted plywood; but if you were a good scrounger you scrounged first, and then found a use for whatever you turned up. We decided to build a sort of barroom at the end of our Quonset hut BOQ. The plywood made a dividing wall and covered the sides and the end. Somebody borrowed a blow torch and ran the flame over the plywood walls, giving, he claimed, a desirable decorator's effect of knotty pine (actually it looked more like burned plywood than anything else). A bar was built in one corner, and a poker table in another, covered with a green blanket that looked, to the casual eye, like green felt. We had everything we needed for a club except liquor.

The quartermaster solved that problem. He heard of an Air Force squadron based in the Philippines that was going home, and he bought the entire contents of their club bar.

"A bargain," he assured us. "You put up ten bucks,

you get five bottles. If you don't want it, trade it for souvenirs.''

"Five bottles of what?" Rock asked suspiciously.

"How do I know? Whatever the Air Force drinks. Don't worry, it'll make you drunk."

Eventually the stock arrived, and was delivered, rather ceremoniously, by the quartermaster and a couple of enlisted men. Box after box marked FRAGILE—GLASS was unloaded outside the Quonset, and as the stock grew we began to feel like millionaires, with all that booze. Then the divvying-up began. There was, we discovered, almost no whiskey; the Air Force types had drunk that before they left. What there was was rum, sauterne, sherry, crème de menthe, curaçao, crème de cacao. Rock got kümmel, in a bottle shaped like a sitting bear. Joe drew rock-and-rye, and stood holding the bottle up to the light, staring in a baffled way at the lumps of rock candy inside.

Some of these liquors we had never seen before, except maybe behind a bar, and we didn't know how you drank them. But they were all we had, and we settled down to find out. The party that night was memorable. There was a poker game that lasted until breakfast, and a fight in the course of which three cots were broken, and Joe invented two new choruses of "Bless 'em All." Even Billy Childers came, with his five bottles, and joined in the singing. When we sang one of our familiar songs, he would decorate the pauses between the choruses with traditional witticisms from his Mississippi country past. We'd be singing, say, a chorus of the endless limerick song, maybe the one about the man from Saint Paul, who went to a fancy-dress ball, and Billy would come in at the end, very drunk, with "Do you wet yo'r hair in the morning, daughter?" "No, mother, I pee through a straw," or "Don't cut no firewood tonight, mother—I'm comin' home with a load.'' And then he'd look around, smiling, as though he'd said something original and funny. It seemed to be a part of the ritual of collective drunkenness, as practiced in Mississippi.

Next morning most of the new stock of booze was gone. Joe's rock-and-rye bottle had only some sticky lumps in the bottom, and the sitting bear, empty now, was on the Quonset hut roof. What was left was mainly things like green crème de menthe, liqueurs that even a drunk man could see weren't drinkable in large quantities. Later on, when there wasn't anything else to drink, we tried the crème de menthe poured over the shaved ice that we got from the mess hall ice machine—Billy called the drink a ''green frappie,'' said it was like what he used to get in the drugstore back home—but nobody could bear to drink enough of it to do him any good.

We went on flying. Sometimes it seemed that we flew simply because we always had flown; that we were a machine that couldn't run down. We flew strikes against islands that now are only names—Gaga Shima, Kume Shima. We hunted Japanese radar installations on the little islands that ran north in a chain toward Kyushu, and attacked buildings and antenna towers with bombs and rockets. We went on flying the interminable antisub patrols, and never saw a sub, though Feeney found a small boat full of men, dropped a depth charge, the only bomb he had, and blew the boat in two. The men were wearing green hats and trousers, he said, but not shirts; but they must have been soldiers, trying to escape from the island, didn't we think so? He was very worried that they might have been civilians, just trying to get away from the Americans, or going fishing or something. We said they were almost certainly escaping Japs. The intelligence officer was

251

pleased to have something new to report, and wrote in his log: "Approx. seven (7) bodies were left lying motionless in the water."

The impulse to do something spectacular, which had almost sent the squadron ship-hunting in the China Sea, was still strong in us. If not ships, well then, the Japanese mainland. Kyushu was barely within range of our planes, and we'd have to hit the extreme southern tip if we were to get back to Okinawa, but we could do it, and we'd have bombed Japan. A target was chosen—an airfield on the southern coast of the island—and a strike was launched. There was no particular reason to bomb that target. Surely the Navy and the Air Force's B-29's had been hitting it for months, and anyway the Japanese were virtually out of aircraft, and their fields were no serious threat to us. The strike wasn't really an attack; it was a sightseeing expedition, something to tell the grandchildren; it was as though we were getting ready now that the war was near its end, to become boring old soldiers, full of interminable war stories and lies.

Everybody was excited by the plan, everybody wanted to go, and I was disappointed and angry when I wasn't chosen, and even felt a touch of satisfaction that the weather was going to be awful; with a little luck, I thought, they won't even find Kyushu. They did, but under a storm front that covered the island with low, solid cloud. They couldn't find their target, headed for another field, couldn't find that one either, and were about to head for home when someone saw an airfield through a hole in the clouds. Any target was better than lugging the bombs home again, and they straggled through the hole and dropped. They had bombed Japan, but nobody could be much more precise than that.

In mid-July the squadron tried another strike against Kyushu. This one was to be led by Jimmy, and all my friends—Rock, T, Joe—went, but once more I was left out. This time there would be an elaborate fighter cover, forty-eight Corsairs over the twelve TBM's; it was going to be a show, something to remember. The fighters took off first and circled in divisions of four, stacked up in the blue summer air above the field. Our planes were delayed, and by the time they were airborne the fighters didn't have enough fuel left to make it to Kyushu and back; and so the strike was diverted to the airstrip at Kikai. We had flown an eighteen-plane strike there the week before, and there couldn't be anything left that was worth bombing, only the patient gunners waiting for a sure shot. But once you have started such an elaborate operation you have to send it somewhere, if only to get rid of the bombs, and Kikai was handy.

I hung around on the hill, watching the squadron take off. It was hot and sunny, and after they had joined up and left I took off my shirt, and brought a chair out into the sun and tried to read. But I couldn't. It was too quiet on the hill—everyone else seemed to be on the strike—and I felt restless, up there alone, waiting for my friends to come back. The ordinary air traffic moved around the field—a P-51 took off, sounding like an intent insect; a night-fighter landed. Down on the line a mechanic ran up an engine, up and up to a high scream like pain, and then suddenly back to a hoarse whisper. Then there was silence, only the hum of summer, and I waited in the sun.

I heard the flight before I saw it, a steady rumble out of the north, and then I could see them, first only a line, at eye level from where I stood on the hill, then separate planes, in tight formation, a column of three-plane V's, close, steady, and formal-looking. But in the last V there were only two planes, and the empty space seemed an enormous emptiness, like a catch in the breath, a skipped heartbeat. One plane was down somewhere—in the sea, or wheels-up on a beach, or crumpled in the rubble at Kikai field.

I waited. I could have gone down to the Operations tent and heard the story, but I stayed on the hill, and put off knowing. The pilots would land, they'd be debriefed by Intelligence, and then they'd come up to their quarters, and I'd hear then.

It was Joe who was missing, and he was dead. He had dived in his turn over the target, and had flown straight into the ground. Not even the beginning of a recovery, just straight in. He must have been killed in the air, Jimmy said, shot dead as he flew; otherwise he'd have got the plane somehow into level flight, and out to sea, as good a pilot as he was. There had been no explosion when he hit, and no fire—just the smash, like a car against a wall, or a tree falling.

In a month the war was over. The atom bombs were dropped, though we got only sketchy and confusing reports of what the bomb was exactly, and what it did to Hiroshima and Nagasaki. We were relieved; we told each other, drinking in our plywood bar, that we were relieved. But we were saddened, too, though we didn't talk about that. Our common enterprise had come to an end; the invasion of Kyushu, and our flaming deaths in combat, would not take place.

Our war ended officially on August 12th, and that afternoon we launched every plane that would fly in what my logbook calls Victory Flight, a sweep out over the fleet anchorage in a huge V-formation. The bay was crowded

with ships, motionless at anchor; they looked very peaceful and tranquil in the August sun, as though they would
never steam out to sea again, or fire a shell, or spray up
tracers against attacking planes. It was a painting of a fleet
that we flew over that hot, late-summer day; the fleet itself
belonged to the past. We finished the sweep and turned,
and the flight leader signaled us into a column. We dove
back toward the ships below us, as though in an attack,
and then, to my astonishment and alarm, the lead plane
pulled suddenly up and heaved itself over into a portly
barrel-roll—a sort of parody of a fighter pilot's Victory
Roll. It was like seeing a fat lady somersault—it seemed
impossible, it was certainly unwise, but she was doing it.
The second plane followed, and the next, and it was my
turn.

The TBM was not built for acrobatics: the wings would
not bear negative stress, and if I faltered in the roll while
the plane was upside down I would surely pull both wings
off, and plunge into the bay. I told my crew to hang on,
pulled the nose up sharply, and rolled. The planed seemed
to resist at first, and then resignedly entered the roll.
A year's accumulated rubbish flew up from under the
floorboards, and I could hear loose gear rattling around in
the tunnel behind me; I wondered how poor Edwards was
surviving back there. Then we were rolling out, swooping
up toward level flight, the horizon returned to its proper
place, and I joined up on the plane ahead of me. So much
for Victory.

It was a stupid thing to have done, but I understand why
we did it—why it was, in a way, necessary. We were giving Death the chance that he'd missed at Kyushu. We had
survived a war, and all the ways that airplanes can kill
you, and we were going one step further, stretching our

luck. Some of the sadness was in it, too; from now on our lives would never be daring and foolhardy again.

That night every gun—every AA gun, every machine gun, rifle, and pistol—seemed to be firing into the sky. Everyone was out in the company streets, outside tents and Quonset huts, firing into the air, drinking and yelling and firing the shells and bullets that they'd never need again. The air was full of noise and the red tracks of tracers, and falling shrapnel. It wasn't safe to be out there, and some prudent pilots crawled under the Quonset hut, regretting that they hadn't dug foxholes. I was ashamed to be so chicken, but I lay inside on my cot, listening to the spent bullets dropping on the tin roof, and thinking how ironic it would be to be killed tonight. Three or four men were killed before the night was over, most of them accidentally, but one—an unpopular Sergeant Major—almost certainly by intention, shot in the back in the uproar. It was an hysterical, frightening night, a purging of war's emotions.

The war was over, but the flying wasn't. The Navy's PBY's, which had flown the night-time antisub patrols, were sent to Japan to fly American prisoners out, and we took over their patrols. Some subs, we were told, were still at sea, hadn't heard that the war was over, might yet sink an American ship. The Seventh Air Force sent down ambiguous instructions—we were to continue to fly armed, but were not to attack unless fired upon, and were not to take shots at Japanese planes or attack ground targets. It was odd, like being halfway in and halfway out of war.

Night searching was a gloomy, fearful business. The weather had turned hot and stormy, the way it does sometimes in August, and every night there were squalls and thunderheads over the sea. The nights were black, without moon or stars or horizon line; even the lightning, which lit the piled clouds with a cold white light, didn't reach the darkness of the sea. My sector was a long triangle over the China Sea—west toward China, then north, then back to the island. As soon as the plane was airborne the lights of the island disappeared, and we entered the blackness. I reported on station, and the voice of the controller came back, but so broken by crashing static that though it was audibly human, it spoke in meaningless syllables: "Hel . . . Four . . . ver. . . . "

I flew among the thunderheads as I would among mountains, watching ahead when the lightning flashed, altering course to avoid the mountains and fly the valleys. (A tall thunderhead is full of violent vertical currents; it will tear a plane apart, hurl the pieces up and down, and scatter them over the sea.) In the tunnel Edwards searched with his radar for submarines, but among such storms it was a useless exercise; only the thunderheads appeared on his scope, as bright as battleships, and more dangerous. In that electric atmosphere the plane itself became charged, and balls of Saint Elmo's fire rolled up and down the wings, and whirled on the propeller. Lightning flashed, and for a time after each flash I could not read my instruments, and had to fly blindly, holding the plane on its course by feel until sight returned.

I was more afraid that night than I have ever been in the air. Fear is probably always there, subliminally, in an experienced pilot's mind; it is a source of that attentiveness that keeps you alive. But only rarely does it thrust itself into your consciousness. This never happened to me on a strike—I felt keyed up, tense, abnormally aware of the plane, but not exactly afraid—but it happened on those night patrols over the China Sea. I felt fear then; but I also felt something else—resentment, outrage that I was out there, with the war over, alone and half-blind with lightning and blackness, that I might die out there, on a pointless exercise in the dark.

I flew my last night patrol on my birthday, August 29th; and when I got back, toward midnight, we had a party—liquor had become a little easier to find by then—and I got pretty drunk. I was twenty-one, I kept telling everyone, and I was old enough to drink. I guess I must have used that line too often, or maybe it was something else, but at the end of the evening I found myself fighting with Rock. We struggled up and down the Quonset hut, over people's cots, and sometimes under them, wrestling (we couldn't really have hit each other), grunting, cursing, until at last he won, and sat straddling my chest the way a fight used to end in school. Then we got up and had a drink. If you have a fancy for symbolism, you could find some there; I had reached manhood and lost a fight on the same night; or, the war was over, and friends turned to fighting each other. Probably either reading would be a bit heavy, but I was sorry I had that fight. I don't think I cared about losing it, much.

Summer turned into fall. The trees on the hillsides above the strip turned brown and gold, and the nights were cooler, but the days were fine and clear, only with that metallic look that blue skies have in autumn. Our lives were aimless, without the momentum of war, and we spent our time mostly just waiting for the orders that would send us home. Flying was only another form of idleness—flying around and around the field testing an engine, or to another field on the island to deliver some mail, or for no reason at all, just to be doing something. Some pilots I knew flew to Japanese-held islands, and landed, and were received with formal courtesy; and there were several round trips to Kyushu, to the airfields we had never been able to find. But I didn't go on any of these tourist trips; I had had enough of islands.

In that fine autumn weather I might have taken a good look at the island on which I had lived for nearly six months. I could have walked over the ruins of Shuri Castle, or I might have driven north, into the steep, quiet valleys that the war had never reached. But I didn't; I stayed there in our tent at Awase, doing nothing, feeling emptied of all motives. A squadron of F7F's arrived—the first we had seen—and I went down to the line to look one over, but I didn't try to wangle a checkout flight. I went on flying Turkeys some, but there wasn't much fun in it anymore. The machine had run down at last.

The Navy announced the system by which we would be returned to the States. It involved an elaborate counting of points—so many for each month overseas, so many for each medal, so many for each dependent. The junior officers in the squadron had all come to the war together, so there was no competition there. And we all had the same medals, earned the same way—five strikes for an Air Medal, twenty for a Distinguished Flying Cross. It was embarrassing to get medals for such humdrum, unheroic actions; but each medal was worth five points in the system. The only variable among us was the number of dependents. Some of us were married and got points for that. A few, like T, had a child (a son, born to his wife in Birmingham in June), and that put them ahead of the rest. It seemed a good enough system, and nobody complained. We just calculated our scores, figured the order of departure, and waited.

Senior pilots began to leave; there were drinking parties

in their tents, and then they were gone, and we became senior, and moved into the tents they had vacated. T and Rock and I moved together, and got a fine tent, with a wooden floor and sides, screens, and electricity—more like a cottage than a tent, with a view of the bay. I thought of the first tent we had shared at Kadena—the dirt floor, the wheat under the cots, the kerosene lantern. Now Bergie and Joe were dead, the war was over, and we had a wooden floor. We found a new partner, an amiable giant from Mississippi named Ed, and settled in to wait for orders.

In the meantime we made ourselves comfortable. That is, we began the process of accumulating and homemaking, partly for comfort's sake, but partly to create a special place to exist in, a place that was marked by the persons who lived there, that wasn't simply something that had been issued. Rock appeared one day with a Seth Thomas clock; he had traded a fifth of whiskey for it, so it must have been important to him. Once it had decorated an Okinawan shop, or perhaps a government office. It had a loud, imperative tick, and was always right, though it never really looked at home hanging on a post in a tent. I found a phonograph, and I traveled the island's chaplains' offices begging phonograph records, ''to help the troops pass the time.'' I accumulated quite a large selection, very random, since I followed the first rule of scrounging and never refused a record; but I remember only one song, Billie Holiday singing ''Travellin' Light.'' We made a bookcase out of shell-cases, and filled it with books. Most of them were government-issue paperbacks, often very peculiar choices for the circumstances (what committee had decided that the troops would want to read Joseph Hergesheimer's *Three Black Pennys?*); but we had a few hardcover books, too, my *War and Peace* from Honolulu, a copy of

The Fountainhead that Liz had sent me, and a New Testament with a steel cover (you carried it in your breast pocket, and Jesus stopped the bullets, but we kept it in the bookcase).

September passed. The days were sunny, and warm at noon, with a haze at the horizon—like good fall days at home. We took books out into the sun, and talked instead of reading, and watched the planes around the field. The P-51's still flew a lot—obviously it was more fun to play at dogfighting and acrobatics in a fighter than to lumber around in a TBM—and we watched them idly, out over the bay, twisting and diving, catching the autumn sun on their silver wings. Two began a dogfight, and we stopped talking to follow their maneuvers, crossing, turning steeply, and diving back toward each other, neither getting an advantage, weaving back and forth as in a formal dance. And then they hit. There was no noise, no explosion or any of the accompaniments of violence; they simply seemed to enter each other for a moment, and to emerge broken. One plane dropped gently into a shallow dive, and flew at that exact and careful angle into the sea; as it dove, a figure fell free, and a parachute whipped out behind it, but the chute did not open, and the figure dropped with the chute-lines streaming, into the shallows of the bay. The other plane broke apart; a wing, separated from the body, fell slowly and weightlessly, like a falling leaf, turning over and over; the rest of the plane began to spin, winding tighter and tighter, the engine winding, too, in a rising whine until it struck the mud flat at the edge of the strip. The water and the mud received the wreckage and the bodies, and in a minute there was nothing to show that two men had died there. Nobody said anything. We had thought the casual dying was over.

On one of those fall days I flew to Kikai to look for the wreckage of Joe's plane—and to say goodbye to him. It was an odd, uncomfortable feeling, to approach that hostile island, and to fly low and slow over the gun emplacements from which my enemies, the careful gunners, had looked up at my squadron's planes, and had killed my friend. The airstrip had not been repaired, it was still what it had been, a heap of useless, broken concrete; but the camouflaged guns had been uncovered, and I was struck by how many there were, a ring of them around the field. As I flew slowly across the field, a man came out of a shed and waved. I rocked my wings. Hell, the war was over.

I found the wreck just south of the field, not far from the beach. The engine was buried in the earth—he must have hit at a steep angle, and at high speed—and the tail stood up in the air, like a monument. The wings had crumpled with the impact, but I could read the number painted on the tail; it was Joe's plane, all right. I felt I should do something; but I didn't know how a man grieves. The reticence that made my father so inarticulate in his loving—I had it too; it was as much a part of my inheritance as my name. I waited for my body to instruct me— to burst into tears, or a howl or a moan of misery—but it did nothing but fly the plane. Down there, under that wreckage, was the disintegrated body of a friend I had loved, a part of my life before the war, and all through it. I felt that part as a vacancy, but I couldn't express how that vacancy felt. There was nothing that I, up there in the plane, could do for him, down there. I flew around the wreck once or twice, very carefully (Nick Nagoda had killed himself flying around the wreckage of his friend's plane), and then turned south and headed home.

Along the northern coast of Okinawa I flew in close to the shore; I would probably never see that part of the island again. It was just as I had first seen it, a bit of peaceful northern landscape—rather like Norway as I imagined it—that had not been touched by the war; its steep wooded hills and narrow valleys were too rugged and too small-scale to interest generals or contain armies. I turned up a narrow, wooded valley, and saw a small house by the stream, and two or three people working in a garden. They looked up, as though they had never seen a plane before, and stood with their hands shading their eyes and watched me out of sight. I went on to Awase and landed, making the squadron approach automatically, the dive to the strip, the steep, impossible-looking bank, wheels and flaps down in the turn, the sharp, last-minute rollout as the plane stalled to the strip. It was still pleasing to land in that extravagant way—if you could make a Turkey behave like a fighter, you could really fly. But there really wasn't any point, any more.

Later on we heard from a Navy unit that had landed on Kikai—maybe to accept the Commanding Officer's sword or something, I suppose somebody had to go round to all those little islands so that they could surrender—anyway, someone had been there, and had seen Joe's grave. The Japanese had removed the bodies from the wreck, had given them a decent burial, and had placed above the graves a marker that read: "In Memory of the Brave American Fliers." That seemed right.

We woke one morning in late September to the sound of wind, the tent slapping, guy wires whistling. It was the typhoon season in the China Sea, and a storm was moving up from Formosa. Aerology said it would reach us in the early afternoon, but it never did, quite, though the edge of the storm that we got was violent, howling, and wet. It broke up some of our planes and beached some small boats; but we rode it out all right, our tent survived intact, and the squadron planes were repaired in a couple of days. Once the sky had cleared and we had dried out, we felt rather proud of ourselves, coming through a typhoon so easily—we were seasoned, Old China hands.

Three weeks later the real storm hit us. It began in the night, with a long, drenching rain; and then the wind began, driving the rain horizontally, with the force of buckshot. We closed and tied down the tent flaps and walked down to breakfast, leaning into the hard, punishing wind, hunched down in our foul-weather clothes. Afterward we sat in the tent, trying to think of what we could do, to be ready. This one was going to be a fierce one, and Aerology predicted that the eye of the storm would pass directly over the island. Already rain was driving in around the tent flaps. We went out into the gale and nailed the flaps to the frame. But still the rain came in, until the wooden floor was slick with mud and drops of water covered the blankets of our bunks like a fine dew. In the bookcase the books warped and swelled. The electric light flickered, brightened, and went out. Somebody stopped at the door to tell us that the anemometer on the control tower was reading one hundred knots and that the planes, which had been tied down facing into the wind, were actually airborne on the gale.

By mid-afternoon the tent was rocking on its pilings, like a small boat in a storm, and we were out in the storm again, putting up braces, ropes, and guy wires to hold the tent down. And still the wind rose—we couldn't tell exactly what velocity it reached, but someone said the anemometer had been registering a hundred and fifty knots when it blew away. The wind was strong enough by then to peel sheets of corrugated tin off the Quonset hut roofs and hurl them through the air like whirling machetes. It could snatch up a tent and whip it off into the storm, and then tear away the plywood flooring and send it spinning after.

Visibility was down to a few yards—our world was our own tent and the Executive Officer's tent next door. Then his went, opening in the air like a parachute and disappearing downwind. The Exec grabbed what he could save and started toward us, and as we watched his progress through the storm the entire plywood floor lifted behind him and struck him to the ground. The giant Ed plunged out into the wind, lifted the flooring, and carried the Exec into our tent. He lay for an hour on a bunk, unconscious, while the wind howled and the rain came in. There was no way of getting him to a doctor, or a doctor to him.

The force of the wind had separated the threads of the canvas in the tent roof without tearing it, and you could stand inside the tent and look up and see a dim light from the sky. Rain soaked in, everything was wet—our beds, our clothing, all the books—the very air inside the tent was a mist of rain. But the tent still stood. We would not have been much worse off without it, but it seemed important that we should win against the storm. The guy wires twanged, and the tent shifted on its pilings; but it stood. It was still a tent and not a scrap of blown canvas; it was the place we had made for ourselves.

When the weather cleared, ours was the only tent in sight. Where the others had stood there were only the pilings of the floors and a few tent pegs. The Quonset hut where we had built our bar had slid down the hill twenty or thirty feet, and lay there at an angle, like a ship aground. The squadron buildings—supply tents, repair facilities, ready room, Operations—were all gone. Of our twenty-four planes, only five were flyable, and some of the others were beyond repairing. The airstrip was littered with wrecked planes and rubbish. Along the edge of the bay, naval vessels and flying boats were beached, some of them wrecked. All communication lines were down; the east coast of the island could not reach the west coast, and we couldn't even speak to our flight line.

The island was once more like a battlefield, the scene of a battle fought against wind and rain. But there was an odd exhilaration in the experience; officers and men had moved together in to the mess hall and were sleeping there on the tables and on the floor, and there was only food enough for two meals a day, but nobody complained. The violence of nature was somehow amiable compared to the violence of war, even though ten men had died in the storm. To survive a war, and then two typhoons—there was a kind of immortality in that.

Ed stole a gallon of airplane paint, and we began to make our tent waterproof again. As I stood on a ladder painting the roof, I thought of the night-fighter pilot and his madness; I too had been driven to paint my tent blue.

My orders came a week later: "When directed by the Commanding Officer, Marine Wing Service Squadron-2, you will stand detached from your present station and duties, and will proceed via first available government transportation to the United States." But there was no transportation—it was on the beach at Buckner Bay, or blown out to sea. We went on waiting—excited at first to be going home, then indifferent, bored, just waiting for the Navy to do something with us, as we had waited so many times before. When a transport ship at last appeared, and we were ordered aboard, the excitement was gone; it was just another move.

There were ten or twelve of us on the orders—married men with two DFC's, I suppose, and no children. We had a party, and the radar officer gave me his last bottle of whiskey as a farewell present, and I was surprised and touched. But it wasn't much of a party. We were ordered to report somewhere at five A.M.—it struck me as a nice Marine Corps touch that my last orders should involve such an unreasonable hour—and we sat up through the night, drinking a little, dozing, feeling bored, and depressed to be bored when we were going home. It was still dark when we drove away from the squadron camp, down Eisenhower Boulevard (or was it Admiral Spruance Drive?) to the coast road, and on south to the landing area.

The ship, we were told, was a converted United Fruit banana boat. The conversion consisted of stacking bunks nine high in the hold for the enlisted men, so close together that a man had to get into a horizontal position first in order to get into bed, and three high, nine to a cabin, in the officers' quarters. We mustered, marched aboard, and waited. And after some delays and confusion, and a lot of roll-calling, the ship sailed. I have no memory at all of the sailing, no nostalgic images of Okinawa receding in the distance, nor even any feelings about the occasion. We just left. But my island had already ceased to exist— it was the island at war, the strikes, the gunfire to the south, Joe Baird laughing and singing, the feeling of a good, working squadron. That was all gone now. I wasn't leaving anything.

The ship was headed east, but nobody knew our exact destination, though there were many rumors. We were going to Pearl Harbor, and would have shore leave there. We were headed directly for San Francisco. We would sail through the Panama Canal and dock in Norfolk. One day followed another, and the ship rolled and pitched in the long Pacific swells, lifting its screw from the water with every swell, so that the ship shuddered and rattled (troops were not as heavy as bananas, though they were packed in nearly as tightly). Everyone was seasick, which was just as well, since there wasn't enough food to satisfy appetites of all the men on board. Officers were all right; we sat down three times a day to well-cooked meals, served on tables with linen cloths and silver cutlery. But the enlisted men were limited to two meals a day, often eaten standing up, or sitting on the deck. Junior officers were assigned as "Mess Control Officers" to see that the men didn't eat more than one serving per meal, or take an extra orange. I took my turn with the rest of the second lieutenants, but I couldn't do the job conscientiously. I just stood at the mess-hall door and tried to look severe as the men came and went, but I never stopped anyone, not even the ones with two oranges.

We were at sea for seventeen days. We didn't stop at Pearl, and we didn't go through the Canal. We went back into the port from which we had left—San Diego. Point Loma on the left, North Island on the right, the circling planes, the berthed carriers, and then the dock—it was all the same, the film run backwards. As the ship tied up, music on the dock below began to play. We surged to the starboard rail, and there below us was a uniformed band and a drum majorette. She marched and twirled and threw her baton in the air, while the band played "From the Halls of Montezuma." It was as though we had won the war all by ourselves. More and more of the troops on board crowded to the rail to see the show. The ship began to list. Over the ship's loudspeaker an official voice spoke: "Now hear this. Now hear this. The starboard head is flooded. The starboard head is flooded." We were moved back away from the rail, the band stopped playing, and the drum majorette moved off to her next docking. We were home. And the starboard head was flooded.

Once more we returned to Miramar. In many ways it was still the same. I roomed with another drunk, who might have been the intelligence officer who introduced me to French 75's, but wasn't. I drank in the bar and tried to put through telephone calls to Liz and to my father, but couldn't, and went on drinking, and went back into the booth from time to time to quarrel with the long-distance operator. The same San Diego tramps were there, in the same low-cut dresses, drinking and talking in low voices to strangers. But it was profoundly different, too. There was no excitement now, no one waiting for orders to the war, no eager young men hanging around some veteran while he told them how it had been at Rabaul. We had all been there, somewhere, and we were through with it. It was like a locker room after a game, a game that you've lost. Or like the morning after a party, when you wake up and realize what you did last night, and how much of it can't be undone, ever.

In a week or so new orders came, and Rock and I and some other pilots checked out and went up to Los Angeles for one last party. Everything was familiar and stale; it was like starting a big evening with a hangover; it was the end of something that had been good, perhaps like the breaking up of a marriage. The train we rode was the same one I had traveled on the year before, with my crutch and my fat ankle; it was just as crowded, with what seemed to be the same people. Sailors sat on their seabags in the aisles and drank from whiskey bottles, and passed them along; babies cried. In Los Angeles the hotel was the same—the Santa Rosa, next to the best in town. We went out to Hollywood, and the same bands were playing in the bars. We drank a lot, and told people that we had just come back from the war, and I tried to teach a bartender to sing "The Fucking Great Wheel." Then I was on the street somewhere, explaining to a Shore Patrol why I was not in the proper uniform, telling him about the two typhoons, and how my dress greens had blown away (a lie, but easier than the truth, when you're drunk). Later we were together in a hotel suite, but it wasn't ours at the Santa Rosa. Everyone was drinking, and there were some girls in the other room. The girls were unhappy, they had expected a party; they wanted to go home, and somebody was saying, in a tired voice, "All right, then, go home. Fuck you." And the girls were crying.

Then it was dawn, another drunk dawn—How many dawns had I been drunk in?—and I was walking alone down some anonymous Los Angeles street that seemed to go on forever. The streetlights were going out along the block, and now and then a car passed, but there weren't any taxis, and I went on walking in the cold November morning.

It was hard to get out of Los Angeles then. The commercial airlines were filled with high-priority bigshots, and every military airbase had a mob of returned troops waiting around for a seat on a cargo or a transport plane going anywhere east. I found another pilot who was headed east, and together we managed to get a two-berth compartment on a train for Chicago. We had no dress uniforms, only or unpressed khakis and flight jackets, and we looked and felt like aliens in that elegant train. But we had our wings, and some ribbons now; and we wore them all above our shirt pockets, as witnesses that we had been there, and were coming home. The working clothes seemed to us worthy. Apparently they impressed others, too; my compartment mate met a California congressman's wife in the compartment next door, and disappeared for the rest of the journey.

I rode out from Chicago on the El, over the slums and the flat empty lots through the gray afternoon, to my parents' factory-town suburb, and took a cab to their house. I hadn't told them I was coming. I imagined a scene of surprise and joy as I turned up unexpectedly, just in time for a home-cooked American supper. But they weren't at the house. It was empty, and their name was gone from the mailbox; they had moved the day before, nobody seemed to know where.

When at last I found the new house, dinner was over, and they were sitting together amid the disorder of packing, looking tired and disoriented. I had to climb over rolled-up rugs and around furniture to reach them. My stepmother kissed me, and my father gripped my hand and said, "Well. Well, well. You're back." Then my stepmother flustered into the kitchen, where everything was still in boxes, and produced my first home-cooked meal—fried Spam. I ate it among the boxes and the piled dishes, while my parents told me that I was looking well. Then we sat in the living room for a while. The furniture was the same stuff I had grown up with—I remembered the sofa, and the oak rocking chair, and the pictures leaning against the wall—but it had grown unfamiliar in this new place. After a while we put a bed together and found some bedding, and I left them sitting there and went to bed.

In the day or two I spent there, my father tried to tell me his feelings. "Son—" he would begin, but then he'd stop. A lifetime of not talking about feelings was too strong a habit to overcome. But I showed him the medals, and he was pleased, almost as pleased, I think, as if he'd won them; and I got out some photographs, and they seemed to make the war more actual for him, and my life credible. Nothing got said, but he managed, just by putting his big hand on my shoulder and saying, "Son—" to express love and pride. We never played the homecoming scene that I had imagined, but it was all right.

But the house wasn't my house, and the town wasn't my town. And I was married. I caught a train for Birmingham, for the other reunion.

Because Liz was waiting in Birmingham, I chose to be discharged from active duty at Pensacola, and we rode down from Birmingham together, on the same slow, dusty train, stopping, as you always did, at Flomaton, and on down to the Gulf. But it wasn't simply convenience that had brought me back to Pensacola. I wanted to return just once, just for a few days, to that place where I had learned the only skill I had, and where I had been happy in that timeless world of young men, before the dying began. Perhaps the impulse to return is a sign that one has grown up, an acknowledgment of the way the good times pass us. We go back in space because we can't go back in time.

Pensacola was peaceful-looking in the winter sunshine; everything was bright with sun—the white-painted buildings, the sandy earth, the palm trees, the quiet waters of the bay. In that mild stillness the sound of planes was as distant and peaceful as the buzzing of insects on a summer afternoon. It was as if the whole place knew that the war was over, that there was nothing urgent left to be done.

I was still on flight orders, and entitled to flight pay if I flew four hours a month; so when I had reported in I went over to the Main Side hangar to look for a plane. There I found another Marine pilot on the same errand, and one plane—an N2S Yellow Peril, the kind I had learned to fly in, back at Memphis. One tank of gas would last, if we stretched it, for just about four hours. We didn't know each other; neither had any particular reason to trust the other's flying; we had nothing to do and barely enough gas to do it; but we took off together to fly somewhere, anywhere, for four hours.

My companion climbed carefully over the lagoon and took a cautious, level course north, over the piny woods. It was the same featureless landscape over which I had navigated two years before, and I felt the same withdrawal from the actual world. He flew on for an hour, made a cautious turn, and flew back toward the field. When it came in sight I took over the controls and headed back out over the pines again. Time passed with excruciating slowness; there was nothing to see but the lengthening shadows of the pines, and we could not communicate from one cockpit to the other, even if we had had anything to say. The plane seemed to move as slowly as the hands of my watch.

As the end of the four hours approached, I turned toward the field, checking my watch nervously against the fuel gauge. It looked as though we could make it, but without much gas to spare. I circled the field, using up the last few minutes. By then it was evening, and the hangar cast a long shadow across the landing mat, and the water of the lagoon was dark. I began an approach to landing,

273

letting down out of the last late sun into the twilight, and landed in shadow, and taxied to the parking ramp and shut down the engine. We both got out and walked silently to the hangar, and separated with scarcely a word. I think we must have had the same feelings. It was all over now, we were at the end of the adventure; we had become men with families and responsibilities and futures. The end of flying had made us mortal.

A Note from
the Naval Institute Press

The Naval Institute Press is the book-publishing arm of the U.S. Naval Institute, a private, nonprofit professional society for members of the sea services and civilians who share an interest in naval and maritime affairs. Established in 1873 at the U.S. Naval Academy in Annapolis, Maryland, where its offices remain today, the Naval Institute has more than 100,000 members worldwide.

Members of the Naval Institute receive the influential monthly naval magazine *Proceedings* and substantial discounts on fine nautical prints, ship and aircraft photos, and subscriptions to the Institute's recently inaugurated quarterly, *Naval History*. They also have access to the transcripts of the Institute's Oral History Program and may attend any of the Institute-sponsored seminars regularly offered around the country.

The book-publishing program, begun in 1898 with basic guides to naval practices, has broadened its scope in recent years to include books of more general interest. Now the Naval Institute Press publishes more than forty new titles each year, ranging from how-to books on boating and navigation to battle histories, biographies, ship guides, and novels. Institute members receive discounts on the Press's more than 300 books.

For a free catalog describing books currently available and for further information about U.S. Naval Institute membership, please write to:

Membership Department
U.S. Naval Institute
Annapolis, MD 21402

or call, toll-free, 800-233-USNI.